Viennese Harmonic Theory from Albrechtsberger to Schenker and Schoenberg

Viennese Harmonic Theory from Albrechtsberger to Schenker and Schoenberg

Robert W. Wason

Copyright © 1985 Robert Wesley Wason

All rights reserved. Except as permitted under current legislation, no part of this work may be photocopied, stored in a retrieval system, published, performed in public, adapted, broadcast, transmitted, recorded, or reproduced in any form or by any means, without the prior permission of the copyright owner.

First published 1985
Reissued by the University of Rochester Press 1995
Transferred to digital printing 2008

University of Rochester Press
668 Mt. Hope Avenue, Rochester, NY 14620, USA
www.urpress.com
and Boydell & Brewer Limited
PO Box 9, Woodbridge, Suffolk IP12 3DF, UK
www.boydellandbrewer.com

Cloth ISBN-10: 1–87882–251–9
Paperback ISBN-10: 1–87882–252–7
Paperback ISBN-13: 978–1–87882–252–9

Library of Congress Cataloging-in-Publication Data

Wason, Robert W.
    Viennese harmonic theory from Albrechtsberger to Schenker and Schoenberg / Robert W. Wason
      p. cm.
    Includes bibliographical references and index.
    ISBN 1–87882–251–9 (hardcover: alk. paper)
      1. Harmony--History. 2. Music theory—Austria—Vienna—History—19th century. 3. Music theory—Austria—Vienna—History—20th century. I. Title.
ML444 .W26 1995
781.2/5/0943613 20

                                                                     94042656

A catalogue record for this title is available from the British Library.

This publication is printed on acid-free paper.
Printed in the United States of America.

To Barbara

Contents

Preface   *ix*

Introduction   *xi*

Part I: Figured Bass and Harmonic Theory in Vienna During the First Half of the Nineteenth Century
1 Eighteenth-Century Theory in Nineteenth-Century Vienna   *3*

2 Foreign Influences on Viennese Harmonic Theory   *11*

3 The Viennese Treatises of the First Half of the Nineteenth Century   *21*

Part II: Simon Sechter and the Fundamental Bass
4 Sechter's First Theoretical Works; the *Grundsätze*   *31*

5 The Fundamental Bass   *37*

6 The Extension of the Fundamental   *45*

7 Progression in Minor; Chromatic Progression   *51*

8 Sechter's System of Harmony: Its Methodological Basis and Historical Origins   *61*

Part III: Viennese Fundamental Bass Theory in the Second Half of the Century
9 Anton Bruckner, the Leading Apostle of Sechter's Teachings   *67*

10 "Romantic Harmony" and the Fundamental Bass   *85*

11 Sechter's System at the End of the Century   *97*

Part IV: The Influence of Viennese Fundamental Bass Theory at the Beginning of the Twentieth Century

12 Systems of Harmony at the Beginning of the Century *115*

13 Viennese Fundamental Bass Theory and the German Function Theory: A Synthesis *121*

14 The Viennese Reaction: Schenker and Schoenberg *133*

Notes *145*

Bibliography *189*

Name Index *197*

Subject Index *199*

Preface

For the American theorist a historical study of Viennese harmonic theory should require no justification, since a continuation of that history is unfolding in America today. Schoenberg himself educated a generation of American musicians in his way of thinking during the 1930s and 1940s, and Schenker's students began spreading their master's word at about the same time. One need only look at any harmony book—or at most any work on music theory, for that matter—published in this country during the last twenty or thirty years to find ample evidence of the American theorist's debt to these giants of twentieth-century musical thought. The history of Viennese harmonic theory is a chapter in the history of *our* thinking about music.

The present study is a critical survey of primary materials: Viennese treatises on harmony (and some unpublished materials) from the late eighteenth through early twentieth centuries. The study does not discuss all of the Viennese treatises on harmony from the nineteenth century, but rather concentrates on the dominant line of fundamental bass thinking which extends throughout the century to Schenker and Schoenberg. It traces the roots of Viennese harmonic theory of the first half of the nineteenth century to eighteenth-century figured bass theory, discusses the mixture of figured bass and Rameauian harmony that characterizes most Viennese theory in the first half of the nineteenth century (part I), and treats Sechter's revival of Rameau's *basse fondamentale* (which he received through Kirnberger's works) at mid-century (part II). This study makes a particularly important contribution in its discussion of Bruckner's reinterpretation of Sechter's system, as well as its examination of the revisions of the system by students of Sechter and Bruckner (part III). Finally, it discusses the early twentieth-century attempts to resolve the crisis in which the theory found itself at the hands of Bruckner (part IV). Aside from the study of primary materials, the work also brings together the results of a large number of recent German and Austrian studies of nineteenth-century harmonic theory, presenting these from the point of view of an American theorist. All translations in this work are mine unless otherwise noted. The original texts are given in the notes; italics are used to indicate varying forms of emphasis in the German texts.

Preface

Viennese Harmonic Theory from Albrechtsberger to Schenker and Schoenberg is a revised version of an earlier work, entitled "Fundamental Bass Theory in Nineteenth Century Vienna." I should like to thank my friend Professor Allen Forte for his invaluable assistance with technical aspects of the study, and for his constant encouragement during the darker hours which seem to be an inevitable part of such endeavors. Professors Jonathan Bernard, David Lewin, and Leon Plantinga of Yale deserve a special word of thanks for their comments and suggestions, many of which have been incorporated into this revised version. Professor Lewin's comments, in particular, often made me think that he knew far better than I did what I really wanted to say, or what I should have said. All of this advice has helped to produce a much better revised version than would have been possible otherwise, and for this I am deeply grateful.

I am also grateful to Professors Arnold Franchetti and Imanuel Willheim of the Hartt School of Music for first awakening my interest in this area of theory, and for introducing me to the Louis/Thuille *Harmonielehre* in particular.

Dr. Anton Porhansl and the staff of the Fulbright Commission in Vienna deserve special thanks for support of my research there. The staffs of the Austrian National Library, the Library of the *Gesellschaft der Musikfreunde* and the University of Vienna Library were most helpful; and the resources of these institutions proved to be vital to my research. In particular, I should like to thank Dr. Günter Brosche of the Austrian National Library for his help, and for permission to quote from unpublished materials in chapters 9 and 11. Thanks go to the New York Public Library for allowing me to quote from the Bruckner manuscript in chapter 9; and also to Professor Victor Fell Yellin for allowing me to use material from his paper on the "omnibus" and to Professor Mark DeVoto for lending me his copy of Yellin's paper.

But undoubtedly I owe the greatest debt to my wife, Barbara, to whom I should like to dedicate this work. Such a gesture is hardly fair compensation for the countless hours spent typing, proofreading, and discussing material contained herein (both in the original version and the revision). She deserves a special word of thanks for preparing both indexes, but most of all for enduring life with an author who was all too preoccupied with a project which often seemed interminable.

Introduction

The history of harmonic theory in the eighteenth century can be viewed as a struggle between figured bass theory and the revolutionary ideas of Rameau. Apparently, Rameau was the victor, for although his ideas met with resistance at first, they had gained considerable support by the end of the century. But in fact the victory was a regional one. For while Rameauian principles were to dominate the further course of German and French harmonic theory, the opposing forces survived, precariously to be sure, in nineteenth-century Vienna.

The history of harmonic theory in the nineteenth century seems at first to be a complex matter. Apparently, we cannot speak of a single theory—or even of two competing theories of harmony. Rather, there appear to be almost as many methodological approaches as there are theorists, and this phenomenon itself has proven to be an interesting line of inquiry.[1] Yet the student of eighteenth-century theory easily detects the ghosts of Rameau and the figured bass theorists lurking behind our nineteenth-century authors. Whether the old ideas are dressed up in the trappings of Hegelian dialectics or legitimized by "modern" empirical science, they are not all that unrecognizable. And thus, a continuation of the struggle between the nearly vanquished figured bass and Rameauian harmony may be seen in the nineteenth century as well, although the lines of battle are redrawn to the decided advantage of the latter.

Rameau's ideas were to play a significant role in German harmonic theory, which, as the nineteenth century drew on, moved further and further from the Viennese view. With Vogler and then Weber, German theory began its century-long preoccupation with chord quality, a concern which might be traced to Rameau's model of the cadence, but which at any rate held little interest for the Viennese theorists, whether they were figured bass theorists (before 1853) or fundamental bass theorists (after 1853). Indeed, Weber, Oettingen, and Riemann revised and "updated" the notation of chord quality at various points throughout the century. German theorists also began to pursue the further implications of Rameau's subdominant, a notion which proved to be most compatible with Hauptmann's dialectic logic. And the notion that minor was the inversion of major, likewise retraceable to Rameau, was given new life by Hauptmann, thereby initiating a development marked first by Oettingen's "dual" harmony-system of "tonicity" vs. "phonicity," and ultimately Hugo Riemann's reinterpretation of "dualism," his unfortunate affair with the undertone series, and his last, desperate effort to justify "dualism" through increasing frequency vs. increasing mass. Both the importance of the subdominant and the dual interpretation of minor were evidence of the main preoccupation of German harmonic theory—again probably given its strongest impetus through Hauptmann's dialectic: the preoccupation with symmetry and elegant logic, often at the expense of musical common sense. Obviously, the search for symmetries could never take as its point of departure something as asymmetric as the diatonic scale. Whether systems were naturally based, philosophically based—indeed, whatever basis they adopted—they all departed from the *Naturklang*. The notion that chords should be derived from the diatonic scale, with all the "inaccuracies" such a process implied, was a mere holdover from the antiquated figured bass, according to Riemann. And in its departure from the *Naturklang* the German theory sought "harmonic" explanations, denying melodic explanations of chords whenever possible. The theory culminated in Riemann's redefinition of "tonality," in which the number of harmonic "functions" was reduced to three, and all vertical sonorities were explained by *direct* reference to the tonal "center," never to local harmonic or melodic contexts. This development is ably described by Riemann in the third book of his *History of Music Theory*[2], a work which is hardly what its title purports it to be, but which nevertheless remains a valuable source from which we may learn the history of the German theory, at least according to Riemann.

In Vienna, on the other hand, a rather different system of harmony evolved. For reasons which are philosophical and sociological as well as musical, Viennese theorists became the trustees of the more conservative eighteenth-century harmonic theory. Here, the diatonic scale continued to reign supreme throughout the century. Despite the incursion of Vogler, the eighteenth-century figured bass treatise continued to flourish during the first half of the nineteenth century in Vienna. And when Rameauian doctrines finally took hold, they never really replaced the figured bass, but were used in conjunction with it. Simon Sechter, whose first works included a *Generalbaßschule*, eventually revived Rameau's *basse fondamentale*, using it essentially as Kirnberger had: as an *interpretive device* in the analysis of harmonic progression. Mitchell[3] has shown the sensitivity to context which was characteristic of figured bass theory; and Beach[4] has shown that this feature was preserved in Kirnberger's synthesis of Rameauian harmony and figured bass theory. Sechter's adaptation of Kirnberger's system, while somewhat mechanical to be sure, nevertheless preserved the notion that some "chords" were explainable by Rameau's theory of inversion, while others were more properly the product of *melodic displacement*. The correct explanation was dependent upon certain preferred harmonic progressions. Thus, unlike German theory, which was preoccupied with chord quality and direct relation of chords to a tonal center by harmonic processes, the Viennese theory was concerned primarily with the allowable progression of the fundamental bass, and the *interpretation* of chords in relation to local contexts of progression.

If Hauptmann and his heir apparent Riemann were to set the tone of German theory, it was Sechter who determined the direction of Viennese theory. Thus, there was no single, international movement towards functionalism, as some would have us believe. If the German theory was truly "progressive," it was the Viennese theory which maintained contact with eighteenth-century thinking and served to counterbalance the motion towards functionalism. Handed down through various interpreters (of whom Bruckner was certainly the most important), Sechter's fundamental bass theory eventually reached the twentieth century, where it influenced harmonic thinking significantly. Whether we speak of modifications of the *Funktionstheorie* which have continued to be important in Europe, or the systems of Schenker and Schoenberg which have had a profound impact in America, each owes a considerable debt to the nineteenth-century Viennese theory of harmony.

Part I

Figured Bass and Harmonic Theory in Vienna During the First Half of the Nineteenth Century

1

Eighteenth-Century Theory in Nineteenth-Century Vienna

The notion of "traditional harmony" which was to become one of the main staples of conservatory education (and which, until recently, continued to be passed on in a relatively uncritical manner) is largely a creation of the progressive theorists and pedagogues of Germany and France during the first half of the nineteenth century. Various forces, among which were the decline in figured bass practice and the demand for a system of harmony that would be teachable to the large classes in the newly established conservatories, conspired to produce a synthesis of Rameauian harmony with simplified figured bass and counterpoint that was appropriate to this new postrevolutionary era. By the end of the nineteenth century figured bass realization was almost completely forgotten in northern Germany, necessitating its historical revival.[1] This, however, was never the case in Vienna, where the style of eighteenth-century music (if not its aesthetic content) survived in nineteenth-century Viennese church music. Throughout the nineteenth century, Viennese music theory remained closely tied to eighteenth-century ideas, as did Viennese culture in general.

Almost all the theorists of the early nineteenth century—German, French and Viennese—considered the style of the Viennese Classic to constitute the basis of the musical language. Throughout the century examples from that repertory would continue to predominate in harmony books, despite changing musical style. But in contrast to France and Germany, where new ideas began to be applied to the music of the Viennese Classic, the eighteenth-century figured bass treatise continued to flourish in Vienna. In a sense, the history of early eighteenth-century harmonic theory was replayed in the first half of the nineteenth century in Vienna: theorists from Albrechtsberger to Sechter remained to a great extent true to figured bass theory; and Sechter ultimately reintroduced Rameau's fundamental bass. The Viennese theorists not only theorized about eighteenth-century music, they did it in an eighteenth-century manner as well.

Manfred Wagner sees the two primary reasons for the conservative nature of Viennese theory in the influence of the church and in what he considers to be the natural tendency towards conservatism of pedagogy.[2] While it could be argued that the latter is certainly variable depending upon other surrounding factors,[3] the Viennese musical life of the time must be deemed at least as influential as the other two. There was no new music, and hence no catalyst for a new music theory. The center of musical "progress" had moved elsewhere, leaving Vienna and the Viennese theorists to reminisce on its heyday, the Viennese Classic. For whatever reasons, the progressive tendencies so typical of the French and German worlds were anathema to the Viennese *Vormärz*. The new German opera, the invention of Weber, met with resistance in Vienna, and the theorists who propounded new ideas also had a difficult time. Weber's teacher, Abbé Vogler, decided to move to Vienna after some considerable success in Prague and the publication of his *Handbuch zur Harmonielehre*.[4] He worked in Vienna between 1803 and 1805, returning also in 1813; but he eventually found more agreeable working conditions elsewhere.[5] Weber described the Viennese reaction to Vogler as follows:

> One group gaped at him in amazement because it was unable to fathom his intellect; the other insulted him because it could not understand him, and saw itself being pushed away from the monopoly of the old "infallible" routine—counterpoint and figured bass—by a fresher view.[6]

The fate of the Czech Anton Reicha was similar. He worked in Vienna between 1802 and 1808, but later found his true home in the Paris Conservatory.

The influence of the church, however, was undoubtedly important. The tradition of Catholic sacred music that had produced Vienna's most important theorist of the early eighteenth century, Johann Joseph Fux, continued unbroken throughout the nineteenth century. With hardly an exception, the Viennese theorists and theory pedagogues were, like Fux, organists and church musicians. This was true of independent private instruction, as well as theory instruction in the Conservatory—the present day *Hochschule für Musik und darstellende Kunst*. This institution engagaged its first theory instructor, Gottfried Salzmann, in 1820,[7] and continued throughout the century to fill this position with church musicians, of whom Anton Bruckner is probably the best-known example. In a manner similar to Fux, who attempted to preserve an earlier style, the early nineteenth-century Viennese theorists attempted to preserve the late eighteenth-century style. But unlike Fux, whose description of *reiner Satz* had a demonstrable effect on the later composers of the Viennese Classic and could easily be interpreted as a *theory* of pure counterpoint—the sources of its appeal to today's theorists—the early nineteenth-century theorists had only slight or problematic influences upon composers of their period or of a later period.

Thomson discusses the contemporary relationship between the Viennese theorists and composers of the early nineteenth century in considerable detail. His conclusions, like Manfred Wagner's, are largely negative. In both cases, the negative conclusions often result from viewing historical development in terms of "progress" and "reaction." Given the significance of this kind of thinking during the period under study, the terms are unavoidable. But they can be dangerous. With Thomson, in particular, they often take on an almost ethical tone, as when he says:

> Every attempt to interpret chordal material functionally must be designated as forward-looking (*zukunftsträchtig*), while the static chord explanation must be labeled Baroque.[8]

Although the preservation of eighteenth-century harmonic theory in nineteenth-century Vienna was not all bad—indeed, it ultimately served as a catalyst for some very interesting thinking at the beginning of the twentieth century—it is undeniable that Thomson's description of the contemporary relationship of theorists and composers is disconcerting. During the 1820s and 1830s in Vienna, what Thomson calls the *Naturalistenstreit* began to flare up. It became fashionable for the members of the *Hofkapelle*—among whom were Sechter and his student Preyer[9]—to designate as "naturalists" those composers who "followed their gift of genius, more than the strict theory of pure composition."[10] The "orthodox," on the other hand, would continually point to the neglect of practice in counterpoint—the approximately 5000 fugues of Sechter's *musikalisches Tagebuch* are indicative of the meaning of "practice" here—as a technical weakness. It may have been partially for this reason that Schubert contemplated study with Sechter, although he expressed fear to Preyer that "Sechter would infect him with the leathery quality of his compositions."[11] A growing interest in the works of Handel has also been advanced as a reason for Schubert's desire to study with Sechter.[12] For whatever reason, the agreement was made that the study would be based upon Marpurg's *Abhandlung von der Fuge* (which Sechter had recently edited).[13] One lesson actually took place on November 4, 1828. Alfred Mann has demonstrated that the subject of that lesson was the composition of the tonal answer, a problem which had vexed Schubert for some time.[14] Schubert was unable to attend the next lesson, scheduled for the next week, because of the illness from which he eventually died on November 19th.

Before 1840, the conservative theorists had considerable influence on Viennese musical life, according to Thomson. But, as a result of unsuccessful attempts to establish careers as composers, their influence began to diminish. Critical reaction to a concert of the works of Gottfried Salzmann on April 21, 1839 resulted in the abrupt termination of his position at the Conservatory. Reaction to the compositions of Joachim Hoffman, a member of the conservative circle and writer of a harmony book to be discussed later, was only slightly more positive: "his compositions support the good old school, in which correct compositions and faultless technique were the primary requisites."[15] Simon Sechter's one attempt to compose a comic opera, *Ali Hitsch-Hatsch*, which was premiered in 1844, was also a critical disaster.[16] The church musicians' attempts to move into the secular areas of opera and chamber music proved to be a serious mistake: neither the theorists, nor the theory, were up to the task.

The Received Figured Bass Theory

A good way to get some idea of the prevalent Viennese view of figured bass at the beginning of the nineteenth century is to examine the work of Vienna's most famous theorist of the latter half of the eighteenth century, Johann Georg Albrechtsberger (1736–1809). Both Albrechtsberger's doctrine of figured bass and his role as a pedagogue and church musician were to be paradigmatic for the early nineteenth-century Viennese theorists.

Albrechtsberger's pedagogy of counterpoint and composition was published as the *gründliche Anweisung zur Composition* (Leipzig: Breitkopf, 1790), part of which has appeared recently in English.[17] Less well-known to the modern reader, however, is his approach to figured bass, which, at the beginning of the nineteenth century, was available in at least two sources: the *Kurzgefasste Methode den Generalbass zu erlernen*, and the *Generalbassschule*.[18] Shortly after Albrechtsberger's death, the *Anweisung* appeared in a new edition together with an essay purporting to describe the master's method of figured bass instruction. This collection, edited by Albrechtsberger's student Ignaz Ritter von Seyfried and known as *J.G. Albrechtsberger's sämtliche Schriften über Generalbass, Harmonielehre, und Tonsetzkunst* (Wien: Anton Strauß, n.d.), extended Albrechtsberger's authority into the mid-nineteenth century, for it appeared in a second Viennese edition (Haslinger, 1837) and two subsequent English translations.[19] The essay on figured bass and harmony (vol.1), however, was actually written by Seyfried, who evidently felt that the two figured bass manuals were insufficient as descriptions of Albrechtsberger's method. In the preface to the second edition, he complains that "the first volume, a thorough-bass school, had to be compiled to a large extent, as only a very small portion of the necessary materials existed."[20]

For our study of the earlier sources, a description of the *Kurzgefasste Methode* will suffice, since the *Generalbassschule* follows it in both content and order of presentation. The only difference is that the latter work offers a greater number of examples and less text, and thus looks even more like the typical Viennese figured bass/harmony book of the early nineteenth century. After examining the *Kurzgefasste Methode* we shall see how Seyfried's essay compares with it.

In the *Kurzgefasste Methode* Albrechtsberger begins by discussing intervals up to the tenth in section one.[21] In the second section he defines the consonant intervals (the unison, major and minor third, perfect fifth, major and minor sixth, octave, and major and minor tenth), and the dissonances—the remaining intervals, and even some of the consonant intervals, if they occur in combination with certain other intervals (for example the fifth when it occurs with a sixth, and the octave when it occurs with a ninth). Also in this section he goes on to combine consonant intervals: three consonant intervals over a *Grundton*[22] produce the "perfect" or "imperfect" chord (*vollkommener o. unvollkommener Acord*), the latter a six-three while the former is a five-three. Albrechtsberger notes here that the six-five is always a dissonant chord (*DisonanzAcord*), and goes on to give further examples of dissonant chords, saying that such chords result when from one to three dissonant intervals are found in a four-voice chord (pp. 2f).

There are only two "perfect" chords: the major and minor triads. But the "imperfect" chords may be formed in three ways: (1) m3+m6+P8, (2) m3+M6+P8, and (3) M3+M6+P8 (p. 4). (The combination of M3+m6+P8, however, belongs to the category of "dissonant" chords.) Albrechtsberger is equivocal with regard to the six-four chord, saying that "some teachers" consider the fourth to be consonant when accompanied by the sixth, and dissonant when accompanied by the fifth (p. 5). Apparently he does not favor this interpretation, since he never speaks of dissonant intervals which can become consonant in combination (cf., six-five, above).

In section three of the work (p. 5) Albrechtsberger begins to deal with doubling in certain problematic three-note sonorities. He says, for example, that in a $^5_2$, the fifth or the second must be doubled. Shortly thereafter he speaks of the augmented sixth, saying that "to the augmented sixth belongs the doubled major third, or only one major third and the tritone ... ,"[23] noting also that the major third and perfect fifth might accompany the augmented sixth, but that such a combination often causes fifths upon resolution (p.10). To the modern reader, the way in which he moves between such apparently unrelated topics as bass-suspension chords and chromatic chords seems peculiar; but of course both are "dissonant" chords, and the issue is merely which intervals are appropriate for accompanying dissonant intervals.

Section four gives more information on doubling and also introduces the first of the "rule of the octave" exercises for keyboard practice (pp. 10ff). The examples illustrate the use of both five-three and six-three chords; later examples illustrate the five to six linear motion in ascent and the seven to six suspension in descent (p. 12). These also serve as an introduction to the second part of the book: "Examples of All Intervals" (*Beispiele über alle Intervallen*) (pp. 17ff). In this part Albrechtsberger includes such sequential exercises as the cycle of fifths, and a sequence of alternating rising fourths and descending thirds (I, IV, II, V, III, VI, etc.)—both of which will later become favorites of Sechter. The book closes with a mention of "ninth chords," all of which are 9-8 suspensions or double-suspension combinations (p. 34).

Obviously, *the Kurzgefasste Methode* is exactly what its title promises: a brief, practical method for learning to play figured basses at the keyboard. Thus it is hardly surprising that there is not a trace of any speculative harmonic theory. Clearly designed as an introductory work, it never gets to the point of discussing more advanced practical topics, such as the organ point, principles of accompaniment, or playing from an unfigured bass. But perhaps the most striking thing about both the *Kurzgefasste Methode* and the *Generalbassschule* is the complete lack of any Rameauian theory whatsoever. After all, by the end of the eighteenth century Rameau's chord categories, or derivatives thereof, had made their way into many practical figured bass manuals. But in Albrechtsberger's work there is no mention of the theory of inversion or the fundamental bass and no preference for stacks of thirds over other interval combinations. Even five-three and six-three chords are not related through inversion theory, but described just as they were in Fuxian counterpoint. Indeed, all chord categories are developed through interval classification and combination, not through inversion theory.

Seyfried begins his essay by discussing intervals just as Albrechtsberger had. And like Albrechtsberger, he combines them to produce the "perfect" chord (the five-three) and the "imperfect" chord (the six-three).[24] He then goes on to say that any chord containing one or more dissonant intervals must be placed in the class of dissonant chords (p. 12). As in Albrechtsberger's discussion, the statement serves equally well in classifying such disparate sonorities as the six-five and the augmented triad. But at this point in the discussion we read the following non sequitur:

> There are in music five principal kinds of chords, viz.:—1st, common chords; 2nd, chords of the seventh; 3rd, chords of the ninth; 4th, chords of the eleventh; and 5th, chords of the thirteenth. (p. 12)

After a digression on keys, Seyfried returns to the "common chord," saying that it is "capable of two inversions," the second of which illustrates the "consonant fourth." Seyfried goes on to say that there are four "common chords" (major, minor, augmented, and diminished), and that the first two are consonant while the latter two are dissonant (pp. 12f). Apparently, he is unaware that the first inversion of the "consonant common chord" duplicates exactly his earlier notion of the "imperfect" chord.

After discussing positions of the soprano, Seyfried turns to the inversions of the seventh chords, and then to the ninth, eleventh, and thirteenth chords. Following Marpurg's practice, Seyfried derives each by the addition of a third, fifth, and seventh, respectively, below a seventh chord (pp.14f). The figures eleven and thirteen are used in examples which illustrate, but they are not to be found in the later keyboard exercises.

After this discussion, the essay once again looks like a figured bass manual. Seyfried treats more difficult chromatic figures, and then goes on to present simple cadence patterns (pp. 22f), rules of the octave exercises (pp. 27f), and the two sequential patterns Albrechtsberger had stressed (pp. 24f). Towards the end of the work he also discusses modulation, defining the "five simple modulations to relative keys" (p. 58). (In C major, the "relative keys" are G major, E minor, A minor, D minor, and F major; in A minor they are C major, E minor, G major, D minor, and F major.) The limitation of modulation to degrees of the diatonic scale would be typical of most of the Viennese theorists down to, and including, Sechter.

Whether Seyfried's invocation of Rameauian theory accurately reflects Albrechtsberger's views is probably impossible to discover with certainty, although evidence certainly speaks against it. Aside from the obvious discrepancy with Albrechtsberger's works, Seyfried's editorial excesses further undermine the credibility of his discussion. There are problems in his edition of his fellow student Preindl's book (see chapter 3), and the discussion of ninth, eleventh, and thirteenth chords in Seyfried's *Beethoven's Studien*, which might be called upon in support of Seyfried, does not come from Beethoven's study with Albrechtsberger, but rather is an inaccurately rendered quote from Türk through Beethoven.[25] Thus there is no evidence to suggest that Rameauian theory played a part of Albrechtsberger's curriculum of figured bass study.[26]

But regardless of whether it did, the contents of both Albrechtsberger's works and Seyfried's essay are typical of the sorts of books produced by the Viennese theorists in the first half of the nineteenth century. Even the uncomfortable relationship between Rameauian theory and the traditional figured bass view in Seyfried's essay would characterize the work of the Viennese theorists. We need only add to this mixture the incipient "romantic harmony" which Vogler imported to Vienna, and the ingredients are ready for the potpourris served up in the Viennese treatises of the first half of the nineteenth century.

2

Foreign Influences on Viennese Harmonic Theory

Many of the important German *Harmonielehren* of the late eighteenth and early nineteenth centuries were available in Vienna. The bibliography which Thomson assembled for his study comprises around eighty works by thirty-two authors (Austrian and foreign), and slightly oversteps the time period 1800-1850 on both ends.[1] A shorter bibliography—sufficient for all but the most specialized purposes—is presented by Wagner.[2] Tittel's article[3] gives a few additional sources which, although not printed in Vienna, were available in the S.A. Steiner *Verlagskatalogen*. The following list of German works is taken from these sources.

> Daube, Johann Friedrich. *Anleitung zum Selbstunterricht in der musicalischen Composition.* Wien: Schaumburg, 1797. *Zweiter Teil.* Wien: Tauvelt/ J. Funk, 1798.
> Kirnberger, Johann Philipp. *Die Wahren Grundsätze zum Gebrauche der Harmonie.* Wien: chem. Drukerey, 1793. Actually written by J.A.P. Schulz.
> _____. *Grundsätze des Generalbasses.* Wien: Musikalisch-typographische Gesellschaft, n.d., probably 1793.
> _____. *Die Kunst des Reinen Satzes in der Musik.* 2 vol. Wien: Musikalisch-typographische Gesellschaft, 1793.
> _____. *Gedanken über die verschiedenen Lehrarten in der Composition.* Wien: 1793.
> Knecht, Justin Heinrich. *Allgemeiner Katechismus. Oder kurzer Inbegriff der allgemeinen Musiklehre.* Wien: Haslinger, n.d. *Neueste, verbesserte und vermehrte Ausgabe.* Wien: Steiner & Co., 1822.
> _____. *Theoretisch, praktische Generalbassschule,* 2nd. edition. Bozen: 1838.
> Tuerk, Daniel Gottlob. *Anweisung zum Generalbassspielen.* Wien: Typo.-Musikalische Ges., 1807. *Neue verbesserte Ausgabe.* Wien: Steiner & Co., 1822. Also, Wien: Haslinger, 1828.
> Weber, Gottfried. *Versuch einer geordneten Theorie der Tonsetzkunst.* Mainz: 1817-24.

It is perhaps debatable whether the Daube *Anleitung* should be considered foreign or Viennese. Daube lived in Vienna after 1770, and this late work, thoroughly in the Viennese tradition,[4] no longer shows the radical traits of the *Generalbass in drey Accorden* (Leipzig: 1756).

French sources appear to have been more limited. Thomson mentions the *Traité d'Harmonie* by Charles Simon Catel (Paris: 1802); several works by

Anton Reicha were published in Vienna by Diabelli. The Reicha works dealing with harmony are the *Vollständiges Lehrbuch der Harmonielehre, des Generalbasses, der Melodie* (Wien: Diabelli, 1833), and the *Vollständiges Lehrbuch der Komposition* (Wien: Diabelli, 1834); the latter is a translation of Reicha's *Cours de Composition* by Carl Czerny. Although not listed in the bibliographies cited, the Reicha *Kunst der dramatischen Composition* (Wien: Diabelli, n.d.; listed by Austrian National Library as ca. 1830) was also available. This six-volume work is also a Czerny translation, beautifully engraved with facing German and French text.

Presumably, the additional sources which Sechter cites (see chapter 8) were also generally available. If so, it would appear that most of the important works on harmony were obtainable. Curiously, very little of the influence of these works is detectable in the domestic product.

Abbé Georg Joseph Vogler (1749-1814)

The most important foreign influence was a German theorist who actually lived and worked in Vienna: Abbé Vogler. Controversy followed Vogler wherever he went; but it must have been at its height in Vienna, where Vogler's cosmopolitan and progressive ideas could only have been met by the most violent resistance from the provincial and conservative Viennese theorists. But despite this controversy, and the brevity of Vogler's stay in Vienna, his influence is unmistakable in a number of Viennese harmony books from the first half of the century.

While the eighteenth-century thoroughbass remained the heart of the usual Viennese system of harmony, Vogler treated the subject in a brief appendix to his *Handbuch*. Here, he assures the reader that "a completely incorrect idea of figured bass is created when it is passed off as some special science, for it is only a practical branch of the theory of harmony."[5] The bulk of Vogler's *Handbuch* deals rather with the practical application of the rationalistic, neo-Rameauian theory which he had developed earlier in *Tonwissenschaft und Tonsezkunst* (Mannheim: 1776).

The core of Vogler's theory of harmony is his notion of *Redukzion:* the process by which a musical texture is reduced to "fundamental" chords *(Stammakkorde).*[6] Unlike many of the followers of Rameau, Vogler reserves the role of "fundamental" chord for the triad, rejecting the seventh chord: "There is only one harmony: the triad. The essential fourth tone [the seventh] is already a dissonance."[7] Of course, the question which then arises is: can any triad be a "fundamental" chord? The answer is quite clear in *Choral-System:*

> ...in *Redukzion,* which breaks down all of the various forms to their fundamental chords,...one must not limit oneself to the most complete harmony (Rameau's *accord parfait),* but rather always return to all harmonies (diminished or augmented intervals may result thereby)...[8]

In fact, the passage just quoted is taken from a lengthy criticism of Rameau and Kirnberger, who are accused of not being true to their "basic principles."[9] Here, Vogler first rejects Rameau's "added sixth" chord, and then Kirnberger's interpretive use of the fundamental bass. Thus, the "basic principles" are really one: the theory of harmonic inversion.

If post-Rameauian systems of harmony are seen in light of ideas stated recently by Carl Dahlhaus (see *New Grove*), they may be divided into those which are primarily concerned with "chord identity," as opposed to those which are further developments of Rameau's *basse fundamentale,* and are thus more concerned with chord progression. By rejecting the fundamental bass and the "added sixth" (in Rameau, the "added sixth" and the later theory of the *double emploi* are a direct result of the rules of fundamental bass progression), Vogler places his system squarely in the "chord identity" camp. Vogler's major "theoretical" achievement—his invention of Roman numeral chord notation[10]—was obviously an important contribution to "chord identity" theorizing. But in rejecting the fundamental bass, Vogler rejected an important means by which to describe local chord-to-chord connections, as well as one of the more contextually sensitive devices in Rameauian theory.[11] Vogler's system was indeed the "wave of the future," as Thomson would undoubtedly say. It was also another step in the direction of the a priori functional thinking that would culminate in Riemann.

If *Redukzion* is essentially the theory of harmonic inversion and the "fundamental" chord is the triad, what of the tones which result from *Redukzion* but do not fit into triads? Such tones are dissonances, which Vogler derives by harmonic means, describing them as the "seventh, ninth, eleventh, and thirteenth."[12] Although the dissonances are described harmonically, Vogler does not speak of them as forming a "chord." Indeed, his rules for the *treatment* of dissonance are quite similar to Kirnberger's: dissonances must be prepared and resolved down by step (thus they are *treated* as suspensions— Kirnberger's "nonessential" dissonances). The exceptions to this are the diminished seventh (which is obviously independent for Vogler), and what he calls the *Unterhaltungs-Siebente*—i.e., the seventh of the dominant seventh chord (Kirnberger's "essential" dissonance), both of which may enter unprepared.[13] Because of this and other reasons, Thomson places Vogler in the Kirnberger camp.[14] In fact, the use of Marpurg's harmonic classification of dissonance together with Kirnberger's melodic rules for its treatment will recur throughout the nineteenth century with Sechter and his followers.

More than likely, it was the work of Vogler's student, Justin Heinrich Knecht, which caused Riemann to accuse Vogler and Knecht of being those responsible for the development of "the schematism of stacked thirds ... to the most absurd consequence."[15] Unfortunately, the statement is a useless oversimplification; nevertheless, it echoes throughout the secondary literature, as we shall see.[16]

The controversy which surrounded Vogler during his lifetime has continued in the attempts to assess his work. Opinions range from Riemann's one-sentence dismissal of his work to the recent resuscitation of Vogler as a forerunner of Schenker. In between he was further criticized for the "improvements" he made in some of Bach's chorale harmonizations,[17] while more recently, he has been seen as a source of what later came to be known as "Romantic Harmony."[18] Indeed, his ideas in this area were both original and extremely influential, as a brief review of them will demonstrate.

After the standard Rameauian derivation of the scale from the triad, Vogler describes his notion of "cadences" *(Schlussfälle)*, again not unlike Rameau:

> The three triads, which are indispensable to the creation of the two scales, embody the original *cadences;* the rules for progression are derived from this cadential quality [*Schlussfallmässigkeit*].[19]

The idea that "progression" is a concatenation of cadences is a typical Rameauian trait. But the notion of cadence, as Vogler understands it, is tied specifically to the dominant to tonic relationship and the resolution of the leading tone:

> A harmony becomes capable of producing a cadence through the major third; without it the harmony will never be decisive, and always remain noncadential.[20]

This means that the "cadence" will not be extended by tonal transposition through the diatonic scale (as it will be later in Sechter); it also means that Vogler's ten allowable "cadences" *all* involve leading tone motion.[21]

The importance of the leading tone in the cadence naturally brings up a discussion of the leading tone itself. While others speak of one leading tone (or, in the case of Rameau, two), Vogler is convinced that there are nine. Like many of the Abbé's extravagant claims, this one also turns out to be a disappointment: the "nine leading tones" are different harmonic settings of two (scale degrees 7 and sharp 4).[22] While not the most successful of Vogler's ideas, it is additional evidence of the nondiatonic character of his system.

The primary means by which Vogler's two-chord cadential model may be extended is what he calls "plurisignificance" *(Mehrdeutigkeit).*[23] To Vogler, "progression" *(Tonfolge)* is a succession of cadences generated by the change of harmonic meaning of one of the two chords. Kreitz believes that Vogler was the first to use this term, which became increasingly popular during the course of the nineteenth century.[24]

Vogler introduces "plurisignificance" through a discussion of the change of meaning of intervals *(Tonverbindungen).* In the chapter on "plurisignificance" he derives the diminished seventh chord, the augmented triad and diminished third/augmented sixth chords from the minor mode and discusses their enharmonic possibilities.[25] His two "species" *(Gattungen)* of this technique clearly reveal his priorities: the *first* of these (and the one which receives the most extended treatment) is the change of harmonic meaning through enharmonic re-spelling; the second is what is generally thought of as diatonic modulation by pivot chord (Vogler's Roman numeral notation is particularly useful here).[26]

If Vogler's concept of "progression" begins to sound like Kurth's notion of "romantic harmony," his definition of what he calls "tonal direction," despite its presumptions of eighteenth-century (or indeed seventeenth-century) "mechanical" aesthetics, only makes the resemblance more apparent:

> *Tonal direction* is the result of an impression, effected gradually through harmony, which the theory of cadences and plurisignificance [makes] upon the ear. Tonal direction gives information about the succession of harmonies, and how the sentiment [*Gefühl*] is excited thereby; that is to say, at times surprised, and at other times disappointed. A not-unclear idea of the musical role of colors comes about in this manner.[27]

"Plurisignificance" also leads to a discussion of the possibilities of modulation *(Ausweichung)*. According to the usual Viennese notion of harmony, modulation is limited to the diatonic *Verwandtschaft*; Vogler, however, has a different opinion:

> There are twelve tones in the chromatic scale [and] I can modulate from each tone to each other one; eleven modulations originate in this manner. From C major, for example, I can go to eleven major and eleven minor keys, and again from C minor, to eleven major and eleven minor keys. Since I cannot call the change from C major to C minor a modulation, this leaves four times eleven, or forty-four modulations.[28]

While most of the Viennese refused to recognize the chromatic scale as a separate entity, Vogler clearly saw it as a kind of master scale containing all tonalities. This point of view is nowhere more apparent than at the end of the *Handbuch* where he gives 132 examples of such modulations as C major to C♯ major; all are one measure long.

Further evidence of Vogler's recognition of the chromatic scale occurs in the brief section on figured bass in the *Handbuch*. Here, he presents some typical *regola dell'ottava* exercises for practice; but along with harmonizations of the major and minor scales, he also gives his harmonization of the *chromatic scale*.

Example 2-1 shows this progression as it appeared in the *Handbuch* (pp. 133f. and table XII); example 2-2 ("Drei Harmonien mit der verminderten Siebente") shows it as it first appeared in his *Kuhrpfälzische Tonschule*

(Mannheim: 1778)—in this case, moving through all three diminished seventh chords.

Example 2-1

The "Omnibus"

A modified version of this progression has recently been called the "omnibus" by Victor Fell Yellin.[29] Yellin, who cites examples of it from musical sources as disparate as Mozart and Scott Joplin, considers the "classical omnibus" to be a succession of five chords, beginning with a root-position dominant seventh and ending with the same chord in six-five inversion. The intervening chords are the product of strict voice leading: two tones are held, while the remaining two proceed by half step in contrary motion (see ex. 2-3).[30]

Example 2-3

Example 2-2

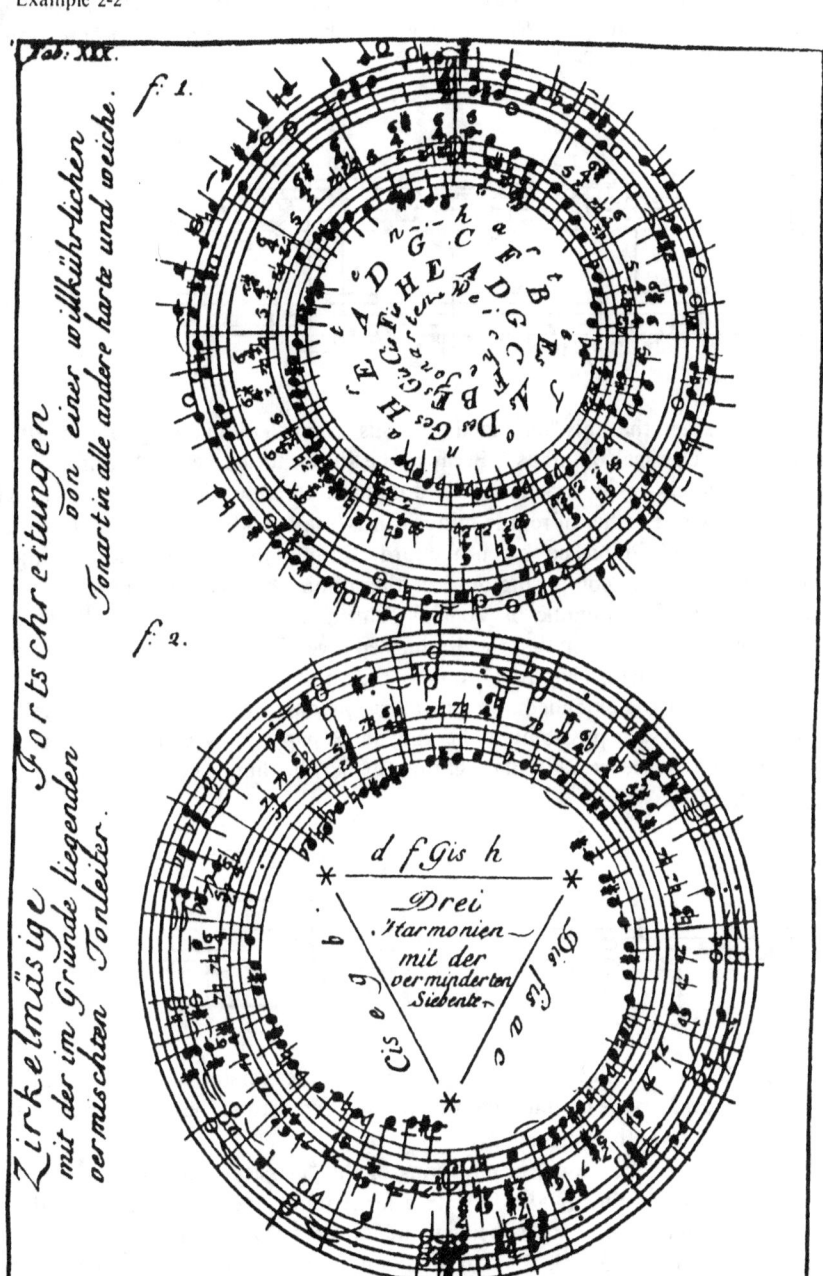

Yellin notes further that if another minor third/major sixth is held, the fourth chord may become the first of a new "omnibus," extending the progression indefinitely (see ex. 2-4).

Example 2-4

It may be seen that this "extended omnibus" is much more ambiguous tonally than the "classical omnibus." Because the fifth chord of each "omnibus" is elided (the chords in brackets), the dominant seventh voice exchange is no longer heard. Furthermore, the minor thirds/major sixths are all components of the same diminished seventh chord, leading the ear to interpret the progression as a "composing-out" of this diminished seventh chord. If we compare the first module of Vogler's "chromatic scale" with the "classical omnibus," it can be seen that the diminished seventh chord subdivision is even more apparent here. The fifth chromatic tone of the upper voice line is already suppressed in the extended version; by suppressing the second tone as well, Vogler removes the possibility of hearing an exchange between the second and fourth chords (see ex. 2-5), highlighting further the diminished seventh chord (see ex. 2-6).

Example 2-5   Example 2-6

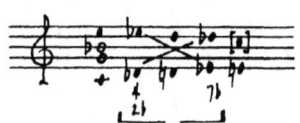   

(Vogler's visual display and description of the earlier version of the "chromatic scale" [ex. 2-2] made it quite clear that he also understood the progression as a diminished seventh chord cycle.)

Given the clear tonal implications of the "classical omnibus," it is not surprising that Yellin is able to cite a large number of examples from the musical literature, the earliest being from Mozart's *Don Giovanni* (1787).[31] (It is certainly not impossible that earlier examples may be found.) Yellin proves clearly that the progression was recognized by the Viennese Classic composers; eventually, it would achieve recognition by the Viennese theorists as well.

Foreign Influences on Viennese Harmony   19

Although it is not cited by the early nineteenth-century theorists, Sechter would later be able to incorporate it into his fundamental bass system (see chapter 7).

But the extended "omnibus" in which the bass is a statement of the complete chromatic scale is another matter. This is certainly not easy to find in the music of the early nineteenth century. On the other hand, it was well known to both the conservative and progressive factions of Viennese theorists. In all cases it was taken from Vogler, who may very well be its inventor. The earliest mention of the progression by a theorist which Yellin cites is in Bonifazio Asioli's *L'Allievo al clavicembalo* (Milan: 1819). His example is in fact a "preludized" version of Vogler's exact progression;[32] Asioli may well have appropriated the progression from the Abbé (who had studied and worked in Italy) just as the Viennese theorists did.

Many examples of the "classical omnibus" may be found in the works of Franz Schubert. The earliest example is in the third movement of the piano sonata, D. 664 (1819). Yellin suggests that Schubert may have gotten the "omnibus" from Beethoven's *Diabelli Variations*[33] (which, however, were published in 1823). Regardless of the origin of Schubert's use of the "classical omnibus," the appearance of the "omnibus" in "Der Wegweiser" (*Die Winterreise,* no. 20) certainly seems to show the Vogler influence (the fact that most of the other Viennese theorists of the time also cite the progression makes it even more likely that Schubert learned of the progression through the theorists).

In "Der Wegweiser" the "omnibus" serves as the ideal harmonic setting for the "road of no return" (see mm. 57ff). Schubert manages to put this apparently atonal progression to tonal use by interpreting it as a "composing-out" of a VII°7/V in G minor (see ex. 2-7). If the harmonic synopsis presented in example 2-7 is compared with the version in Vogler's *Handbuch* (ex. 2-1), the similarity is striking—but the subtlety of Schubert's version is also immediately apparent: while the first composed-out third in the bass lasts four measures (mm. 57-60), the ascending voice arpeggiation to B♭ (and crescendo dynamic) is accompanied by an acceleration in harmonic rhythm. Thus, through subtleties of tonal meaning and rhythm a mechanical figured bass exercise is transformed into a powerful compositional device.

Example 2-7

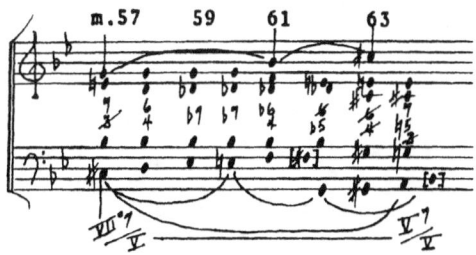

3

The Viennese Treatises of the First Half of the Nineteenth Century

Emanuel Aloys Förster (1748-1823)

Förster, whose *Anleitung zum Generalbass* (Wien: A. Steiner, 1805) went through five editions by 1858, was clearly one of the most widely read and influential theorists. He was also a notable exception to the rule, being neither organist nor church musician. A friend of Beethoven's, Förster propounded the traditional view of the figured bass theorist, and seems to have been a confirmed anti-Rameauian. Speaking of the origin of suspension chords, he writes to his publisher:

> Today I am sending you in advance a list of suspensions with the necessary preparation[s]. Moreover, I am of the opinion that these chords originate in the creative imagination of the composer in this manner—*not* through all possible inversions of the Rameauian system.... I am convinced that none of the great composers thought of Rameau's system.[1]

This opinion, so reminiscent of C.P.E. Bach's famous letter to Kirnberger, is an indication of Förster's theoretical stance as well as the direct style of writing of the *Anleitung*. Förster's system is diatonic in the most conservative sense. This often results in thinly veiled attacks on Vogler's efforts to concentrate on chromatic and enharmonic techniques:

> ...in present-day music there is neither a *chromatic* nor an *enharmonic* scale, although [there are] certainly individual [cases] of non-essentially [*zufällig*] raised or lowered tones which can be called *chromatic*....[2]

The diatonic major and minor scales thus form the basis of the system. In typical eighteenth-century manner, the related keys *(Verwandtschaft)* are the scale degrees of the initial scales: in the case of C major, they are A minor, G major, E minor, F major, and D minor; in A minor they are C, G, and F major, and E and D minor. Like most of the Viennese theorists, Förster only grudgingly admits the existence of the parallel major-minor relationship:

> The scales of the same name, such as C major and C minor ... also have a certain relationship between them, as may often be found in composition.[3]

Although acknowledged, this relationship plays no further role in Förster's system.

The discussion of minor brings up a paradox: the natural minor scale, which was used to generate the *Verwandtschaft*, is not the model scale for the minor mode. Förster introduces an example in minor without the leading tone, which he finds most unsatisfying.[4] He goes on to conclude that the seventh of every minor scale must therefore be raised; since he considers this leading tone to be essential *(wesentlich)* to the scale, he refuses to call it chromatic. Clearly in reaction to Vogler's theory of nine leading tones, Förster maintains that there is only one, and that it is always diatonic:

> I repeat that according to the ideas presented here only the seventh step of every scale is the *leading tone;* the remaining non-essentially [*zufällig*] raised tones are merely chromatic tones which do not alter the scale. The G♯ in A minor or the D♯ in E minor, etc., is diatonic—that is, essential [*wesentlich*] to the scale.[5]

Förster accepts the customary two "fundamental" chords *(Stammaccorde)*: the triad and the seventh chord. The $^6_3$ and the $^6_4$ chords are derived through the theory of inversion, and both are said to be consonant. Although derived by the theory of inversion, the use of the $^6_4$ is clearly described in figured bass terms: it may occur over scale degrees five or one, followed by a $^5_3$ over the same degree. The obligatory diatonic triads make an appearance in the text, but Förster makes no real use of them. Probably because of his view of minor, Förster accepts the augmented triad (as III in minor), thus making four qualities of triads. Other possible triads are of no interest to him:

> I shall pass over all remaining triads—which are merely considered as such because they can be constructed from thirds, fifths, and octaves—since they are of no use.[6]

The only exception is the diminished triad with lowered third, which Förster sees as the origin of the augmented sixth chord (though he notes that it is useless as a triad).[7]

One of the most personal features of Förster's system is his organization of seventh chords, the four classes of which are: (1.) "characteristic chords": the dominant sevenths; (2.) "enharmonic chords": the diminished sevenths. Förster regards their proper place as scale degree seven in minor; he also discusses their enharmonic use. The diatonic seventh chords are also placed in category two. Like the scale degree triads, they serve no further use; (3.) "amphibolous chords" *(zweideutige Accorde)*: according to Förster, these chords differ from the "enharmonic chords" because they are equally at home in minor or in major. The only one discussed is VII7 in major which may be II7 in minor; (4.) "all remaining seventh chords, which deserve no further attention."[8]

The list of possible chords derivable by stacking thirds ends with the seventh chord. All other chords, including the ninth chord, are derived by stepwise displacement of triads or seventh chords and are discussed in his fourth chapter, "Of the Remaining Chords."[9]

The general idea of Förster's definition of chromaticism—that all chromatic structures reduce to diatonic ones—is implicit in most of the Viennese systems of harmony:

> Thus, every note is *chromatic* which, on account of its nonessential alteration, does not belong to the scale, and for which a diatonic note may be substituted.[10]

But Förster's insistence that the leading tone is always diatonic leads to further confusion here: whenever an alteration is interpreted as the leading tone of a related key it is *not* chromatic. Thus, in Förster's system, the notions of diatonic modulation and chromatic tonicization are not distinguished from one another. This leads him to propose two harmonizations for the chromatic fragment (ex. 3-1): the first is diatonic (ex. 3-2), while the second is chromatic (ex. 3-3).[11]

Example 3-1

Example 3-2

Example 3-3

Example 3-4

24 Viennese Treatises Before Sechter

Example 3-3 is said to be chromatic because it is replaceable by example 3-4. Of course, it might be asked if a version of 3-2 with accidentals removed might serve to replace 3-2. This difficulty is later avoided by Sechter, who would consider both harmonizations of the chromatic fragment to be "chromatic."

The previous examples also illustrate Förster's analytical notation, which he seems to have invented. The notation marks an interesting transitional phase between figured bass thinking and Rameauian harmony. Although Förster derives $^6_3$ and $^6_4$ triads by the theory of inversion, this theory is not used in analysis—it is simply a device for chord classification. The Arabic numerals indicating scale degrees under the bass line do not change due to the influence of a theoretical chord root; the conventional harmony book I6 chord receives a 3 under the bass note.

In the matter of modulation, Förster is far more perceptive than his primitive notation might indicate. After defining the Neapolitan sixth as a $^6_3$ chord on the fourth degree of the scale in minor in which the sixth is "nonessentially" lowered, he presents example 3-5 to show its more extended use.[12]

Example 3-5

Förster continues in the manner of the typical eighteenth-century figured bass manual by introducing *regola dell'ottava* exercises. However, one of these turns out to be Vogler's chromatic scale harmonization, which Förster calls the "Devil's Mill" (ex. 3-6):

Example 3-6

Förster, who introduces the progression in order to illustrate the enharmonic use of diminished seventh chords, credits the Abbé with it, saying, however, that:

> In his *Handbuch zur Harmonielehre*, etc., Herr Abbé Vogler calls this passage the chromatic scale; I, however, cannot conceive of it as a scale.[13]

Förster's version corresponds to the 1778 version of Vogler; that is, to the "regularized" version in which the meter signature agrees with the harmonic rhythm. While Förster is able to invoke his chord categories, his attempt to analyze the progression diatonically only obscures the fact that it cycles atonally through a diminished seventh chord.

Between Förster and Sechter

In some respects, Joseph Drechsler's *Harmonie- und generalbass-Lehre* (Wien: 1816) resembles Förster's work, a fact which the latter did not fail to note (caustically, of course) in the introduction of the 1828 edition of the *Anleitung*. Drechsler, an organist at St. Stephen's, shows only the milder features of Vogler's ideas. His book is one of the first of what was to become a long line: a simplified harmony book designed for use in teacher training schools. Thus, in its purpose it has something in common with the German *allgemeine Musiklehre* of the same period, though the resemblance stops there.

The *Einleitung* emphasizes the importance of the organ, clearly divulging the author's profession. The importance of figured bass is stressed right at the outset—clearly at variance with Vogler's cursory treatment of the same subject. Yet Vogler's influence is there in the use of Roman numerals for chord notation. In his explanation of ninth, eleventh, and thirteenth chords, Drechsler follows Marpurg by subposing thirds.[14] He also quotes the "omnibus" from Vogler.

Undoubtedly, the most radical of the Viennese books from this period is the *Harmonielehre* (Wien: 1828) by August Swoboda, another student of Vogler's. The title itself is already an indication that Swoboda stands much closer to Vogler's point of view than most other Viennese. In the introduction he writes:

> Under harmony (incorrectly thoroughbass) one understands the theory of *all* intervals [*Tonverbindungen*] which may occur in the realm of music. ... He who wishes to lay claim to the title of thoroughly educated harmonist must know *every* harmony, its *origin*, its *use* and its *tendency* (goal, direction).[15]

The paraphrase of Vogler is obvious. In his view of the chromatic scale, Swoboda also follows Vogler when he says that in addition to the major and minor scales, there is another "in which such intervals or modulations have their foundation, and this is the chromatic scale."[16]

Considering Swoboda's emphasis on chromaticism, it is curious that he is one of the few Viennese theorists to defend the natural minor scale. In fact, he shows what would appear to be a perceptive understanding of the relationship between chromaticism and the minor mode:

> The nonessential raised seventh of the minor scale is only a hidden component of the chromatic scale..., for the minor key sounds much softer [and more minor-like] if the seventh step is not raised, since a hardness [*Härte*] clearly arises thereby, which, to an extent, is necessary at the close, in order to effect a complete cadence.[17]

This view leads him to place the diminished seventh chord in the category of "Artificial Chords," which also contains the augmented sixth. Swoboda is particularly free with the latter, saying that it "can be used on any degree of the scale where a major sixth and major third occur."[18]

He presents a series of chords which he says result from the process of suspension; and recommends the term "Suspension Chords" *(Auf- oder Vorhalte Accorde)* and the elimination of the term *zufällig*.[19] The chords beyond the seventh are not in this category however; they were generated earlier by sub-posing thirds, as Drechsler had done.

Easily one of the most radical aspects of the work—again, probably due to Vogler—is Swoboda's advice on modulation. The theory of modulation presented in almost all of the Viennese books of the period combines Förster's *Verwandtschaft* with a short discussion of enharmonic modulation by diminished seventh chord.

Swoboda, however, defines three types of modulations: "Simple," which are modulations to the keys of the *Verwandtschaft;* "Extended" *(weitläufige),* which refers to the continuation of this process (i.e., from the direct relations to new direct relations not in the original key); and "Sudden," indicating modulations done "quickly and unexpectedly to an extremely distant key."[20] Swoboda warns of the overuse of the second of these:

> One also goes to distant keys by means of the "extended" modulation, when one progresses from one degree to the next.... But this type of harmonic passage is long outmoded and totally banished from our music of more modern taste.[21]

A footnote to the above text says that this sort of technique is only heard with organists "when they are supposed to close in a distant key, and know no other way except to go from key to key."[22] Swoboda chooses to concentrate on the third technique instead.

For the "Sudden modulation," Swoboda's recommendations frequently demand the change of mode. For example, we are told that one may go immediately to any related key. Implicit is the fact that the mode may change, yielding such progressions as: C major-A major-D minor-B♭ major-D major-G minor, etc. Progressions based upon changing the third of the first chord are discussed, yielding the possibility of D minor-D major-F♯ major. The pivot on the single tone is also mentioned.[23] Examples given for this technique are, in elementary harmony book notation,

$$C:I - \\ A\flat: V_3^4 - I, \quad \text{and} \quad C:I - \\ D\flat V7 - I$$

(cf. Vogler, above). The discussion is not terribly systematic and there is frequent confusion between chromatic and enharmonic modulations. Nevertheless, Swoboda is the *only* Viennese theorist to attempt to deal with chromatic modulation to keys outside of the diatonic *Verwandtschaft.*

According to Thomson, Joseph Preindl's *Wiener-Tonschule*[24] first appeared in 1827. A student of Albrechtsberger's (and his successor as *Domkapellmeister* of St. Stephen's), Preindl takes the expected conservative point of view. The first volume is essentially a figured bass book, with chapters corresponding to the various figures. The second deals with counterpoint. The size and detail of the work are probably the most ambitious found before Sechter's.

The 1840s saw the appearance of a number of books by the organist-theorists. The first of these was the *Elementar-Lehrbuch der Harmonie- und Generalbass-Lehre* (Linz: 1841) by Johann August Dürrnberger. The Linzer Dürrnberger is remembered primarily as one of Anton Bruckner's theory teachers. His book, with its use of such terms as *Mehrdeutigkeit* and *Tonverbindung,* shows some influence of Vogler, albeit in a highly diluted form. Its pedagogical organization had a definite influence on Bruckner's teaching, which will be discussed later (chapter 9). The *Lehrbuch der Tonkunst* (Wien: 1842) by Gottfried Salzmann credits the author on the title page with being "Professor der Tonsetzkunst—Konservatorium," although by this date he was apparently self-employed. Salzmann uses a Roman numeral notation, but as in Förster's notation, the numerals are unaffected by theoretical chord roots. Here again the theory of inversion serves only as a means of cataloging figured bass chords. Salzmann goes on to generate chords beyond the seventh by sub-position of thirds, as Drechsler and Swoboda had done.

Apparently Tittel was unaware of the Salzmann *Lehrbuch.* Clearly, his opinion that the Viennese Conservatory was the first institution which taught Rameauian theory in preference to the figured bass is untenable.[25] On the contrary, the Viennese Conservatory was probably one of the last to preserve the figured bass.[26]

Franz Krenn, who later (1862) became *Kapellmeister* at St. Michael's and taught theory and composition at the Conservatory, published his *Generalbass-(Harmonie-) Lehre zum Selbstunterrichte* in 1845. A curious mixture of old and new, Krenn's book on one hand held to the eighteenth-century practice of using *Grundton* to mean bass tone (as had Dürrnberger), while on the other hand it recommended the treatise of A.B. Marx.[27] The Marx influence is apparent in his discussion of modulation, where he says that after a full cadence, the next phrase may begin "without transition..., so to speak, as though a new piece were beginning."[28] The example which follows shows a cadence in C major with the next phrase beginning in F# major. The *Harmonie (Generalbass-) Lehre* (Wien: 1846) of Joachim Hoffman, who was mentioned earlier in regard to his unsuccessful career as a composer, is in most respects derived from Förster. Among the many personal characteristics of Förster's work in Hoffman's book are Förster's analytical notation and his classification of seventh chords.

Harmonic Theory in Decline

The first years of the nineteenth century were a time in which the eighteenth-century musical values of Vienna came into direct contact—and conflict—with the revolutionary ideas of Vogler, the prophet of the romantic musical language. Förster and Vogler—clearly the dominant personalities of the period—represented two irreconcilable points of view. The vitality of this debate is to a great extent the result of the clearly opposing positions that the participants took on matters of the musical language that continue to interest us today. Förster, the conservative, presents an extremely convincing defense of the traditional figured bass viewpoint, supported by many examples drawn from the works of his friend Beethoven. Vogler, on the other hand, emphasizes features of the musical language which would become more and more characteristic of nineteenth-century music.

The influence of Vogler and Förster continued to be felt for some time, but the vitality of the debate gradually disappeared as the theorists retreated more and more into the artificial style of church music. The books of the 1840s, the titles of which consist of every permutation of *Harmonielehre* and *Generalbasslehre,* are the results of this dilemma. Scholastic in the most pejorative sense of the word, they consist mainly of watered-down tenets drawn from both camps. They never seem to fuse into a unit, and are never tested in musical analysis. Thus, it is against a background of decline—both of the theory and of the influence of the theorists—that what Thomson calls Sechter's "rescue attempt" must be seen.

Part II

Simon Sechter and the Fundamental Bass

4

Sechter's First Theoretical Works; the *Grundsätze*

Simon Sechter (1788-1867), "Vienna's most famous music theorist after the death of Albrechtsberger,"[1] was born in Friedberg, in what was then southwestern Bohemia.[2] As a boy he studied with Johann Nepomuk Maxandt, a teacher and chorus master, before coming to Vienna in 1804. He spent the rest of his life in Vienna, active in a variety of teaching positions ranging from his early work as a private teacher to his eventual appointment at the Conservatory. He continued studies in Vienna with Hartmann and Leopold Koželuch, but none of this early study appears to have had much effect on the system of harmony expounded in his major work, *Die Grundsätze der musikalischen Komposition* (Leipzig: Breitkopf und Härtel, 1853-54).[3]

During the 1820s, Sechter began to gain quite a reputation as a contrapuntist, to the extent that Abbé (Maximilian) Stadler called him Vienna's greatest living contrapuntist.[4] These years also saw the first of his didactic works, which marked the beginning of his career as a theorist. Appropriately, the first of these was a practical theory of fugue composition. As with all of his works before the *Grundsätze,* there is no explanatory text other than an introduction. The point is to teach through example. The *Fugenlehre* is a combination of fugue and variation techniques, presenting what Sechter calls a *Grundthema* and elaborating it through rhythmic variation and embellishment. Example 4-1 shows the *Grundthema* and two variations:

Example 4-1 (p. 21)

32   *The* Grundsätze

The work appeared in three installments,[5] and the Foreword to the third installment reads in part as follows:

> Both the Opus 7 as well as the Opus 12 are part of the same idea. Together with the present work they form a totality, which was written by the author in order to show how every complex fugue theme must have a basic theme. Thus, these three works form, so to speak, a practical system of fugue....[6]

The most general feature of Sechter's theoretical method is already evident here: i.e., the belief that the complexities of art are an assemblage of simple components. The corollary—that the process may be reversed—is essentially Sechter's pedagogical method. The slow, clear, and even progress of the *Fugenlehre*—a less benevolent assessment might call it prolix—illustrates this for the first time.

Sechter published his *Generalbassschule* in 1830. It too teaches through example alone. Although the fundamental bass is never mentioned, all progressions can be interpreted according to the rules of the *Grundsätze*, reinforcing Zeleny's opinion that Sechter's system of harmony was already well established by 1830.[7] The *Generalbassschule* clearly places Sechter in the line of Viennese theorists of the first half of the century. Yet, at the same time, its implicit recognition of the fundamental bass is an indication of the direction which Viennese theory would take in the second half of the century.

The *Praktische und im Zusammenhange anschauliche Darstellung, wie aus den einfachen Grundharmonienen die verschiedenen Bezifferungen im Generalbass entstehen* (op. 59: 1834) combines characteristics of both the *Fugenlehre* and the *Generalbassschule*. In the form of a didactic composition (variations again), it starts with a progression of simple root position triads and gradually introduces all the common chords of figured bass practice.

Although the use of the fundamental bass in the later *Grundsätze* would cause a number of departures from eighteenth-century style, Sechter was apparently unaware of this. He clearly believed that his system was consistent with the figured bass practice he had demonstrated in the *Generalbassschule*, and continued to defend it against the ever-growing number of attacks throughout his life:

> I believe to have proved through my work "The Correct Succession of the Fundamental Harmonies" that I have endeavoured, and continue to endeavour, to place the basic principles of harmony in an understandable system; [and this I have done] without it appearing necessary to me to banish the thoroughbass.[8]

The first volume of the *Grundsätze* appeared when Sechter was sixty-five years of age; thus, the treatise as a whole is the product of many years of teaching experience. After an earlier unsuccessful attempt at gaining a teaching position at the Conservatory,[9] Sechter finally received an appointment in 1851. This event may very well have provided the incentive necessary to the writing of the work. There is, however, little doubt that the substance of the *Grundsätze* formed the core of Sechter's private teaching long before the work's eventual publication.

The Correct Succession of the Fundamental Harmonies; or, of the Fundamental Bass, its Inversions and Substitutes

While German and French theorists were searching for a new starting point for a theory of harmony—concentrating on such matters as the chord itself and the leading tone—Sechter held resolutely to the traditional Viennese starting point: the diatonic scale. The laws of progression held little interest for the German and French theorists; for Sechter, on the other hand, these laws are the "basic principles." As the title of volume one of the *Grundsätze* clearly states, the essence of a theory of harmony is the knowledge of the allowable successions of degrees of the diatonic scale, each of which acts as the theoretical root of a chord. In Sechter's theory, such matters as the theory of key relations and the theory of chromaticism are also retraceable to the diatonic scale.[10]

The result is what has been termed a *Stufentheorie*.[11] It should be emphasized however that Sechter's version is one of the purest of the genre: seldom has the diatonic scale received such importance. If, for example, Sechter's theory is contrasted with Weber's, a theory which has also been characterized by the above term,[12] the difference is clear. An important aspect of Weber's theory—and one which clearly had the greatest effect on later systems of harmony—is his chord notation. This notation has the effect of concentrating attention on chord quality, something which always remains unimportant for Sechter, just as it is unimportant in figured bass. For Sechter, analysis consists merely of the notation of chord fundamentals; the succession of the resulting diatonic roots is always the main issue.

The purity of Sechter's theory made it the logical choice for Ernst Kurth in his discussion of the relative merits of the *Funktionstheorie*, as opposed to the *Stufentheorie*. But it is precisely for this reason that his opinion that "almost all commonly used textbooks or treatises on harmony are based upon the first volume of his [Sechter's] *Grundsätze*..., to the extent that they do not follow Riemann's opposing theory"[13] is misleading. Sechter's theory was not the only alternative to the *Funktionstheorie*. The preoccupation of the nineteenth-century theorists with the "chord" had an effect that was inescapable. Weber's notation of chord quality, or modified versions of it, gained wide acceptance; more important, concentration on the "chord" and a conception of progression as an attraction of force between two chords (not a succession of fundamentals) is equally pervasive. Clearly, the influence of Sechter—at least of the most personal and identifiable aspects of his work—is more limited than Kurth's opinion allows. It survived mainly in the work of Bruckner and his students, in a relatively small Austrian circle.

The Acoustical Basis

In spite of the obvious neo-Rameauian character of Sechter's treatise, there is no discussion of any physical or numerical basis of a theory of harmony. Neither ratios and proportions, nor the overtone series, play any role in the work, although there exists in manuscript form an "Abhandlung über die musikalisch-akustischen Tonverhältnisse" which, together with another study, "Vom Canon," were probably intended as volume four of the *Grundsätze*.[14] Implicit throughout the *Grundsätze*, however, is the assumption of a tuning system which approximates just intonation.[15] This accounts in part for Sechter's conservative position on modulation and chromaticism, and it causes him to regard the fifth of the II chord as a dissonance requiring downward resolution. It also accounts for the obvious reticence that comes through in his discussion of the enharmonic. Speaking of those who "place too much stock in enharmonic modulation," and who consequently would like to simplify the notational system to twelve pitch symbols, he concludes that "these do not want to retain the inner essence, but merely the outer appearance."[16]

Details of the System

In the opening section on elementary principles in major, Sechter recognizes the familiar two "fundamental" chords: the triad and the seventh chord. He enumerates the diatonic triads, emphasizing the scale as *Grundlage* from the outset.

In spite of the attack by Gottfried Weber, the discussion of consonance and dissonance remained a required subject for all Viennese theorists.[17] Here, Sechter shows a chordal orientation, deriving consonant intervals from the consonant triads (major and minor), and dissonant intervals from the dissonant chords (the diminished triad, its inversions, and the seventh chords).[18] Sechter's opinion on this matter is the opposite of Kirnberger's, who defines a consonant chord as one which contains intervals consonant to the bass and to one another. Sechter's dissonant diminished triad is considered to be consonant by both Kirnberger and Marpurg. Later, in the discussion of minor, Sechter, like all of the other Viennese theorists after Albrechtsberger, accepts the augmented triad, the existence of which Kirnberger had refused to acknowledge.

In the discussion of the syntactical roles of the various diatonic triads, the tonic is placed first. Next on the list is the dominant, followed by the subdominant. In the prominence given to the latter, Sechter departs somewhat from the conventional Viennese party line.[19] But his notion of the subdominant is completely unrelated to its use as *dominant preparation.*[20] This is clear from the subsequent example of its use: I-V-I-V7-I-IV-I-V7-I, which illustrates the "reciprocal effect" *(Wechselwirkung)* of tonic, dominant, and subdominant. Because of the eventual prohibition of stepwise progression, IV as dominant preparation is impossible.

The role of the minor triads in a major key is clearly stated and relatively unproblematic. They may be: (a) mixed with the more important major triads, as in progressions which descend a third from a major triad. The first example given is V-III; fortunately, the next two—I-VI and IV-II—have more than a theoretical existence; (b) ordered so that they imitate the cadence. At this point Sechter introduces the VII chord, giving the possibility of the seven triads of the major scale "in an order similar to the cadence."[21] Rameau's "imitation of cadences" becomes Sechter's main pedagogical device, and will appear countless times throughout the *Grundsätze.*[22]

Later on (p. 19), Sechter introduces sevenths into the chords of the falling fifth sequence. Only the seventh of the dominant may enter unprepared; all other sevenths are treated as passing tones.

All descending progressions by third or fifth are allowed without exception. But because Sechter regards the fifth of VII and the fifth of II (see "Acoustical Basis") as dissonances which must resolve down by step in the next chord, certain rising progressions are forbidden (V-II, VII-IV; II-IV, II-VI). Thus, there is no sequence of rising fifths.

5

The Fundamental Bass

In his long and productive career as a theorist, Rameau set forth ideas which continued to be important in subsequent systems of harmony. The mixture of Rameauian theory and the remnants of figured bass thinking fueled a debate which lasted into the twentieth century.

But contradictions in Rameau's theories caused considerable disagreement. The theory of the fundamental bass was an especially controversial item. As Shirlaw has pointed out,[1] there are really two kinds of fundamental bass: the one which results from the theory of chord inversion (which gained nearly universal acceptance), and the one from the second book of the *Traité,* which Rameau uses in his discussion of the laws of harmonic progression:

> The entire progression of the fundamental bass should involve only these consonances [the fifth and its inversion, the fourth; the third and its inversion, the sixth]. Dissonance may sometimes oblige us to make the bass ascend only a tone or semitone. In addition to the fact that this arises from a license introduced by the deceptive cadence... we may note that this ascending (but not descending) tone or semitone is the inversion of the seventh heard between the two sounds forming the tone or semitone.[2]

Obviously, the idea is to derive the rules of chord progression from the structure of the chord itself. But here, Rameau's belief that "the seventh is the first and so to speak the source of all dissonances"[3]—that is, that stepwise motion ("the inversion of the seventh") is "harmonic"—leads him to include the rising step in the list of allowable fundamental bass progressions. But if only the descending step is disallowed, then according to this definition the second type of fundamental bass differs little from the first.

Yet, after informing the reader that "the ascending... tone or semitone is the inversion of the seventh" (above), Rameau immediately goes on to say that "except in the case of the deceptive cadence, the progression of a third and a fourth may be understood here." Presumably, Rameau means that the rising step progression may be seen as the combination of a descending third and rising fourth—precisely the way in which Sechter will explain example 5-2.

38 The Fundamental Bass

Although Rameau presents two contradictory explanations, it seems that he would prefer to limit the progression of the fundamental bass to fifths and thirds, their inversions, and combinations thereof. In Rameau's later work the theory of the *double emploi* would allow him to read this more limited fundamental bass; ironically, the same notion would serve to support the primary role of the subdominant in the works of some later theorists, and thus would ultimately hasten the demise of the very theory it was designed to support.[4]

After Kirnberger, and his student J.A.P. Schulz who supported the more limited fundamental bass (see below), the idea was essentially dead. All that remained of it was the explanation of diminished seventh chords as incomplete ninth chords that can be seen in a few theorists, such as Weber or Marx. The new breed of theorists began to see the essence of harmony embodied in the leading tone; to them the fundamental bass was useless.

The fundamental bass played no role in Viennese harmonic theory before Sechter. Under attack by Vogler, it was ignored by the Viennese neo-Rameauians, who were Vogler partisans; and it was obviously irrelevant to figured bass theory. Sechter's "rescue attempt" was the reintroduction of the limited version of Rameau's fundamental bass, in which the only allowable fundamental progressions are by third or fifth. Essential to Sechter's conception of harmonic progression is the notion of the "harmonic connective" *(harmonisches Bindungsmittel)*: in every connection of two chords, at least one tone must be in common. If it is not literally there, it must be inserted analytically.

The "Intermediate Fundamental"

In order to explain the ascending stepwise progression, the "harmonic connective" must be interpolated between the two chords:

> Progressions which appear to rise by step must also be modeled after the cadence. For example, in order to normalize the progression from the triad of the first scale degree to that of the second, the seventh chord of the sixth degree must either actually occur, or be imagined in between.[5]

Example 5-1   Example 5-2

"Notated in C major:"   "or with concealment of the second fundamental:"

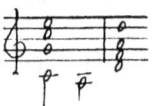 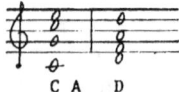

This use of the fundamental bass to explain stepwise progressions—Sechter's theory of the "intermediate fundamental" *(Zwischenfundament)*—is an obvious example of Sechter's ultimate debt to Rameau. However, as we shall see later, Sechter only knew Rameau's ideas through later German interpretations, and thus the most likely *direct* source of the "intermediate fundamental" is the following passage from the Kirnberger/Schulz "True Principles...,"[6] upon which David Beach comments as follows:[7]

> Schulz, however, proceeds to point out that many root progressions which appear to be by step are really not. He then offers the following astonishing observation: If the first chord of such a progression permits the addition of a sixth above its supposed root, then its real root is a third lower. This cancels the stepwise progression to the following chord, and changes it to one by descending fifth! As proof of this observation he provides the following example.

Example 5-3

The fundamental bass for this example, says Schulz, is not example 5-4 but is more correctly example 5-5.

Example 5-4   Example 5-5

Schulz's "astonishing observation" is, in fact, one of Sechter's "basic principles."

The similarity between Sechter's "intermediate fundamental" and Schulz's example is apparent; but even more apparent is the vastly different use to which the example is put in Sechter's system. Beach remarks that Kirnberger makes only limited use of the fundamental bass, resorting to it only in some dozen examples in the entire *Kunst des reinen Satzes*.[8] The fundamental bass appears most prominently in "The True Principles," leading both Beach and Cecil Power Grant to imply strongly that Schulz was responsible for its greater use.[9]

The limited use of the fundamental bass is a result of Kirnberger's empirical method of theorizing. In discussing the laws of harmonic progression, Kirnberger considers each case individually and turns to the fundamental bass only on rare occasions when it seems to explain the aural logic of the particular case in question. He does not categorically forbid progressions by step, but rather suggests precautionary measures in some of the more problematic ones. In the case of the progression VII-I, Kirnberger regards the VII as a rootless V7;[10] but this one isolated case does not become the model for all stepwise progressions.

The "intermediate fundamental," on the other hand, is the clearest evidence of the essentially rationalistic character of Sechter's method. Derived from Kirnberger and Schulz, the device is nevertheless used in the manner of Rameau or Marpurg. Thus, Sechter banishes all stepwise progressions a priori, and then invents the "intermediate fundamental" to justify their return. The principle is used to explain all ascending progressions and later on (see below) a number of descending progressions as well.

Various uses of "inferential" basses in Rameau and Kirnberger have recently been discussed by Grant, who claims that Marpurg's term "interpolated bass"[11] has been used indiscriminately for all of them. Grant distinguishes between a usage which he calls the "implied fundamental" (e.g., in the progression I-VII-I, the VII is seen as a rootless V7) and one which may be more properly "interpolated" (ex. 5-5 illustrates this usage).[12] The latter is considerably more abstract, for a single chord is subjected to two interpretations in order to normalize the progression. Grant demonstrates that both usages may be found in Rameau and Kirnberger; it may be added that both were taken over by Sechter, the latter being characteristic of the "intermediate fundamental."

From the former usage arises another of Sechter's "basic principles": the notion of "substitutes" (*Stellvertreter*). Upon permitting the progression VII-I, Sechter calls the VII chord the "substitute" of V7 (*Grundsätze*, p. 49). The "substitute" is the chord which is actually present; according to Sechter, it results from the "concealment" of the "real" root. In contrast to Riemann's later use of the term, the designation of a particular chord as a "substitute" is entirely dependent upon the context of progression.[13] This results in conflicts with Riemann: IV is a "substitute" for II in the progression IV-V (*Grundsätze*, p. 116); and, in the minor mode, II may "substitute" for V (Sechter gives an example in A minor of a B diminished triad moving to an A minor chord; the fundamental bass is E-A [*Grundsätze*, p. 82]).[14] Thus, the notion of "substitutes" is designed to serve the same purpose as the "intermediate fundamental": to prove that all progressions move by third or fifth, whether they appear to do so or not.

These are the only "inferential" basses used by Sechter. The use of "inferential" basses (and chords) by Kirnberger and Schulz, besides being more judicious and context-oriented, is yet more abstract. Aside from the above two, Schulz also resorts to the notion of harmonic elision or ellipsis: for example, in order to explain an unresolved seventh, Schulz assumes the elision of an intermediate chord which not only resolves the seventh, but also displaces (eliminates) the first chord.[15]

Assuming that one can accept Schulz's explanation of example 5-3, Sechter's extension of this principle to other scale degrees (and hence, his derivation of all ascending stepwise progressions), while over-generalized, is not completely unconvincing. The descending progressions are another matter, however. The main problem here is one of voice-leading. For Schulz's explanation to be at all plausible, the "imagined" seventh (or ninth) should behave like the real thing and resolve down by step. Otherwise, the melodic derivation of both the seventh and ninth chord[16] is ignored, and the explanation weakened to the point of meaninglessness.

But the strict resolution of these "chordal" dissonances is not as easy to accomplish in descending stepwise progressions, which in most cases require a considerable amount of ascending stepwise motion in order to avoid parallels. While the ascending stepwise progression of two root position triads proved to be no problem at all, the inversion of this progression can only result in parallels or nonresolution of "imagined" dissonances (see ex. 5-6 and 5-7).[17]

Example 5-6

Example 5-7

Sechter nevertheless insists upon explaining the descending stepwise progressions in a similar manner (*Grundsätze*, p. 34). He begins by discussing the progression of a root position triad to a first inversion triad (see ex. 5-8).

Example 5-8

Example 5-9

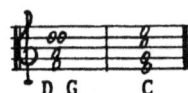

All transpositions of this progression are permitted except for two: IV-III6 and VI-V6. In the case of the former, the root of the IV chord becomes the dissonant fifth of the "imagined" VII7, and the incorrect resolution of this tone is impossible to avoid. Because the fifth of II is "dissonant" in Sechter's system, the latter progression is forbidden for the same reason. In the progression of the first inversion to another first inversion triad (see ex. 5-9) the same restrictions hold (assuming the root doubling, as in ex. 5-9). The forbidden progressions are permitted (that is, all transpositions are allowed) when only three real parts are present (see ex. 5-10).

Example 5-10

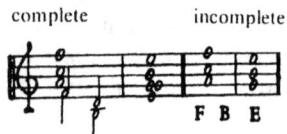

complete   incomplete

F B E

Had Sechter stopped here, he might have prevented much later criticism. Unfortunately, he did not. Apparently unaware of how tenuous his reasoning had become, he decided to discuss "irregular progressions." Example 5-11 shows an innocent-looking ascending progression, this time involving two first inversion chords:

Example 5-11

C A D

But upon closer inspection it is clear that the doubled fifth of the first chord is the "dissonant" seventh of the "imagined" chord; obviously, one of these "sevenths" resolves incorrectly. And it is equally obvious that Sechter cannot forbid this perfectly common progression. Rather than admit that his explanation does not work here, he destroys the last shred of credibility left in it:

> This freedom... never occurs in the bass voice, and is only permitted in the remaining voices under the following conditions: that the fundamental is *not* heard, [and] thus the seventh cannot be perceived as such.... [18]

Fortunately, this is the only "exception" of this sort discussed in the first volume of the *Grundsätze*. But near the end of the second volume there is a passage which is even more embarrassing. By way of introduction to the notion of "strict composition" *(strenger Satz)* which he will present in volume three, Sechter speaks briefly of the harmonic progressions characteristic of the style. He insists upon seeing a contrapuntal style through the eyes of the fundamental bass theorist. The result is that the simplest progressions imaginable become the most refractory "exceptions."

Progressions consisting only of root position triads are characteristic of the style, Sechter notes, but unfortunately:

> The number of correct fundamental progressions is so small [in root position triads, that is] that in this style one must take refuge in the artificial progressions, to which, in particular, the stepwise succession of triads belongs; here it is allowed that a seventh whose fundamental is not heard may also ascend [to resolution], or even leap....[19]

At this point Sechter shows the customary chord connections in such progressions as A minor-G major, G major-F major, etc.[20] Each is interpreted according to his "intermediate fundamental." As might be expected, the sevenths are not the only "dissonances" to skip to resolution; the "ninths" must do likewise.

Sechter's "intermediate fundamental" was already in need of further refinement in the discussion of "common practice" music--the music to which Sechter could speak with some authority. Here, it is completely absurd. Thus, it was Sechter who invented the "exceptions" which would later contribute to the destruction of the system. (They would become all the more apparent when they reappeared as norms in Bruckner's system.)[21] But the problem is not simply, as Tittel would have it, *"thinking with nonexistent tones"*[22] (italics in the original). Musical memory does exist,[23] and the ear does hear apparently different progressions in similar categories. The problem with Sechter is more properly the nonthinking with nonexistent tones; that is, the dogmatic and uncritical extension of "principles" with no empirical checks.

6

The Extension of the Fundamental

Because all progressions are derived from the model progressions by fifth or third, the stepwise progressions are only "apparent" (Sechter does not even mention the "deceptive cadence"). So too are combinations of stepwise progressions with progressions by fifth or third. In such cases, more than one chord may be related to a single fundamental.

As we shall see, Sechter develops a number of techniques which, in effect, extend the duration of a single fundamental. But unlike the case of the "intermediate fundamental," Sechter fails here to coin a general term to describe the process; the phrase "extension of the fundamental" is mine, not Sechter's.

The Melodic Analysis of "Chords"

Arpeggiation and the Passing Seventh

Having discussed the use of seventh chords in the falling fifth sequence, Sechter presents a version of the progression in which bass arpeggiation occurs simultaneously with the passing 8–7 (see ex. 6-1).[1]

Example 6-1 (p. 21)

By reversing the "intermediate fundamental" technique Sechter avoids reading a chord in the second half of the measure (and thus acknowledging the illegal stepwise progression). In effect, a passing chord—the result of the coincidence of the soprano passing seventh and the bass arpeggiation—serves to extend the fundamental. (The full implications of this will later be recognized by Mayrberger.)

Suspension

Sechter defines the suspension as the delay (*Verzögerung*) of a natural melodic resolution. Among the various examples of suspensions are the following:

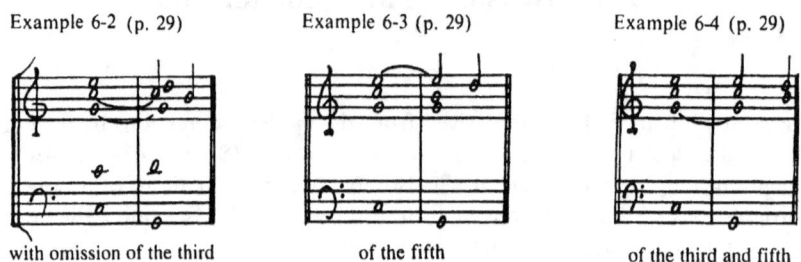

Example 6-2 (p. 29)   Example 6-3 (p. 29)   Example 6-4 (p. 29)

with omission of the third   of the fifth   of the third and fifth

Sechter calls the $^6_3$ and $^6_4$ chords formed, respectively, at the beginning of the second measure of examples 6-3 and 6-4 *gekünstelt*. When such verticalities are read as "chords" (i.e., with fundamentals determined by the theory of harmonic inversion), they are termed *natürlich*. The terms are clearly Sechter's version of Kirnberger's *wesentlich* and *zufällig*. The idea that certain "chords" result from melodic processes allows Sechter to read such progressions as II "I^6_4" V according to his rules of progression (as II V^{6-5}_{4-3}).

To a surprising extent, Sechter manages to make his system of fundamental bass compatible with figured bass practice. However, the treatment of the six-four is an exception. Admittedly, Sechter defines clearly the *suspension six-four* (above), the *passing six-four* (see "Voice Exchange") and the *auxiliary six-four* (see below). But the problem is that there is no real limitation on the *consonant* six-four: essentially, any six-four is admissible, because of the possibility of supplying mentally the missing root with the fundamental bass. The result is that the defined dissonant six-fours function mainly as a means of avoiding certain forbidden fundamental progressions. Meanwhile, other six-fours which appear to be of vaguely melodic origin—and seem to have a rather questionable relation to compositional practice—are legitimized by the fundamental bass. In such cases the bass need only resolve by step:

Example 6-5 (p. 63)

The Voice Exchange

Another clear debt to Kirnberger is the *voice exchange*.[2] Sechter defines it as follows: "During the duration of one and the same fundamental chord, the voices may exchange their components."[3] Sechter introduces the passing tone as a means of elaborating the exchange, giving the following examples:

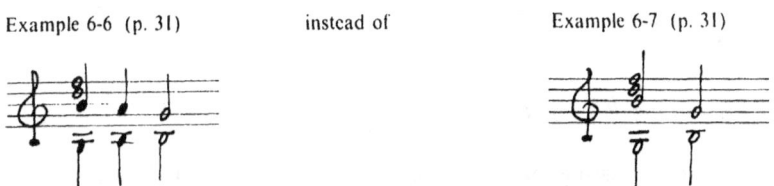

Example 6-6 (p. 31)   instead of   Example 6-7 (p. 31)

The exchange may occur together with the passing 8–7, as the following example shows (ex. 6-8). It may also be elaborated with contrary motion passing tones, together with the 8–7 (ex. 6-9).

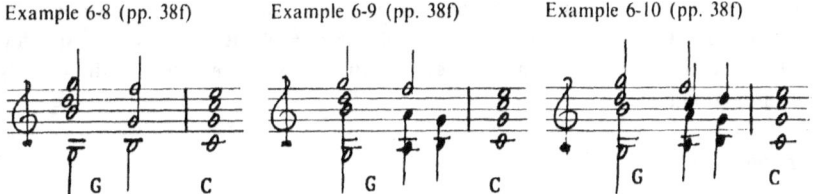

Example 6-8 (pp. 38f)   Example 6-9 (pp. 38f)   Example 6-10 (pp. 38f)

After this definition of the passing six-four, Sechter notes that the fifth may move to the fourth and back again (ex. 6-10), thus defining a passing six-three chord. All of these progressions are transposed through the sequence. If viewed in terms of fundamental progression, the passing chords may appear to violate the earlier rules of correct progression. However, Sechter reminds us that the third quarter of each bar of the sequence (the passing chord) is "not essential."[4]

The "Irregular" Passing Tone

"The passing tone which only appears with the entrance of the new fundamental (instead of before it) is called irregular."[5] Examples 6-11 and 6-12 show the derivation of another dissonant $^6_4$ which may be added to the list of "artificial" harmonies. In effect, Sechter has relaxed Kirnberger's strictness with the suspension six-four, allowing it to enter with stepwise preparation as well.

Example 6-11 (p. 42)

Example 6-12 (p. 42)

The "Returning Passing Tone"

The "returning passing tone" (*zurückkehrender Durchgang*) is Sechter's term for the common neighbor note or auxiliary. As with all devices discussed from the suspension onward, "artificial" chords are always formed. Here, two neighbor notes form the *neighbor note* or *auxiliary six-four* chord. For Sechter, the so-called nonchord tones prove to be a method of generating chord progressions melodically which are harmonically impossible in his system. The more conventional idea of a "nonchord tone"—as sub-metrical embellishment—is encountered only rarely in volume one of the *Grundsätze*; Sechter reserves this for discussion later on in the sections which deal with counterpoint.

Tonicization

The term "tonicization"—Roger Sessions' translation of Schenker's *Tonikalisierung*[6]—is an appropriate heading here, since essentially the same process was first described by Sechter (who failed, however, to introduce any new terminology or notation for it).

In the previous "suspension chords," either one or two voices were viewed as the result of melodic displacement; in the case of the "voice exchange," the "passing chord" was seen as an entirely melodic event surrounded by two fundamental chords. Sechter describes a related process towards the end of the discussion of chromatic progression in major when he shows the means by which the fundamental may be extended at another level of harmonic interpretation. This occurs when, with the exception of scale degree seven, the remaining scale degrees temporarily assume the role of tonics.[7] True to his pedagogical method, Sechter presents a series of "Variations" (*Veränderungen*) on an eight-measure harmonic pattern: I–V–III–VI–IV–II–V–I (later called the "extended cadence" by Bruckner). Each variation consists of one of Sechter's model progressions transposed according to the harmonic scheme of the "theme"; for example, variation one shows each "tonic" moving to its dominant and back, while in variation two the "tonic" moves to its subdominant and back. Finally, each measure of the last variation contains a transposition of the complete "theme" in eighth-note rhythm. Sechter explains:

> The capital letters [one per bar] indicate in all variations the main fundamentals which are in force at the beginning and end of the bar; those which lie between are only subordinate fundamentals, which are related only to the first and last fundmental—the tonic of the bar. Thus in this variation there are subordinate scales, which all relate to the main C-major scale.[8]

The consistency of this technique with the general goals of Sechter's system is obvious. It is also quite compatible with Sechter's other ideas on chromaticism: for Sechter, all chromaticism arises from the technique of tonicization. Moreover, except for the duration of the "temporary tonics," the idea differs little from his theory of diatonic modulation.

This same passage from the *Grundsätze* was first cited by Morgan[9], who considers it important to the history of reduction analysis. Caplin, in his insightful discussion of the relationship between Sechter's ideas on rhythm and harmony, brings in related material from volume two of Sechter's treatise, where similar "reductions" can be found.[10] He shows that Sechter's most important principle of harmony and meter—that each bar be marked by the appearance of a new fundamental (a "decisive" harmonic change)—is the most likely cause of the one-measure limit on Sechter's reduction technique.[11]

Modulation

Considering the scope of the *Grundsätze*, the discussion of modulation is surprisingly short: a mere sixteen pages. Sechter recounts the usual eighteenth-century *Verwandtschaft*, offering two new possibilities which are the result of his theory of minor. Both entail a pivot on the raised sixth; for example, C major–G minor, and A minor–G minor. But essentially, the notion of modulation differs little from that of tonicization.

Modulations beyond the initial *Verwandtschaft* are handled by giving specific instructions for each as the distance from the starting key increases by fifth each time. The keys are displayed on a line rather than a circle, showing the assumption of nontempered tuning. The procedure is the usual "extended" diatonic modulation: each new key generates a new *Verwandtschaft*, and so on. The idea is an exhaustive exploration of *pure* diatonic possibilities; the results are what Swoboda had considered "outmoded and totally banished from our music of more modern taste."[12]

The Extension of the Fundamental and the *Stufentheorie*

Among Sechter's most obvious debts to Kirnberger are the two means by which he accounts for "apparent" fundamental motion by step: the interpolation of a chord between two chords in stepwise relation ("intermediate fundamental") and the relating of more than one "chord" to a single fundamental.[13] While the former technique accelerates the harmonic rhythm, the latter results in an extension of the fundamental. If to this extension of the fundamental we add the further "levels" of harmonic analysis represented by Sechter's implicit recognition of tonicization and his allied definition of modulation, then it is clear that the term *Stufentheorie*—if it indicates a system in which scale degree chords are never subsumed by higher level phenomena—is inadequate to describe Sechter's system. Rather, it should be noted that at many points Sechter's system is also a *Funktionstheorie*, in which "function" is not arrived at a priori, but through the local context of progression.

7

Progression in Minor; Chromatic Progression

The Minor Mode

The most distinctive feature of Sechter's system in minor is the equal prominence which he gives to all forms of the minor scale. The hegemony of the harmonic minor, so characteristic of the average nineteenth-century *Harmonielehre*, contravenes his eighteenth-century point of view:

> Are they not hypocrites, who purport to have great reverence for Bach, Handel, Haydn, and Mozart, and yet criticize that in which these masters are in complete agreement? Each of them used the sixth and seventh degrees of the minor scale in the natural form descending, and in the raised form ascending. But ever since Gottfried Weber preferred to see the seventh step always raised and the sixth step always natural, some respect the reputations of these masters less, and lament that they lived in a time when prejudice yet reigned. Some even flatter themselves that if these masters were still alive, they would also comply with the modern view.[1]

This is not to say that the harmonic minor scale is eliminated; in fact, Sechter discusses it first, calling it the first and "natural" type. His definition cleverly avoids the problem of the augmented second by saying that the scale "proceeds from the first step to the sixth in ascending direction, and from there back to the first, after which the half step below the scale follows, returning immediately to the first step."[2] Thus, there is no connection between scale degrees six and seven in the harmonic minor. Sechter proceeds to define the two remaining minor scales: the ascending and descending melodic minor. Sechter considers the leading tone in minor to be an alteration (*erhöhte Stufe*)—yet he considers the harmonic minor "natural."

The variable sixth and seventh steps lead Sechter to postulate the existence of thirteen diatonic triads in minor. The possible seventh chords are somewhat more limited: although Sechter accepts the augmented triad with major seventh on III, the minor triad with major seventh on I does not exist, since its seventh may not be resolved in the manner of a chordal seventh.

Minor Mode; Chromatic Progression

Fundamental Progression in Minor

Correct progression of the fundamental bass in minor combines the principles already discussed in major with careful observation of the melodic tendencies of the sixth and seventh degrees of the minor scale. To this end, Sechter gives the following examples:

Example 7-1

a

b

c

In each case, his attention is primarily drawn to the voice containing the sixth and seventh degrees. He points out the soprano descent in example 7-1a, its ascent in example 7-1b, and, as an example of the use of the harmonic minor, he notes that in example 7-1c the alto moves from scale degree 5 to 6 and back again. In his attention to these details Sechter shows his affection for the early eighteenth-century style, as well as his determination to preserve pure diatonicism, even in the minor mode.

But the major subdominant and minor dominant never quite achieve the status of their opposites: if I moves to V or IV with the intention of returning immediately, V must be major and IV minor—the latter termed by Sechter the "true" subdominant. During the discussion of minor, the new dissonant triad—the augmented chord—is introduced; the dissonant fifth must be prepared, and consequently it may only be preceded by V or VII.

Sechter's attempt to avoid chromaticism was directed only at the voice leading of the melodic parts—not at the succession of chord fundamentals. A problem is already present in major (where IV–VII is derived from the model V–I). But in minor it only becomes worse: since Sechter uses both the harmonic minor and the ascending melodic minor interchangeably with the natural minor, the system not only tolerates progression by diminished fifth (VI–II: IV–VII), but also progression by augmented fifth (VII–III).[3] Thus, by the end of the nineteenth century, one of the main objections to the system was that it apparently gave equal status to root progressions by perfect fifth (or fourth) and those by diminished or augmented fifth (or fourth).

Chromatic Progression

The main assumption underlying Sechter's theory of chromatic progression (*chromatische Fortschreitung*) is essentially that which was implicit to most Viennese systems of harmony of the first half of the nineteenth century: every chromatic structure, without exception, is reducible to a diatonic one. However, it is the means by which this reduction is accomplished that is important.

The traditional figured bass view, as exemplified by Förster, views the chromatic tone as an "alteration" which requires no harmonic justification. In discussing the origin of the augmented sixth chord, Förster gives the following progressions and explanation:

Example 7-2

The natural *sixth* D of scale degree six F from A minor is shown in example 7-2a. In example 7-2b the *sixth* D is chromatically raised to D♯, and thus transformed into an augmented sixth, [which] allows itself even to be taken into the *major* scale [ex. 7-2c].[4]

Implicit is the idea that the alteration—the *zufällig erhöhte Sexte*—does not change the interval structure above the bass. To the extent that this interval structure is "harmony" in figured bass theory, chromatic alteration remains outside of it: "chromatic harmony" does not exist in figured bass theory.

Sechter's conception of chromaticism, on the other hand, is completely harmonic. Yet, as we shall see, it remains questionable whether his ideas present any more of a theory of chromatic harmony (whatever that may be) than figured bass theory does.

Like everything else in Sechter's system, chromaticism is dependent upon the laws of the fundamental bass. These laws remain exactly as they were in diatonic harmony:

> The use of tones *foreign to the scale* may not be extended to the fundamentals; consequently, all fundamentals in the chromatic C-major scale remain just as they were in the diatonic [scale]....[5]

54   Minor Mode; Chromatic Progression

Thus, the familiar progressions of diatonic thirds and fifths—foremost being the sequence of descending fifths—continue to serve as models for chromatic progression as well. Precisely what Förster had refused to call chromatic becomes the core of Sechter's theory of chromaticism: the leading tones of the related keys (*Verwandtschaft*). The available chromatic tones in any key are, in fact, strictly limited to these tones; thus, the progression which Förster refused to call chromatic[6] becomes a model chromatic progression for Sechter. The different emphasis is clear: rather than conceiving of chromaticism as the alteration of a diatonic intervallic succession (as Förster does), Sechter sees chromatic progression (note the chordal emphasis) as a type of contracted diatonic modulation.

According to Sechter, the discussion of minor served as an introduction to chromaticism. He notes that the variable sixth and seventh steps are evidence that the minor keys "supply the greatest amount of material for chromatic progression."[7] But this is the full extent of this line of reasoning: chromaticism is *not* promoted by mixing major and minor (as with Hauptmann). Even in the discussion of chromaticism the distinction between major and minor remains as rigid as it was earlier. Speaking of the diminished seventh chord (which he regards as an incomplete ninth chord), Sechter describes the simple progression of $B°7-C$ major as follows:

> The harmony of the fifth step of the C-major scale can be made into that of the fifth step of C minor through the alteration of the ninth, after which the tonic of the C-major scale follows nevertheless.[8]

Although Sechter returns to some more specialized observations regarding minor towards the end of the chromaticism discussion (pp. 182ff), the bulk of his theory of chromaticism is concerned with the usual secondary dominants (he does not use the term) in major, and their possible transformations.

The progressions of secondary dominants to secondary tonics are called by Sechter the "simple chromatic progressions." In such progressions a minor triad may be altered to major, or a major triad altered to augmented. The possibility of a progression of two or three chords in a row from outside of the key is offered by the "compound progression" (*zusammengesetzter Satz*) which consists of II7, V7, and I of a related key, and which, like the "simple" progression, may be extended sequentially.[9]

The diminished seventh chord—Sechter's incomplete dominant ninth—is also extended sequentially. When the fundamental bass is removed, the result is a succession of diminished seventh chords descending by half step, which are nevertheless still interpreted as fundamental bass motion of descending fifth.

The "Hybrid-chord"

Because the laws of the fundamental bass forbid stepwise progression, Sechter must view all of the traditional augmented sixth chords as being either complete or incomplete forms of II7 or II9 in minor:

> [If] one alters the third to a major third without changing the diminished fifth, such a chord (whose major third is found in a different scale from its diminished fifth) has a *hybrid-nature*;...therefore, it is an authentic *chromatic* chord which cannot be found in any diatonic scale.[10]

The "hybrid-chord" (*Zwitteraccord*) is Sechter's last desperate effort to prove that all of chromatic progression may be explained by the techniques of diatonic harmony. It is the last contraction of related diatonic keys—this time within a single chord itself. The common augmented sixth chords of the late eighteenth-century were almost universally referred to as "altered." By defining the "authentic chromatic chord" as the sum of diatonic components, Sechter clings tenaciously to his belief that the source of all chromaticism is diatonic and chordal.

Later on, the "hybrid-chord" would cause problems for even the most confirmed Sechter partisans. Although the term itself (and the explanation) would find only limited acceptance, the idea certainly did much to promote the concentration on these chords as paradigmatic chromatic sonorities, a feature typical of late nineteenth-century *Harmonielehren*. The explanation may also be seen as the source of the "chord combination" explanations of chromaticism that reemerged in the early twentieth century.

Sechter's formalization of the "hybrid-chord" effectively extends the use of the traditional augmented sixth far beyond that discussed by any theorist before him. Once these chords are introduced into the falling fifth sequence, any secondary dominant may become a "hybrid-chord". Moreover, because of the fundamental bass (which is there even when it is not), they may be used in any inversion. Examples 7-3 and 7-4 show a diatonic sequence and its subsequent transformation through the introduction of "hybrid-chords".

Example 7-3

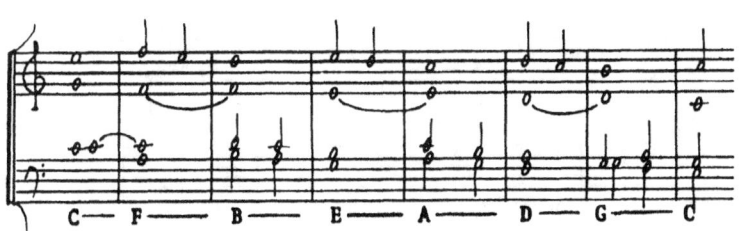

56   Minor Mode; Chromatic Progression

Example 7-4

Not only is the actual sounding of the fundamental bass optional, but in the case of the so-called German sixth (which Sechter considers an incomplete II9), we are told that the root is usually left out "in order to take the harshness out of these ninth chords."[11] At this point one cannot help wondering what connection remains between the fundamental bass and these chromatic chords.[12]

The Abbreviated Sequence: the Cadence

Most of the *Grundsätze* is concerned with one progression: the falling fifth and its extension to all degrees of the diatonic scale. But during the discussion of chromaticism, the "primary chord model" plays an important role.[13] Example 7-5a shows the diatonic model with fundamental bass analysis:

Example 7-5

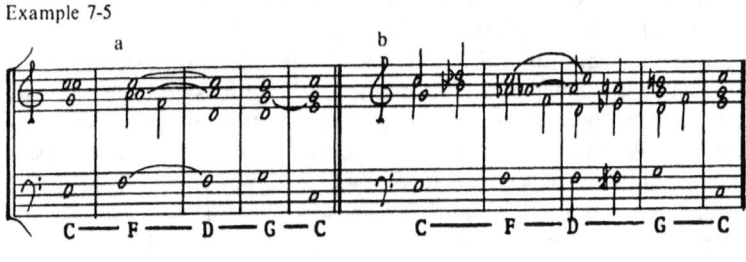

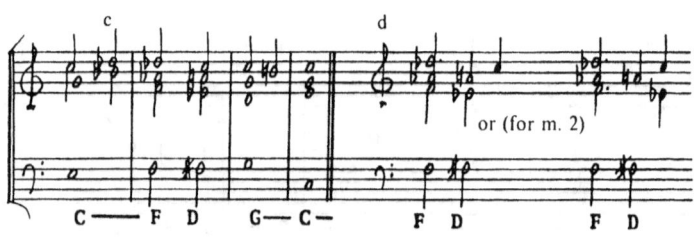

Example 7-5b is the first elaboration of example 7-5a, and is painstakingly explained as a series of modulations. Further extensions of example 7-5b all involve various suspensions[14] creating new chords (see ex. 7-5c and ex. 7-5d). For all the wealth of examples which Sechter introduces here, at no point does the Neapolitan proceed directly to the dominant, or indeed, even to the six-four of the dominant. Such a progression would of course break one of Sechter's two rules of progression and chromaticism: he would either have to acknowledge fundamental progression from IV to V, or extend chromatic alteration to scale degree two.

The Chromatic Bass and the Chromatic Passing Chord

Curiously, the voice exchange and its embellishment through chromatic passing tones—and consequently chromatic passing chords—is missing in the *Grundsätze*. But earlier, in the *Generalbassschule*, Sechter had included an exercise which shows the chromatic elaboration of the voice exchange:[15]

Example 7-6

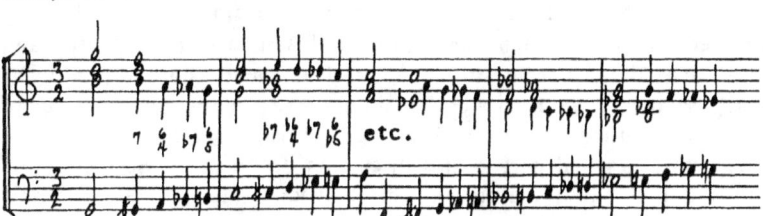

Sechter has clearly taken a segment of Vogler's chromatic scale harmonization and modified it so that the progression results in the exchange of components of a dominant seventh chord—Yellin's "classical omnibus." However, the modification results in a radical change of emphasis: the chromatic octave scale of every two 2/3 bars is divided unequally (and tonally) so that it fits into the fundamental bass system, instead of equally (and atonally), as it is in Vogler.

All other techniques for harmonizing the chromatic scale involve continual change of fundamental. Example 7-7 is another chromatic progression taken from the *Generalbassschule*.[16] With its combination of "artificial" six-fours and "intermediate fundamentals" it shows how abstract—and questionable—Sechter's chromatic analyses can become.

58   Minor Mode; Chromatic Progression

Example 7-7

C A   D B   E C   F   D   G E   A

The appearance of chromatic bass lines in the earlier *Generalbassschule* and their later absence in the *Grundsätze* show their derivation from traditional *regola dell' ottava* techniques.

The Enharmonic

The reticence with which Sechter speaks of the enharmonic is evident throughout his discussion. Forced to admit the necessity of tempered tuning here, he goes on to discuss the customary enharmonic modulations by diminished seventh and augmented sixth chord. With evident resignation and displeasure he allows a progression of diminished seventh chords ascending by half step, saying, "one does not bother about the explanation by succession of fundamentals, letting it be excused through 'plurisignificance'."[17]

The most original part of this discussion occurs when Sechter shows methods of modulating "diatonically" through equal interval cycles. Example 7-8 shows a series of modulations through the cycle of major thirds:

Example 7-8

```
C: I
e : VI II7 V7 E: I
        G♯: VI II7 V7 A♭: I
                    c: VI II7 V7, etc.
```

Examples are given for the major second and minor third as well, but the section on the enharmonic ends with the not altogether unexpected warning:

> The enharmonic modulations in extended usage are the natural enemies of sound melody; thus, their effect is mysterious and surprising. They are the image of the world at large, in which family life founders and disappointments often occur, and in which the unimportant appears to have a certain splendor. But then, one cannot recognize what is important or unimportant.[18]

The Significance of Sechter's System of Chromatic Progression

Sechter's system of chromatic progression is undoubtedly the most original aspect of the *Grundsätze*. Here, chromatic possibilities are extended considerably beyond those offered in the more or less perfunctory discussions of that topic in other books of the period. But the extreme limitations of Sechter's ideas are also obvious: they result from his insistence on the complete reduction of all chromatic phenomena to a diatonic basis.

Sechter's theory of modulation is a case in point. Modulation was one of the very few means that theorists of the past had to discuss long-range tonal procedures. It is undeniable that chromatic modulation and the important structural usage of secondary tonalities not in pure diatonic relation to the initial tonic were realities, both in the musical and the theoretical literature of the time.[19] But here Sechter is caught in his own pedantic categories: his theory of modulation does not transcend the *Verwandtschaft*, and thus he has no possibility to discuss chromaticism beyond chord-to-chord motion. Moreover, because of his limited diatonic point of view, Sechter's system ignores almost completely the mixture and interchange of parallel major and minor modes as a source of chromaticism.

Finally, Sechter's concept of chord-to-chord motion presents serious problems in itself. Properly speaking, his chromatic progression is merely the chromatic alteration of the surface of a composition; the controlling structure—the eternal falling fifth—remains unaffected. But is the fundamental bass really the controlling structure? Aural evidence speaks to the contrary. Probably the most primitive image of the essence of "romantic harmony" is the leading tone moving to resolution; that is, motion to rest, or a less harmonic (or perhaps melodic) event moving to a more harmonic one. But Sechter's analyses make everything harmonic, resulting in a radical conflict with the actual sound of the music. (His "German sixth chord" demonstrates this problem particularly well.) This is not to say that there are no diatonic resting points in chromatic harmony; such points do exist and are of great structural importance. But the attempt to interpret every verticality diatonically results in a flattening of harmonic dimensions: the melodic motions of "romantic harmony" are transformed into the placid falling fifths of the diatonic system.

In fairness it should be remarked that the leading tone and the nondiatonic aspects of "romantic harmony" received more than equal time in the German treatises, as did modal mixture. Many of these works were as insistently chromatic and atonal as Sechter was diatonic and tonal. The truth of the matter lay somewhere in between: chromatic harmony is not completely unrelated to diatonic procedures, but it is certainly more than the mere surface alteration of an essentially undisturbed diatonic structure.

Sechter's system at least provided the tools to relate some chromatic progressions to larger tonal considerations, something which many other systems could not do. Consequently, it is not surprising that his followers, who attempted to provide the empirical support which his system so badly needed,[20] were the first to come up with analyses of Wagnerian harmony that were in any sense coherent.

8

Sechter's System of Harmony: Its Methodological Basis and Historical Origins

Of all the systems of harmony of the period, Sechter's has perhaps the most problematic relation to contemporaneous music and thought. Descended from Kirnberger to some extent, it is essentially a theory of "pure" composition. But one of the most attractive features of Kirnberger's work is his attempt to relate his theory of *reiner Satz* to the musical practice of his day. Sechter's work, on the other hand, contains no such attempt.[1] Other *Kompositionslehren* of the period (Marx, Lobe, etc.), with which Sechter's work might be compared, all comment upon well-known compositions;[2] Sechter's *Grundsätze* contains not one example from the musical literature. These other works are written in a manner which might be called critical; Sechter's can only be called dogmatic. The other important work which appeared in the same year as Sechter's—Hauptmann's *Die Natur der Harmonik und der Metrik*—equals or surpasses Sechter in abstraction and in its aloofness from the music of the time, but its basis in the thought of the period is obvious. Sechter's work, on the other hand, can only be seen as an anachronism, for its philosophical basis is early eighteenth-century rationalism (which of course had also survived in Vogler) transplanted to mid-nineteenth-century Vienna.[3]

Sechter's personality and attitudes were formed apart from the strife and revolutions of late eighteenth- and nineteenth-century Europe. He was a product of the comparatively tranquil and somewhat provincial environment of *Biedermeier* Vienna. Here, the spirit of the Austrian Baroque continued to live in sacred music (as it still does); the belief in eternal ideas and the identification of religion and art were basic to Sechter's personality and thought.

In an essay "Etwas über mein Studium," Sechter recalls general works which influenced his thinking. Chief among these are the Old and New Testaments of the Bible, and the classic works of Schiller, Goethe, and Herder. "Lighter" works, and those which smacked of heresy, were avoided:

> I only came to know Voltaire to the extent that I knew he would make me discontented, and [then] I asked nothing more of him. Indeed, I read many novels in my youth, but I did not find that they contributed to my contentment; on the contrary, it was these which made the more serious books necessary to me.[4]

Religious faith was a way of life for Sechter; and as was so typical in the Baroque, it was closely related to art. In a characteristic aphorism Sechter says:

> God is also the Creator of that which man has been able to produce, for everything comes from him. Oh artist, you have not bestowed your most beautiful ideas upon yourself, for they come from Him....[5]

Obviously, this attitude placed Sechter squarely at odds with the Faustian image of the romantic artist—the cult of the individual. He fought continually against what he called the "search for originality," promoting instead a simple and "universal" musical style.

The *Grundsätze* is primarily a pedagogical work, not a theory. The fundamental bass is, for Sechter, revealed truth, reflecting his belief in an orderly universe based upon eternal principles which are not to be questioned. But all is not optimism. Sechter's "sociological" analysis of the enharmonic, like so many parts of the *Grundsätze*, shows the threat that Sechter felt from the "disorderly" world around him.

Further on in "Etwas über mein Studium" Sechter also recalls the music-theoretical works which he had read:

> Textbooks which I studied are: Marpurg's *Treatise on the Fugue*, his book on harmony, and his *Temperament;* Kirnberger's *Art of Strict Composition*, [and] his *True Principles of Harmony;* Emanuel Bach's "Essay on Accompaniment"; Albrechtsberger's books on thoroughbass and composition; Mattheson's *Complete Conductor;* Türk's book on thoroughbass. More recently I also read: Gottfried Weber's theory, the treatise on composition by Reicha, a few parts of the system by Herr Marx from Berlin, and a few other small textbooks. I almost forgot that I also read Riepel's works.[6]

Conspicuously absent from the above is Marpurg's translation of d'Alembert's *Elémens de la Musique,* which was the nearest thing to "pure" Rameau in the German-speaking world. Sechter apparently learned Rameauian theory from second-hand sources. Moreover, Sechter does not mention Fux's *Gradus*. Marpurg's book on harmony is most likely his *Handbuch bei dem Generalbasse und der Composition* (Berlin: 1755–60).

The last section of Zeleny's book is devoted to the question of the influence of the above sources on Sechter's system. With a knowledge of Sechter's personality and his system, Zeleny's conclusions are not hard to guess. He rapidly dismisses the works which Sechter read "more recently," since they disagree with Sechter's work both philosophically and technically, and were read by Sechter at a point when his system was already substantially complete. The "almost forgotten" Riepel, who places melody over harmony in importance, clearly exerted even less influence. Commenting on Sechter's list of books, Zeleny concludes:

> In this list of textbooks studied, the dominant role of Marpurg and Kirnberger—who are first on the list and represented by a number of works—is immediately apparent. Also, it is essentially these two theorists who have given the most to Sechter. Sechter, the logician, has thus rendered judgment on these works by the order of their mention—at least in regard to the meaning they had for him.[7]

As Zeleny shows, the influence of C.P.E. Bach, Albrechtsberger, and Mattheson upon Sechter is minimal.[8] In addition, Türk may only be considered an influence to the extent that he passed on the doctrines of Marpurg and Kirnberger. It is from Kirnberger in particular that Sechter took many of his ideas.

Because Sechter always remains unclear on just why he accepts the two "fundamental" chords, he may be allied with either Marpurg or Kirnberger on this issue. But on many other points he clearly follows Kirnberger rather than Marpurg. Like Kirnberger, he rejects tempered tuning. He also rejects Marpurg's ninth, eleventh, and thirteenth chords formed by supposition, following Kirnberger in discussing only the ninth chord as the result of melodic suspension. He coins the term *gekünstelte* for Kirnberger's *unwesentliche* dissonance.[9] Here, he is substantially in agreement with Kirnberger, viewing all suspensions and suspension chords as the result of melodic processes. The discussion of the voice exchange and passing chords comes from Kirnberger and Schulz. In essence, Sechter rejects Rameau's *double emploi* by emphasizing that the seventh of a seventh chord is always the dissonance, regardless of inversion. The progression II_5^6 –I never occurs in Sechter, so we cannot be absolutely sure that he would follow Kirnberger in considering the 6 to be a passing tone. However, it seems most likely, since the chord quite clearly could not be read as "II." Sechter's explanation of the augmented sixth chords also resembles Kirnberger, who reads the Italian sixth as the "second inversion of the third essential seventh chord."[10] Schulz, like Sechter, reads the German sixth as an incomplete ninth chord. Marpurg, in rejecting the fundamental bass of these chords, grants them independent existence as well as invertibility in his category of "fantastic" chords. In general design Sechter's treatise resembles Kirnberger's *Kunst:* both start with harmony before counterpoint. The similarities of Sechter and Kirnberger were noted by Bruckner, among others, who claimed that Sechter's theory was an "abstraction from Bach's works."[11]

In matters of detail, Sechter's relationship to Marpurg is not nearly as close.[12] Yet, for all of this affinity to Kirnberger, Sechter could hardly be more remote from him in general approach. Gone is Kirnberger's empiricism, replaced by Sechter's penchant for immediately raising particular cases to general laws based upon empirical evidence which varies from slight to nonexistent. In this also lies much of the originality of Sechter's work: the importance attributed to all scale degrees, as well as the highly generalized theory of chromaticism, are direct results of this way of thinking. Unfortunately, so too are the problems which ultimately contributed to the system's demise. It is this hybrid of eighteenth-century sources—what could be called Kirnberger "rationalized"—which became the nineteenth-century Viennese system of harmony.

Part III

Viennese Fundamental Bass Theory in the Second Half of the Century

9

Anton Bruckner, the Leading Apostle of Sechter's Teachings

The Bruckner biographers are united in their description of the relationship between Bruckner (1824–96) and his most important teacher: in Bruckner, Sechter found both the perfect student and a man of strikingly similar temperament. Both men came from simple, provincial environments; and despite the difference in their ages, the attitudes and beliefs of both were products of the tranquil *Vormärz*. The piousness of the teacher was reflected in the student; perhaps the most oft-encountered word in descriptions of Bruckner's character is *Autoritätsglaube*—an unquestioning faith in authority which obliged Bruckner, while working with Sechter, to a regimen of harmony and counterpoint exercises often requiring six and seven hours a day. The relationship between Bruckner and his students would never be quite as comfortable. By the 1870s modern Europe finally reached Vienna; and Bruckner's students inhabited a world which he—a last remnant of the eighteenth century—would never quite understand.

Without Bruckner it is questionable whether Sechter's authority in theoretical matters would have survived much beyond his death. But the stature which Bruckner eventually acquired as a composer, coupled with his obvious belief in the validity of Sechter's ideas—which can be seen in his many respectful bows to the "Professor," as Bruckner referred to him in his University lectures—made Sechter's system something that could not be dismissed lightly. The facts were undeniable: Bruckner was indeed an important, if controversial composer; and Sechter's teachings were to him the indispensible *Wissenschaft* of composition. When asked about the amount of time that should be devoted to the study of harmony in the curriculum for young composers, Bruckner replied that three years were absolutely necessary (for harmony according to Sechter, of course), while for composition a few months would do, since composition was not really teachable anyway.[1]

Bruckner taught throughout his lifetime in capacities ranging from early experiences in small town schools to his later position at the Vienna Conservatory, his private students in Vienna, and his lectures at the University of Vienna. But never did he teach composition as we know it. His influence as a composer was unrelated to his pedagogical activities and thus, although influential, he created no school of composition. In Bruckner we see the inevitable end result of the ever-widening gap between theory and compositional practice which extended throughout the nineteenth century. In his pedagogical activities Bruckner once again shows his eighteenth-century outlook. However, due to the problematic relationship between the theory he taught and the music he wrote, it can only be seen as an anachronism.

The division between theory and practice also means that the influence of Sechter's theory upon Bruckner's composition—if indeed there really is any—is difficult to determine.[2] That imposing topic—appropriate to a more specialized Bruckner study—will not be discussed here. Rather, the present study views Bruckner as the most influential transmitter of Sechter's system to a later generation. The discussion will thus be confined to Bruckner's system of harmony, its historical origins, and the somewhat different form which Sechter's system began to assume in Bruckner's presentation of it.

The Historical Origins of Bruckner's System

Almost all of Bruckner's system of harmony is retraceable to sources which he studied as a student, which, according to Ernst Tittel,[3] are complete in the following list:

> Dürrnberger, Johann August. *Elementar-Lehrbuch der Harmonie- und Generalbass-Lehre.* Linz: 1841.
> Türk, D.G. *Anweisung zum Generalbassspiel.* According to Tittel, the edition is the "neue verbesserte Ausgabe" (Wien: Haslinger), which he claims appeared between 1832 and 1837.[4]
> _____. *Von den wichtigsten Pflichten eines Organisten.* Halle: 1787.
> Marpurg, F.W. *Handbuch bei dem Generalbasse und der Composition.* Berlin: 1755-60.
> _____. *Abhandlung von der Fuge.* Berlin: 1753-54, and Simon Sechter, ed., Wien: n.d.
> Sechter, S. *Grundsätze* (vol. 1-3).
> Marx, A.B. *Die Lehre von der musikalischen Komposition.* 4 vol. Leipzig: 1837-47. (Only vol. 3 studied)

Bruckner first studied theory at the age of eleven with a cousin, Johann Baptist Weiss. Upon completion of his early education at the monastery of St. Florian, Bruckner spent a year in Linz to pursue the teacher-training program he had chosen. It was here that he studied with Dürrnberger, at about the time that the latter's harmony book was published. After finishing school in Linz, Bruckner worked first in Windhaag and then in Kronstorf. According to Tittel, he continued his theory education on his own during this time (1841-43), studying the copy of Marpurg's *Handbuch* which Dürrnberger had given him. In 1843, while still in Kronstorf, Bruckner began study in neighboring Enns with a well-known organist and choir director, Leopold Edler von Zenetti. This study may have lasted well beyond 1845, the point at which Bruckner secured a position at St. Florian and moved there. With Zenetti, he worked through the Türk sources listed above; it was also during this time that he compiled the notebook entitled *Kurze Generalbass-Regeln* which has been preserved.[5] The year in which Bruckner assumed the post of cathedral organist in Linz (1855) also marked the beginning of his monumental correspondence course with Sechter. At this time he studied Sechter's edition of Marpurg's *Abhandlung* (which he had been studying on his own) and all three volumes of the *Grundsätze*. Upon finishing Sechter's exhaustive course in 1861, Bruckner—at thirty-seven years of age still the perennial student—seems to have felt the need for a less abstract form of study: with Otto Kitzler, he worked primarily on form and instrumentation. During study with Kitzler (1861-63), he worked on the third volume of Marx's treatise; it was Kitzler who introduced him to Wagner's music.

From the surviving evidence of Bruckner's harmony teaching,[6] it is clear that Sechter's *Grundsätze* (I) and, to a lesser extent, Dürrnberger's *Elementarbuch* were most influential. The Marpurg *Abhandlung* and the Marx *Lehre*—concerned respectively with counterpoint and instrumentation—are irrelevant to the present discussion; and it is difficult to detect any direct influence of Türk on Bruckner's teaching.

The Marpurg *Handbuch* appears to have been held in some esteem by Bruckner; a reference to it appears in Eckstein's notes.[7] Although not included in Tittel's list, there is a chance that Bruckner may have known some Kirnberger. On two pages of Eckstein's unpublished notes from the University lectures of 1884-85 there appear to be references to Kirnberger. The first says "Lehrbuch von Dürrnberger, Wien 1841"; "Dürrnberger" is penciled over as "Kirnberger." While this could very well refer to the Dürrnberger *Elementarbuch* (Linz:1841), the next reference clearly states "vgl. *Kirnberger rein* [sic] *Satz*, 1842 [1 written over 2] Hofbibliothek." But whether or not Bruckner had read Kirnberger, there is no doubt that the influence of Marpurg is far more prominent in his system.

A vivid picture of Bruckner, the teacher, survives in a number of amusing anecdotes, all of which testify to the fact that he remained the small-town schoolmaster throughout his life. Not surprisingly, his theory teaching appears to have been thoroughly practical. According to one of his Conservatory students, he never dealt with any speculative theory, and had no knowledge of Riemann.[8] He also appears not to have known the ultimate source of many of his neo-Rameauian ideas: Eckstein guarantees that he had never read any Rameau.[9] Concerning the sources of his University lectures, he was curiously inconsistent, claiming at the beginning of one series of lectures that because of his extensive experience in the subject at hand he had decided "not to be bound to any of the presently available works with my lectures, but rather to lecture *freely.*"[10] Yet Schwanzara quotes him on May 16, 1892 as saying that "all of this is presented according to Sechter, Book I."[11]

All sources make it clear that volume one of Sechter's treatise formed the basis of Bruckner's teaching, but his opinion of the rest of Sechter's work and the extent to which he used it in his teaching are more complicated issues. The comparatively small amount of surviving counterpoint material appears to follow Sechter,[12] but there is disagreement regarding Bruckner's use of the rest of Sechter's *Grundsätze.* Decsey, for example, claims that the section entitled "Vom einstimmigen Satz" was for Bruckner "absolutely the holiest of the holy."[13] But Friedrich Klose (who had studied privately with Bruckner) says that Bruckner, the creator of the "most wonderful melodic structures of all time," knew that Sechter could not explain melody, and hence he avoided this chapter completely. Klose goes on to say that Bruckner also avoided Sechter's *Von den Gesetzen des Taktes.*[14]

Aside from the Sechter influence, Bruckner's University lectures also show the influence of his earlier teacher in Linz, Johann August Dürrnberger. Dürrnberger's *Elementarbuch* begins with an extensive section (pp. 22–40) entitled "Tonverbindung oder Intervallenlehre" (remember that *Tonverbindung* is Vogler's equivalent for "interval"). Here, forbidden interval progressions are discussed before the definition and discussion of chords. This is quite different from Sechter, who gives only the most cursory discussion of intervals. (He instead derives the notions of consonance and dissonance from chords, and returns to a discussion of forbidden interval progressions only after the close of the complete section on progression in major [*Grundsätze*, pp. 42–45].) Here, Bruckner follows Dürrnberger rather than Sechter: not only does he teach elementary voice leading rules through interval progressions, but he goes on to describe consonance and dissonance in intervallic rather than chordal terms.[15] Bruckner's discussion of the six-four chord is an excellent case in point (see p. 77 below).

Another clear instance of Dürrnberger's influence may be found in Bruckner's instructions for the connection of root position triads. Indeed, one of the most famous of Bruckner's pedagogical laws, passed on to later generations by Schoenberg[16] among others, is the "Gesetz des nächsten Weges"—a phrase which originated neither with Bruckner nor Sechter, but with Dürrnberger. Shortly after his discussion of intervals, Dürrnberger gives the laws of *Verbindung:* (1) retain oblique voices; (2) those voices which do not remain oblique follow the "law of the shortest way"; and (3) if there are no notes in common, choose contrary motion according to the "law of the shortest way" (*Elementarbuch,* p. 53). Bruckner's voice leading rules are reduced to the first two, since he chooses to treat stepwise progressions only much later in his system.[17] Throughout his University lectures, Bruckner notated all musical examples on a four-stave system: the lowest staff contained the bass line (and the fundamental bass notated in black note heads, as Sechter often did), while the upper three staves illustrated the three possible positions of the soprano in close position. The *praktischer Teil* in Dürrnberger's book is set up in precisely the same way (without the fundamental bass, of course).

Not all of Bruckner's system of harmony is derived from Sechter, but neither is there anything in it which conflicts with Sechter.[18] The pedagogical approach (certain aspects of which come from Dürrnberger) was undoubtedly influenced to an extent by the nature of Bruckner's teaching. In his University lectures, he was faced with the task of teaching students with very little prior musical experience, and it may be for this reason that he chose Dürrnberger's simpler presentation as a model.[19] The demands made upon Bruckner as a teacher may have influenced the more theoretical aspects of his system as well. As we shall see shortly, Sechter's system of harmony became considerably more "harmonic" in Bruckner's hands. Counterpoint, both as a separate discipline and as a component of harmony, became much less important. The result was a system of harmony which, although questionable, was probably quite efficient (as oversimplifications frequently are) for the teaching of large lecture classes.

Bruckner and the Ninth Chord

The "theoretical"—or perhaps it might be better to say the "systematic"—aspects of Bruckner's system are derived from Sechter, but there *are* differences. The most important of these is undoubtedly Bruckner's position on the ninth chord. For Sechter, the chord was derived through change of bass upon resolution of a 9–8 suspension. With evident reluctance Sechter admits that

> to the ninth, which is introduced here arbitrarily and really only delays the entrance of the octave, one can attribute an (admittedly inauthentic) independence, in that one calls the simultaneous sounding of root, third, fifth, seventh, and ninth a ninth chord.[20]

For Bruckner, on the other hand, the ninth chord is elevated to the position of one of the three fundamental chords:

> The three-, four-, and five-note chords are the three fundamental chords of music. The six- and seven-note chords only occur incidentally.[21]

This statement, taken from one of the earliest in a sequence of lectures recorded by Schwanzara, occurs long before any mention of the suspension (which, incidentally, receives a one-sentence definition and no musical examples).[22]

Clearly, Bruckner attributes considerable independence to this "fundamental harmony," while acknowledging as well the existence of the "six- and seven-note chords, which occur only incidentally"; to Sechter, the latter were not chords at all.

According to Schwanzara, Bruckner spent considerable time on "difficult" resolutions of the ninth chord and its figured bass representation.[23] In Eckstein's notes from his private study, the inversions of the ninth chord are given the following names: (1) 7 chord with a 6; (2) $^6_5$ with 4; (3) $^4_3$ with 2; and (4) 2 with 7. Eckstein goes on to say that with inversions of the ninth chord the ninth may not be next to the root or below it. Consequently, the first three inversions work well, but the last is unusable.[24] In another set of notes from the University lectures of 1879–80 we are told that inverting the ninth chord with the sounding root is incorrect. But the writer of these notes follows the statement with: "Strange that one does not do it; *Bruckner* wants to do it, and *Wagner* [already] has."[25] In taking up the cause of Bruckner's beloved ninth chord, Schoenberg ultimately would fulfill Bruckner's repressed desire. After complaining that "...theory has the tendency, whenever it has no example for something, to declare it bad, or at least [to dismiss it as] impossible," Schoenberg finds the requisite example: a "last-inversion" ninth chord from *Verklärte Nacht*, in which all voices proceed by half step to resolution, the "root" and "ninth" moving up by half step (in parallel sevenths), while the other voices descend by half step.[26]

The existence of scale-degree ninth chords in major, while strongly implied, is not actually stated. But this is clearly because Bruckner felt it unnecessary to do so; in the discussion of minor, he enumerates the various scale-degree ninths possible through use of the variable sixth and seventh degrees.[27]

On the matter of the six- and seven-note chords it appears that Bruckner was not terribly consistent. In his private lesson notes, Eckstein has written:

> Difference between the *eleventh* and *thirteenth*, as opposed to the *seventh* and *ninth*: The eleventh and thirteenth must resolve over the same fundamental, while the seventh and ninth can be resolved over *different fundamentals;* therefore, the eleventh and thirteenth are not independent dissonances.[28]

Yet, there are certainly passages in Bruckner's music which seem to suggest that he thought of such dissonances as producing a "chord," at least on the dominant. Measures 103–23 of the first movement of the Seventh Symphony[29] certainly seem to suggest such a sonority. Moreover, a surviving page of Bruckner's manuscript[30] shows him experimenting with possible inversions of six- and seven-note chords on the dominant:

Example 9-1

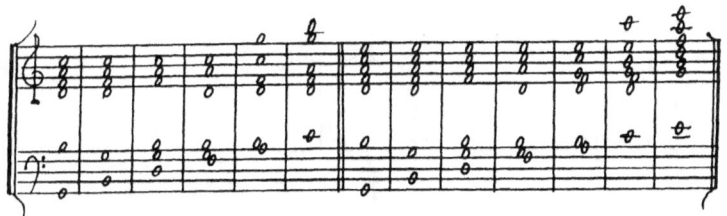

In regard to his own music Schwanzara quotes Bruckner as saying: "In the Ninth Symphony I use seven-note chords with omission of the third and fifth, and complete resolution."[31] And Josef Vockner, the only student known to have taken Bruckner's complete theory course privately, has notated the chords of the "ninth, eleventh, and thirteenth." However, no resolutions for these chords are given,[32] and at another point in his study, the eleventh and thirteenth are once again treated as suspensions.[33] In Loidol's University notes we read that the third is usually left out of the "seven-note chord,"[34] while in Schwanzara's later University notes the subject is avoided completely. The most likely explanation for the apparent contradiction is that Bruckner regarded the use of these chords as an advanced technique and preferred to be somewhat more conventional with his less-advanced students.

Marpurg's classification of dissonance found widespread acceptance in the nineteenth century. However, as we have seen with Vogler and Knecht, this does not mean that the "dissonances of the ninth, eleventh and thirteenth" necessarily form "chords." The opinions of Sechter and Bruckner on this matter are really quite different, although Riemann's "third-stacking" accusation has caused considerable confusion here as well.[35] A brief summary will serve to set matters straight. In Sechter's system, the ninth is always the product of suspension, there are no inversions of the ninth chord, and scale-degree ninth chords can only occur in the sequence through delayed resolution of a suspension beyond the change of bass. Moreover, the dissonances of the eleventh and thirteenth do not form chords. In Bruckner's system, on the other hand, the ninth chord is a "fundamental harmony"; the eleventh and thirteenth are on some occasions the result of suspension, while on others they are part of a six- or seven-note chord on the dominant.[36]

Bruckner's acceptance of the ninth chord as a "fundamental harmony" has important ramifications throughout his system of harmony. For one thing, the ability to conjure up five-note chords at will enables him to explain progressions harmonically which Sechter had explained melodically. Example 9-2a is one of these.[37]

Example 9-2

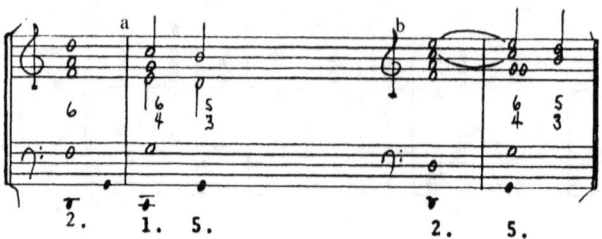

This is precisely the same progression—with exactly the same metric setting and voice-leading—which Sechter had used to illustrate his "irregular passing tone," defining thereby one of his model "artificial" six-four chords: the cadential six-four prepared by step (see chapter 6, p. 48). But as the fundamental bass indicates, the very same chord is "natural" for Bruckner, and thus represents a root-position C chord. Bruckner's choice of the very same example seems hardly fortuitous, but rather a self-conscious revision of Sechter's system. The increase in the number of fundamental readings from two to four is typical of Bruckner's readings; the "fundamental" ninth chord increases greatly the possibility of fundamental readings.

Example 9-2b is recorded by Schwanzara immediately after example 9-2a. It shows the "artificial" six-four over the dominant, and is quite revealing of the effect that the "fundamental" ninth has had upon Sechter's system. An "independent" II9 outside of the context of change of bass 9-8 suspensions and the descending fifth sequence is unthinkable in Sechter. But in Bruckner, the stack of thirds has been increased by one, and consequently the "II9" becomes a canonical preparation of the cadential six-four.

Stepwise Progressions and the "Intermediate Fundamental"

For Sechter, the "intermediate fundamental" had served primarily as a means to explain progressions which *ascend* by step. The problems which began to develop with the *descending* stepwise progressions (which demanded the ninth chord in all cases) finally culminated in the embarrassing "exceptions," the worst of which were hidden at the end of the second volume of the *Grundsätze*. For Bruckner, on the other hand, the exceptions become norms; the "fundamental" ninth chord leads him to treat the ascending and descending stepwise progressions equivalently.[38]

Bruckner gives Sechter's first example of an ascending progression (see ex. 9-3):

Example 9-3

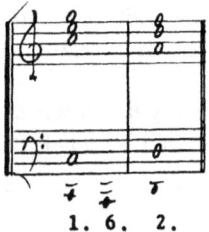

His explanation makes it clear from the outset that he is merely paying lip service to Sechter's theory of "imagined" dissonances:

> The G... is called an inaudible seventh. Because it is not a real seventh, under [certain] circumstances it can often ascend, just as an inaudible diminished or impure fifth [the fifth of II] [may do].[39]

Having thus disposed of the ascending stepwise progression of two root position triads, what could be more logical than to tackle the same progression in descending motion? Bruckner gives the following examples and explanation:

Example 9-4

> But because the G [in ex. 9-4b] is not supposed to leap, I shall put in a passing tone. Then the G resolves downward to F and the E is a passing seventh which resolves correctly to D.... The descending stepwise progression starting in the soprano position of the *fifth* [9-4c] is very interesting and seldom found in textbooks.... The inaudible ninth G is in the soprano, and so that it does not leap as in [ex. 9-4a], I shall put in a passing tone, this time in ascending motion.[40]

In offering an explanation akin to the idea that embellishing parallel fifths somehow eliminates them, Bruckner appears to believe that sub-metrical embellishment can somehow resolve chordal dissonance which clearly does not resolve. But this sleight of hand simply will not do. How can the G remain the ninth of the F chord when it "resolves" to the F during the time of that chord? If the G "resolves," is the actual progression not I–IV$_3^4$–VII? If we grant the "resolution" of the G to F (as a sub-metrical embellishment), it does appear that the eighth-note E is a "passing seventh which resolves correctly to D"; but what of the soprano E which is of far greater duration and does not resolve correctly? No amount of sophistry can cover up the fact that these chordal sevenths and ninths simply do not resolve.

Thus the device which already bordered on the illusory in Sechter has become completely absurd with Bruckner. Not only is it "inaudible," but it is no longer even the result of intelligent interpretation.

Less Controversial Features of the System

In most other regards, Bruckner's system follows Sechter's very closely. There are differences of terminology, as for example, when Bruckner coins the terms *Ganzschritte* and *Halbschritte* for progressions by fifth and third, respectively,[41] and the term *Doppelschritte* for the stepwise progressions. The latter are explained as combinations of the former: the ascending step consists of the descending third and descending fifth, while the descending step is a combination of two descending fifths.[42] This idea is implicit in Sechter's system, but stated explicitly only by Bruckner.

Like Sechter, Bruckner teaches that the fifth of II is impure, although he later ignores this at many points. However, in the University lectures he appears to have justified this by speaking of tuning, while in his Conservatory teaching Decsey claims that he cited neither tuning nor the "subdominant function" of II, but merely said that the tone was often treated as though it were impure (and thus resolved down by step) in practice.[43] The idea of "substitutes" (*Stellvertreter*) which Sechter had considered important enough to make part of the title of his work, was, according to Schwanzara, ignored by Bruckner completely.[44] But some evidence exists to contradict this.[45]

There is, however, a distinctly different emphasis in Bruckner's discussion of progression when he defines the "characteristic cadence."[46] The "three most important scale degrees" are necessary in order to determine the tonality, according to Bruckner;[47] but since one may not proceed directly from IV to V, the acceptable cadence form is, in Bruckner's notation, 1.4.2.5.1. Of course, this is the same as Sechter's cadence (see chapter 7, p. 56), but it is interesting to note that the cadence is discussed at a relatively late stage in Sechter's system.[48] Bruckner, on the other hand, works by building up successively larger progressions of chords; the next progression discussed after the "characteristic cadence" is the "extended cadence": 1.5.3.6.4.2.5.1. Only somewhat later does he arrive at the fifth sequence of all scale-degree chords, for which he coins the term *Tabulatur*. The primacy of the cadence over the sequence in Bruckner's[49] system may be attributed to pedagogical considerations (again, this is from the University lectures). But it is also undoubtedly a reflection of the general view of the time: the cadence began to assume ever greater importance in most *Harmonielehren* throughout the nineteenth century. As with the ninth chord, Bruckner appears to be embracing "modern" notions.

While Bruckner's treatment of chord inversion is essentially the same as Sechter's, the excesses of fundamental bass thinking are even more apparent in his discussion of the six-four chord than they were in Sechter. The category of "artificial" six-fours has shrunk to minute size and importance in Bruckner's system; in contrast to Sechter, the idea is first mentioned very late, and the small number of examples occurs even later.[50]

Almost all six-fours are of the "natural" type, concerning which Bruckner says the following:

> The fourth in itself is a consonance. Likewise, the sixth in itself is a consonance. But when the fourth and sixth sound *together*, the fourth no longer sounds consonant. Thus the six-four chord has a double-nature.[51]

Here we can see the peculiar results of Bruckner's attempt to blend Dürrnberger's notions of intervallic consonance and dissonance with Sechter's fundamental bass theory. Why are the fourth and sixth consonant? And why are they dissonant when they sound together? These would seem to be important questions which must be answered if we are to determine just what the "double-nature" of the six-four really is. Unfortunately, they are left unanswered, followed merely by Sechter's rules for the treatment of six-fours, which state that either the bass or the fourth above must be prepared by common tone and that subsequently either tone (whether prepared or not) may resolve by step. The result in Bruckner's exercises, as in Sechter's, is the appearance of many six-fours that seem questionable. Klose, for example, claims that Bruckner's "I_4^6" alone admitted of fourteen different resolutions to various triads, seventh chords, and their inversions.[52] Bruckner's idea of the six-four is clear from his explicit recommendation that the theoretical root be doubled (resulting in the resolution by skip, or by step upward, of the doubled fourth from the bass).

The "harmonic" character of Bruckner's system is very much in evidence in his discussion of the seventh chord, which, it will be remembered, Sechter derived from the 8–7 passing motion. Mentioning that the seventh chord can be derived from the triad, Bruckner cautions that "according to their *essence*, however, the seventh chords are not *derived* from triads, but independent...."[53] His first examples support this view; the sevenths are of equal duration to other chord tones, and thus the canonical preparation of the seventh is by common tone. The 8–7 occurs only much later with the examples of "artificial" chords.[54]

78   *Anton Bruckner and Sechter's Teachings*

Analysis

Like Sechter, Bruckner was possessed by the desire to present the eternal truths of harmony. To this end, he generally confined the discussion to textbook examples generated specifically to prove particular theoretical points. Schwanzara claims that his examples had such "general validity" that he used exactly the same notes throughout his twenty-six year career of lecturing.[55] All sources are in agreement that he never discussed his own compositions; according to Decsey, he also avoided "licenses" from the scores of Liszt and Wagner.[56]

The most extensive example in Schwanzara's notes is the following "kleines Präludium," composed as a model for the University class.[57]

Example 9-5

In the first measure we see the typical passing VII6, used to linearize the voice exchange progression, I-I6. Since the progression is a near transposition of Sechter's V7-IV6-IV$_5^6$ passing chord progression (see chapter 6, p. 47), Sechter most likely would read the whole bar over a single C fundamental (especially considering voice leading and the unaccented position of the passing chord). If this reading were not chosen, the most likely alternative would be to consider the VII6 to be a *Stellvertreter* of the dominant (see chapter 5, p. 40), resulting in the fundamental reading (in quarters) C-G-C. Bruckner's reading of five fundamentals in one bar seems most contorted and unlikely.

The bracketed numbers refer to voice leading which Bruckner thought to be at least somewhat exceptional, and thus needful of explanation. The text to number one points out that the ninth of the *Zwischenfundament* rises. This is, of course, one of Sechter's "exceptions" from the second volume of his

Grundsätze. Number two notes that the seventh is a "passing tone" and thus needs no preparation, (remember that most of Bruckner's sevenths are *not* passing). Number three notes that the ninth of the *Zwischenfundament* leaps. This is the progression which Sechter only allowed in three parts, precisely so that this would not occur. Numbers four, five, and six are noncontroversial, noting respectively that the solution in parenthetical note heads avoids the problem of number three, that a triad was chosen before the seventh chord in measure six, and that the skip from the third of I to the third of V is permitted. But seven speaks to the apparent "license" in the preparation of the six-four: neither the bass nor the fourth of the six-four is prepared by common tone. The example is, of course, Sechter's "irregular passing tone" in a different metric setting. For Sechter, the chord would have been "artificial," and thus exempt from the previous voice leading requirements for "natural" six-fours. Bruckner is unable to explain away the obvious contradiction.

Examples from the actual musical literature are only slightly less scarce than Decsey's opinion would indicate; nevertheless, they do exist. Examples drawn from the Mozart Requiem and "Jupiter" Symphony, the Beethoven Ninth Symphony, and Wagner's *Meistersinger* may be found in Loidol's notes from the earlier University lectures (leading Flotzinger to speculate that Bruckner may have simplified his approach in the later series).[58] An interesting example may also be found in Eckstein's notes from private study:[59]

Example 9-6

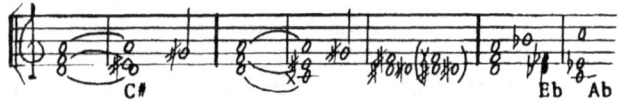

The example shows an enharmonic reinterpretation of the "Todesverkündigung" motive from the second act of *Die Walküre*. (Underneath the example in Eckstein's manuscript appear the scratched-out remains of "Walküre, Todes.") This is taken from a demonstration of enharmonic modulation by respelling triads, a subject generally ignored (and certainly not mentioned by Sechter), but evidently of interest to Bruckner. Bruckner clearly reads the fundamental of the second bar as C♯ (in the first version); the apparent D minor chord is thus "artificial," resulting from melodic displacement of the C♯ seventh chord (of the hypothetical next bar—not shown). This example may well have provided inspiration for the researches of Bruckner's student Josef Schalk, who cites the same example in his work on Wagner's harmonic practice (see chapter 11).

Chromatic Harmony

Because most of the surviving records of Bruckner's system of harmony are student notes from the University lectures, there is little material dealing with more advanced topics. Schwanzara's notes, for example, contain a mere two pages concerning chromaticism. "Chromatic harmony" is defined exactly as Sechter had defined it, but in addition there is a definition of "chromatic modulation" (*chromatische Tonwechslung*): "In chromatic modulation, the transition is effected with chords *foreign* to the key."[60] This, of course, is the standard meaning of the term; but it should be remembered that the idea of "modulation" is incompatible with Sechter's theory of chromaticism, which is based upon "tonicization", and thus still tied to the diatonic *Verwandtschaft*. Bruckner gives a brief example: a modulation from C major to E♭ major with a pivot on a C dominant seventh chord. He remarks that the pivot is foreign to both keys.[61]

Bruckner clearly followed Sechter in demanding that the fundamentals of all chromatic chords always be diatonic.[62] Moreover, Sechter's distinction between "simple" and "compound" chromatic progression is maintained by Bruckner, and the "hybrid-chord," whose ultimate origin Bruckner attributes (incorrectly) to Marpurg, is also mentioned repeatedly. Thus, with the exception of the previously mentioned definition of "chromatic modulation"—which, unfortunately, receives no further explanation—the theoretical aspects of Bruckner's teaching of chromaticism follow Sechter exactly.

The idea of modal borrowing, a pervasive feature of German *Harmonielehren* which was incompatible with Sechter's strict division between major and minor, is nevertheless dealt with by Bruckner, who goes on to describe modulations in major by use of the borrowed minor subdominant.[63]

In spite of apparent disagreement, Bruckner's thoughts on the enharmonic do not differ substantially from Sechter's.[64] However, in Sechter's system the enharmonic was kept quite separate from the techniques of chromaticism, while Bruckner, on the other hand, gives a number of examples which combine both. Example 9-7 presents the opening measures of four sequences which appear in Eckstein's notes under the heading "Enharmonic by means of the hybrid-chord."[65] In each of the four, the first two measures involve chromatic motion, while the sequential transposition involves the enharmonic. Example 9-7d, which may well have been derived by Bruckner from 9-7c by harmonic ellipsis and the enharmonic, shows the resolution of an augmented sixth chord (here a diminished third) to a dominant seventh. Although certainly common in the musical literature, the progression is relatively rare in *Harmonielehren* of the period. Louis and Thuille would later coin the term "back alteration" (*Rückalterierung*) for the characteristic motion of $\sharp\hat{4}$ to $\flat\hat{4}$.[66]

Example 9-7

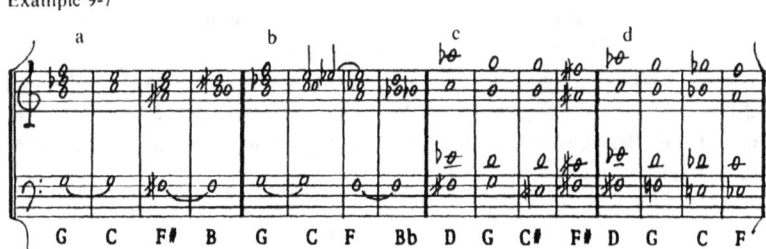

According to Eckstein, Bruckner's first exercises in chromatic writing utilized contrary motion chromatic scales.[67] Eckstein's examples are mainly exercises in chromatic spelling, the technique of which is close to the usual practice: sharps (or naturals) are used in ascending motion in major (with the exception of the seventh degree), and flats (or naturals) are used in descending motion (with the exception of the raised fourth degree). In minor the spellings are less variable: the usual spellings of the sixth and seventh degrees are used in both directions, and the Neapolitan (lowered second) is also invariable. The raised third in ascending motion is spelled as the lowered fourth in descending motion; the raised fourth and lowered fifth work similarly. The contrary motion technique is clearly derived from the usual diatonic contrary motion scales: the alignment of the two scales is according to letter name. While the choice of certain of the spellings would appear to be harmonic in origin (raised fourth, Neapolitan, etc.), this aspect remains unclear because Eckstein gives no harmonic interpretation.

The Chromatic Bass and the Chromatic Passing Chord

Eckstein's contrary motion scales, which are essentially alterations of diatonic structures, may have served as preparation for more thoroughly chromatic techniques; there is evidence that Vogler's chromatic scale (the "omnibus") played a role in Bruckner's teaching.

A Bruckner manuscript entitled "Chromatische Anmerkungen"[68] illustrates most of the chromatic procedures described by Sechter: "apparently" chromatic pitches drawn from the *Verwandtschaft* are placed between diatonic whole steps, thirds and fifths of chords are altered (but never roots), and the diminished seventh (the dominant ninth) occurs frequently. There are slight deviations from Sechter's practice: the progression of an F dominant seventh chord to a B dominant seventh occurs in two examples; although the fundamentals are diatonic within C major-A minor, the questionable enharmonic (E♭-D♯) and the fact that the F7 is not a secondary dominant make the progression unlikely in Sechter.

In addition, the manuscript gives examples of Bruckner's use of Sechter's "artificial" chords and confirms that Bruckner remains loyal to Sechter here too. A few selected examples will illustrate. Example 9-8, the first on the manuscript, shows contrary chromatic motion in bass and alto supported by two fundamentals; the diatonic II^6_4–V^6_5 is embellished by the "artificial" B♭ seventh chord. Bruckner notes that the harmonic reading is the same whether the B♭ is present or not.

Example 9-8

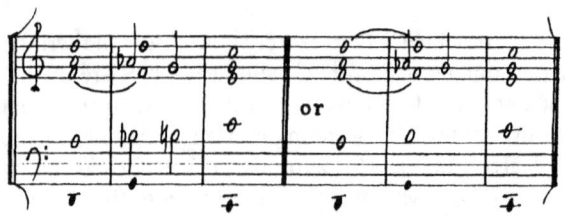

(Courtesy Music Division, New York Public Library)

Examples 9-9a, b, and c appear consecutively in the manuscript. Example 9-9a, which shows contrary chromatic motion over a single fundamental, is quite similar to Sechter's version of the "classical omnibus" (see chapter 7, p. 57), the only difference being the diminished third chord on the second beat. Example 9-9b—another variant of the "omnibus"—favors the diminished seventh, while 9-9c shows the possibility of the "artificial" IV6 through neighbor note motion in the upper parts. This may be compared with one of Sechter's examples of the voice exchange (see chapter 6, p. 47). Example 9-9d appears somewhat later when the examples deal with chromaticism in the minor mode. It, too, illustrates IV6 as an "artificial" chord and shows that at least on some occasions Bruckner does not read the motion of V–IV with a change of fundamental.

Example 9-9

Example 9-9 (continued)

(Courtesy Music Division, New York Public Library)

Example 9-10, the longest on the manuscript, is an elaboration of Sechter's famous fifth sequence. Beginning with the fourth fundamental (E), each fundamental is elaborated through quadruple counterpoint: two voices have the chromatically embellished voice exchange, one voice has a chromatic elaboration of an 8–7 motion, and one voice remains stationary. Each pattern is stated in each voice during the fundamentals E, A, D, and G; the "inversions" of the "artificial" chords change accordingly.

Example 9-10

(Courtesy Music Division, New York Public Library)

Thus the harmonic techniques first described by Vogler and Kirnberger/Schulz survived through the nineteenth century in the Sechter/Bruckner system.

The "Bruckner Problem"

The more controversial features of Sechter's system (the "intermediate fundamental," the assumption of just intonation) drew considerable criticism—but not from Bruckner, who accepted them unquestioningly. Yet, ironically, it was he who brought the system to its breaking point. Despite his attempts to preserve Sechter's system, it simply could not be made to accept the "fundamental" ninth chord without dire consequences. With the parity of ascending and descending progressions, the "intermediate fundamental" became the result of mere mechanical routine rather than analytical interpretation. And both the greater freedom in the voice-leading of dissonant chords and the near extinction of "nonessential" chords placed a far greater emphasis on "harmony" (the fundamentals). If, as Dahlhaus asserts, "Schenker denied the concept of the 'essential' dissonance and Schoenberg that of the 'incidental',"[69] there can be little doubt that, in Bruckner's hands, Sechter's notion of harmonic progression had moved considerably closer to Schoenberg's "theory of root progressions."

By the end of the nineteenth century, Sechter's *Grundsätze* was long out of print and nearly forgotten. The "basic principles" lived on mainly in the works of later interpreters, of whom Bruckner was certainly the most influential. A new generation came to know Sechter's system only in Bruckner's revision. Moreover, their opinion of the system was colored by their regard for Bruckner as a composer and pedagogue. Thus Schoenberg's sympathy for the "older theory" is perfectly consistent with his sympathy for Bruckner the composer. And Schenker's criticisms result partially from his opinion of Bruckner's music, but also from such famous utterances of Bruckner the "theorist" as, "Segn's mein Herrn, dass ist die Regl, i schreib natirli not a so." (Look gentlemen, this is the rule. Of course, I don't compose that way.) "What marvelous snarls of contradictions!" Schenker observes, "one believes in rules which should be laughed at."[70] And indeed, when one reads Bruckner's explanation of the descending step progression, the ironic mockery of "rules" is apparent.

The "Bruckner Problem" is a complex one: both what he said about harmony and what was left unsaid contributed to it. From the former it was clear that the system was in drastic need of reform, while from the latter it was equally clear that much of what Bruckner the composer did was inexpressible—at least in the system he taught. Indeed, Bruckner personified the critical state in which music theory in general found itself at the end of the nineteenth century. And the importance of this image should not be underestimated: when, at the beginning of the next century, music theory finally moved a bit closer to practice, a number of harmony books which appeared were clearly reactions to the paradox of Anton Bruckner.

10

"Romantic Harmony" and the Fundamental Bass

Despite its down-to-earth, pedagogical nature, Sechter's *Grundsätze* remains an "abstract" work when viewed in the context of nineteenth-century compositional practice. Moreover, Bruckner's apparent separation of composition and theory could only have made the system seem more irrelevant. The task of demonstrating some relationship between Sechter's ideas and the music of the period fell to the students of Sechter and Bruckner. Karl Mayrberger, (1828–81), a student of Preyer's,[1] was the first to use the system in the analysis of a contemporary work: the Prelude from Wagner's *Tristan und Isolde*. Wagner himself took an interest in Mayrberger's monograph, recommending it for publication in the *Bayreuther Blätter;*[2] and it was undoubtedly this pioneering work which served as the main stimulus for the later efforts of two Bruckner students, Josef Schalk and Cyrill Hynais (see chapter 11).

Besides his Wagner monograph, Mayrberger is also the author of a brief work on the diminished seventh chord[3] and a treatise on harmony[4] which remained unfinished at the time of his death. Like Hasel's *Harmoniesystem* (another late nineteenth-century version of Sechter's system; see chapter 11), Mayrberger's treatise was designed for use in a teacher-training school, and is a thoroughly practical (and rather pedantic) work. The completed portion of the book is, in essence, a highly expanded version of Sechter's system of progression in major (385 pages are spent on what Sechter had covered in a little over fifty pages). Most of it shows an almost medieval dependence on Sechter's authority (even going so far as to repeat Sechter's dubious advice on nonresolution of dissonance resulting from the "intermediate fundamental" when such dissonance "is not heard as such"[5]). However, Mayrberger has some original thoughts in two areas: the distinction between chordal and intervallic consonance, and the explanation of passing chords.

The *Lehrbuch:* Consonance and Dissonance

In the introduction to the *Lehrbuch* Mayrberger claims that his work rests upon a precise definition of chordal consonance. Indeed, we soon find that he has done much to eliminate the confusion between the notions of intervallic and chordal consonance which plagued Bruckner, in particular.

"Chordal consonance" is the property of those tones which "[when] *related to a scale-step, form a perfect octave, a perfect fifth, a major or minor third, or a perfect unison.*"[6] Mayrberger cites Hauptmann as the inspiration for this idea. Indeed, the definition is certainly derived from Hauptmann's three "directly intelligible intervals,"[7] but Mayrberger's inclusion of the minor third (not "directly intelligible," according to Hauptmann) clearly indicates that he would not accept Hauptmann's "dualistic" derivation of the minor triad. For the notion of intervallic consonance Mayrberger suggests the term "consonant sounding intervals" (*consonirend klingende Intervalle*); these are "viewed in isolation" rather than "related to a scale-step"; and include the major and minor thirds, the perfect fourth and fifth, and the major and minor sixths. Thus Mayrberger draws a clear distinction between Sechter's chordal approach and Bruckner's intervallic approach to consonance.

Unlike Bruckner's, Mayrberger's ideas about chordal *dissonance* fall right in line with those of Kirnberger and Sechter. The difference between melodic and chordal dissonance is that the former

> *can resolve over their own fundamental, as opposed to those which have been learned up to this point—that is, the diminished fifth and the seventh, which can never resolve over their own fundamental, but rather need a new fundamental for their resolution. On that account these are also called the true chordal dissonances.*[8]

In order to understand properly Mayrberger's Wagner analyses, it is necessary to be quite clear on the limitations he imposes on "chords." Again, his explanation (in italics) comes straight out of Kirnberger:

> *It is evident that the chordal dissonances are essential components of their chord, which cannot be separated from it. The dissonance of the suspension, on the other hand, is a contingent phenomenon whose existence does not alter in the least the essence of the chord to which it is related.*[9]

Mayrberger's opinion of the "ninth chord" comes as no surprise:

> [*If*] *the suspension is not an essential chord tone,* [*then*] *neither is the ninth in our example. Thus, to speak of a ninth chord as a fundamental harmony—as so many textbooks incorrectly designate it (Marx, p. 168)* [*Volume I of Marx,* Die Lehre von der musikalischen Komposition, *Leipzig: 1837*]—*is out of the question.*[10]

And of course the dissonances of the eleventh and thirteenth may not form chords either.[11]

In discussing the 7–6 suspension—a troublesome "exception," since Mayrberger has categorically declared the *descending* seventh to be a "chordal dissonance"—his reason for demanding compound interval notation of "suspensions" emerges. Mayrberger gives examples 10-1a-b and explains:

Example 10-1

From these two examples... it is clear that only when the chord tone sounds simultaneously with the suspension does the suspension configuration emerge beyond any doubt, while, if this... is not the case, it is at least very questionable whether a seventh chord on the sixth step might be meant during the first two quarters.[12]

Mayrberger goes on to lament the fact that the "older scores" were not figured with the necessary scrupulousness. While this problem of interpretation is most pronounced with the seventh (which is usually a chordal dissonance but may be a suspension), Mayrberger demands the compound notation for all "suspensions." His reasoning is certainly overly literal, but in any event it is clear that he regards the ninth, eleventh, and thirteenth as melodic displacements of triadic tones, not as "chord tones."[13]

Passing Chords

Mayrberger begins this discussion unassumingly enough with the idea of "harmonic figuration," which he may have gotten from A.B. Marx.[14] Example 10-2a is, in a sense, equivalent to example 10-2b because "what can happen with one voice can also happen simultaneously with two or more."[15]

Example 10-2

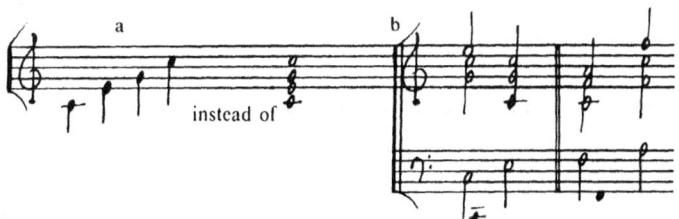

88 "Romantic Harmony" and Fundamental Bass

While on the surface this might appear to be nothing more unusual than the theory of harmonic inversion, the idea allows Mayrberger to get close to defining the *consonant six-four:*

> Here it should be noted that when one and the same chord is harmonically figured, a simultaneously attacked fourth from the bass is allowed.[16]

The example which illustrates this statement shows a C major chord with the bass arpeggiating from C to G, creating a six-four. This six-four, in which the fourth from the bass may be approached by skip, differs from both Sechter's "natural" six-four (in which either the bass or the fourth must be prepared) and his "artificial" six-four. Mayrberger fails to make further use of the idea, however.

Mayrberger's ideas on "passing chords" (*Durchgangsaccorde*) are much more developed. After defining passing tones (*Durchgangsnoten*) in a more or less conventional manner, he goes on to show how they may be used simultaneously in two and more parts, and finally remarks, "to the passing tones, harmonic figuration may be added simultaneously in another voice."[17] The combination of passing motion and arpeggiation was implicit in Sechter;[18] yet he did not develop the idea further, perhaps because the exact processes involved were not defined clearly. Mayrberger, on the other hand, ultimately reaches an extremely sophisticated notion of "passing chords"; to the processes of arpeggiation and passing motion he adds a third: the changing tone. Example 10-3a illustrates simultaneous changing tone motion in three parts;[19] example 10-3b shows the combination of changing tone motion and harmonic figuration, example 10-3c the combination of passing and changing motion, and example 10-3d the combination of all three.[20]

Example 10-3

The discussion of the previous examples leads directly to the complete definition of the "passing chord":

> Until now, we have constructed two chords such that each was based upon its own individual fundamental.

Now we wish to become familiar with another type of chord formation in which two chords, and in fact various chord tones, are built upon one and the same fundamental, whereby the latter chord is of course always built upon the fundamental of the former.

For this chord relationship we will require the techniques of harmonic figuration, the passing tone and the neighbor tone, all of which have been discussed previously.

According to our needs, we shall use each of these devices separately or together, and call the resulting chords...*passing chords.*[21]

From this point on, the "passing chord" becomes an important part of Mayrberger's system of harmony. Example 10-4a is of course Sechter's example, but examples 10-4b-c show Mayrberger's further development of the idea. As is apparent, the idea of "harmonic figuration" allows him to use the second and third chords in inversion. Oblique tones are not simply held, as in Sechter; they may be introduced by skip as well. The use of two passing tones and "harmonic figuration" allows Mayrberger to account for the progressions II–(IV7)–V and II–(VI)–V in a similar manner.[22]

Example 10-4

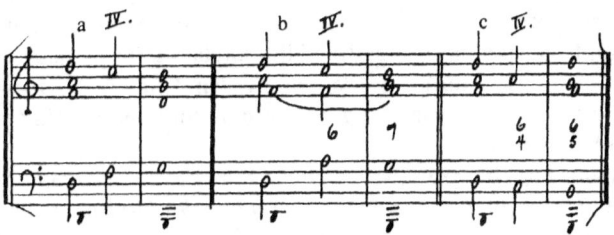

It is undeniable that most of Mayrberger's work is a mere footnote to Sechter: all of Sechter's ideas are there—even the most dubious ones.[23] Nevertheless, Mayrberger's attempt to distinguish between both intervals and chords which are "related to a scale-step" (as opposed to those which are "consonant" but not "harmonic") begins to suggest the notion of "scale-step" which Schenker will present later in his *Harmonielehre*. It would be going too far to ascribe any real influence to Mayrberger's ideas about diatonic harmony (this is not true, however, for his ideas about chromatic harmony; see below). More than likely, Mayrberger's *Lehrbuch* was unknown outside of his classroom. But it is interesting to see the different directions in which varying interpretations of Sechter's system may lead: while the "fundamental ninth chord" and the greater use of the "intermediate fundamental" necessarily lead to frequently changing fundamentals in Bruckner's system, Mayrberger's conservative position on chords and his use of "passing chords" results in a broader notion of harmony.

Mayrberger's Analysis of *Tristan*

Perhaps no work has ever excited the reaction from music theorists that Wagner's *Tristan und Isolde* has. The debate began some fourteen years after the opera's premiere (Munich: 1865) with Cyrill Kistler's analysis of the "Tristan Chord." By the time Mayrberger wrote his study two years later, it was already clear that *Tristan* had become the touchstone for any system of harmony aspiring to legitimacy. At the turn of the century the Riemann partisans attempted to apply his system to *Tristan*,[24] and even Capellen's *Streitschrift* (the content of which is really a general attack on Sechter's whole system) claimed to be an inquiry into the "suitability" of Sechter's system for "Wagner research."[25] Twenty years later the enigmatic language of *Tristan* would become the model for Ernst Kurth's researches in chromatic harmony,[26] and recent writings show that *Tristan* continues to be as provocative as ever.[27]

Kistler, a born-again Wagnerite,[28] is the author of the first practical harmony book which assumes the Wagnerian style as a norm.[29] Essentially, the book consists of practical advice (including many progressions which capture the style rather well, and—in the second edition—quite a number of examples from the literature) supported by Hauptmannian theory. Kistler's explanation of the "Tristan Chord" is based upon a personal interpretation (or perhaps a misunderstanding) of Hauptmann's "overlapping system" (*übergreifendes System*), a theory by which Hauptmann sought to account for tonicizations of the dominant or subdominant.

The normal minor key (for example, C minor: F a♭ C e♭ G b D) can be shifted by one third to the right, resulting in the *übergreifendes Mollsystem* (a♭ C e♭ G b D f♯).[30] Using this scheme one may construct the new seventh chords: D f♯/a♭ C or f♯/a♭ C e♭ from the extremes of the chain of thirds. Hauptmann denies the possibility of b D f♯/a♭, claiming that the chord is "untrue" and "discordant" because it contains two leading tones (b and f♯) which must create parallel fifths upon resolution.[31] The possibility that one of the leading tones might be retained in the chord of resolution (precisely what happens if one chooses this interpretation of the "Tristan Chord") does not seem to have occurred to Hauptmann. This is the interpretation which Kistler chooses, making him the inventor of the idea that the "Tristan Chord" is the "minor triad with diminished seventh" on scale degree VII.[32]

This was the entire extent of theory connected with *Tristan* when Mayrberger entered the fracas. A true Sechter disciple, Mayrberger attempted to apply Sechter's norms of harmonic progression to *Tristan*. The diminished third/augmented sixth chords have only one place in Sechter's system: they must be derived from II7 or II9. Accordingly, Mayrberger considers the "Tristan Chord" to be Sechter's "hybrid-chord," and thus becomes the author of the other interpretation of the "Tristan Chord"—the one in which the G♯ is nonchordal,[33] and the one which Lorenz later calls "the most significant step" in the analysis of the "Tristan Chord."[34]

Example 10-5

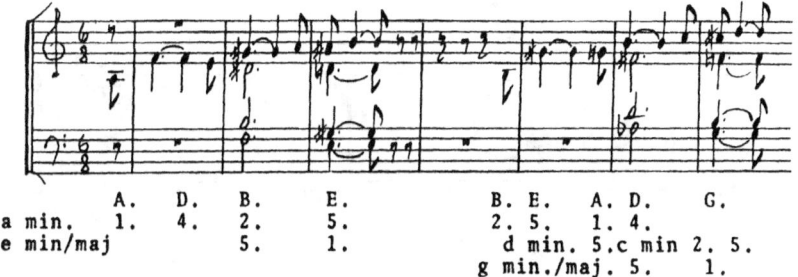

```
              A.   D.   B.   E.          B.  E.   A.  D.   G.
a min.        1.   4.   2.   5.          2.  5.   1.  4.
e min/maj               5.   1.          d min. 5.c min 2. 5.
                                         g min./maj. 5.     1.
```

Regardless of the reaction one might have to Hauptmann's *übergreifendes System* as an explanation of the "Tristan Chord," there does seem to be a grain of truth in Kistler's idea. If we were to view the work from the perspective of a present-day analyst, we might call upon the voice exchange B–G♯/G♯–B as evidence that the G♯ is *not* nonchordal.[35] However, a chordal G♯ presumes a view of "harmony" which is considerably broader than that of any nineteenth-century theory. That is, if we dismiss Kistler's solution as mere labeling, and yet believe that the G♯ is chordal in both the "Tristan Chord" and the subsequent E7 chord, then we are forced to conclude that there is no harmonic progression between these two chords. (In fact, even if Kistler's label is retained, the motion of VII to V is essentially no progression—according to both the step and function theory.) This is obviously something which early analysts—accustomed as they were to accounting for most chord-to-chord motion in harmonic terms—were unprepared to accept. Consequently, Mayrberger's analysis of the "Tristan Chord" was one of the most influential aspects of his work. This is one point where the German and Viennese theories agreed, and thus the vast majority of later commentators also see the "Tristan Chord" as some sort of "B7" chord; the only question remaining is whether it is an alteration of a diatonic II7—a subdominant "function" (Lorenz)—or of V7/V (Kurth).[36]

Just as the hybrid-chord is a response to Sechter's system, so too is Mayrberger's analysis of the first complete measure. When Mitchell says that this bar represents I, but that the opening cello solo has been misinterpreted in the past as outlining VI or IV,[37] the responsibility again may well be Mayrberger's. If the "Tristan Chord" is "II," the previous measure cannot possibly be "I"; it *must* be VI or IV.

92 "Romantic Harmony" and Fundamental Bass

So far, Mayrberger has encountered few problems. The real trouble begins, however, with the next transposition of the "Tristan Chord."

Mayrberger gives the following analysis of these measures (ex. 10-6a):

Example 10-6

```
              A.   (F#) B.         A.   (F#) B.
a min.        1.
e min.        4.   (2.) 5.
```

The second two rather complicated measures, we are told, may be reduced to the simpler structure of example 10-6b. Here, we must quote Mayrberger's explanation exactly:

> D is the free [unprepared] suspension of the eleventh, which, in order to ascend, becomes a chromatic passing tone, D#.
>
> G# is the suspension of the rising seventh, which becomes a ninth over the imaginary fundamental F# and later resolves to the seventh of the dominant over B.
>
> F is the suspension of the thirteenth, which resolves according to the rules. E# in the upper voice is the melodic-chromatic lower neighbor of F#.[38]

If we can trust what Mayrberger has had to say on these matters in his *Lehrbuch*, the "free suspension of the eleventh" (D), the "suspension of the ascending seventh"[39] (G#), and the "suspension of the thirteenth" (F) are "nonessential" dissonances; that is, the first chord is a *melodic* suspension chord.[40] Vogel, however, claims that "he [Mayrberger] calls the verticality C–F–G#–D a hybrid-chord from A minor:I and E minor:IV."[41] But Mayrberger never calls *this* verticality a "hybrid-chord"; in fact, he never says that these dissonances form a chord at all. Once again, the misunderstanding is probably due to Riemann's familiar third-stacking accusation.

In his attempt to account for these difficult measures, Mayrberger reaches for a familiar progression from Sechter: the phrygian half cadence with Sechter's obligatory "intermediate fundamental." If his analysis seems less than convincing, it is interesting that one of the first attempts to apply Riemann's theory of harmony to *Tristan* agrees exactly with Mayrberger at this point,[42] and that later attempts to account for these measures have not been trouble-free either. Kurth's analysis, for example, seems even less convincing than Mayrberger's.[43] Even if local harmonic problems are deemphasized by concentrating on long-range features, difficulties remain: the clear voice exchange which is essential to Mitchell's reading of the "Tristan Chord" becomes a somewhat more obscure chromatic exchange here (F–D/D♯–F♯).[44] It is precisely at this point that the symmetrical minor third transposition scheme of the first two phrases (excepting the opening A) gives way to the demands of the tonal system: the B7 chord, creating the middleground arpeggiation of the dominant. Some tension between these two contradictory phenomena is bound to assert itself in the analysis.

Although Mayrberger's study is supposedly confined to the *Leitmotive* from *Tristan*, he nevertheless manages to cover a considerable amount of the Prelude,[45] and in the second installment he deals with passages from Act I as well. The chromatic passing and suspension chords, while perhaps not as prominent as one might expect, continue to play an important role in his analyses. Two notable examples are the passing six-four in the second half of measure 18 of the Prelude (the "Glance" motive; see ex. 10-7a),[46] and the analysis of the first statement of the "Deliverance by Death" motive (mm. 63–70 of the Prelude),[47] in which all chords other than E7 are read as "nonessential."

Example 10-7

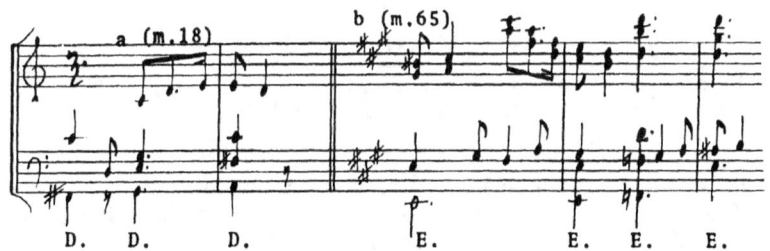

In the second section of the monograph Mayrberger also has more to say regarding his "new" theory of the *harmonic ellipsis*, the basis of which is his belief that dissonances need not be resolved if they merely have the possibility of resolution.[48] This notion serves conveniently to explain away a multitude of harmonic freedoms, such as unresolved sevenths. And if resolutions can be elided, Mayrberger reasons, why not whole chords as well? This is precisely the way in which he accounts for troublesome chromatic root progressions: the motion of C major to D♭ major, for example, is explained by interpolating an imaginary C°7 between the two chords,[49] proving once again the versatility—if not the usefulness—of this time-worn idea.

One of the most loyal of Sechter's followers, Mayrberger accepted Sechter's system almost unquestioningly, and thus its deficiencies are inherent in his analyses. Sechter's rigid rules of progression and the rapid harmonic rhythm resulting from their application already seem incompatible with the musical language of *Tristan* in the first eight bars (ex. 10-5). And the charge of "too many modulations" would later become a familiar criticism. Mayrberger deserves to be defended here, however. Although he accepted Sechter's limited definition of a key, he was able to see beyond the succession of swiftly changing keys and make broader connections—at least on some occasions. Example 10-8 shows a passage derived from the "Glance" motive as it appears in the second scene of Act I.[50] Although Mayrberger is forced to call upon three different keys to explain a four-measure passage, his analysis also makes it quite clear that the excursions into G and D minor act as a means of prolonging the dominant of C:

Example 10-8

It should also be noted that many of Mayrberger's "modulations" result from the lack of any notation for tonicization in Sechter's system. But although the system failed to distinguish between "modulations" of extreme brevity and those of longer duration, it seems likely that Mayrberger himself was aware of this distinction; that is, the "modulations" in example 10-8, for instance, could hardly have been as significant to Mayrberger as the present-day definition of the term might suggest. The most important failing of the system in regard to modulation is undeniable, however: it provided no real means by which to account for modulations which transcended the diatonic *Verwandtschaft*.[51]

The question which naturally arises is what, if anything, did Mayrberger accomplish with his efforts? His subordination of the "Tristan Chord" to a model of harmonic syntax (albeit, a somewhat primitive one) was certainly an important and influential contribution. Furthermore, he was probably the first to distinguish clearly between three types of chromaticism: the true chromatic chord (Sechter's "hybrid-chord"), the chromatic chord resulting from melodic processes, and chromaticism of a purely melodic (embellishing) sort.[52] This would later be taken over by Louis and Thuille.

Mayrberger's effort to retain the eighteenth-century theory of harmony as a kind of *reiner Satz* against which to gauge the apparent freedoms of *Tristan* differed considerably from German attempts to grapple with the piece. At the very end of the century a slim volume entitled *Melodik und Harmonik bei R. Wagner* by Salmon Jadassohn appeared.[53] Jadassohn, the author of one of the favorite harmony texts of the later nineteenth century,[54] was a student of Hauptmann's, and (like his teacher) a thoroughgoing verticalist. According to Jadassohn, the harmonic language of *Tristan* is characterized by Wagner's use of "passing altered tones" which have a "chordal meaning."[55] Example 10-9 shows his analysis of the opening of *Tristan:*

Example 10-9

Jadassohn contends that chordal meaning—no matter how farfetched—is always chosen by the ear above melodic meaning; and the analysis which results shows the most extreme concentration upon chordal identity at the expense of harmonic syntax. Jadassohn's implicit definition of melodic dissonance is so narrow as to leave no room for interpretation, or for the existence of "apparently consonant" structures which function as dissonances:

> one cannot speak here of suspensions which enter freely and resolve upward, or of passing tones; for the characteristic of suspensions as of passing tones is not that they form components of a chord, but that they dissonate against it.[56]

Jadassohn may be an extreme case—his ideas certainly seem to have had little further influence—but his assumption that contrapuntal explanations of Wagnerian harmony are arbitrary and unsatisfactory has continued to survive.[57] In studying the continuing battle between harmonic and contrapuntal explanations of *Tristan* one cannot help but be reminded of the words of a far more influential spokesman for the conservative faction:

> Then Wagner came along! His formations of passing tones, appoggiaturas, neighboring notes, suspensions were so biting to the ear that because of their highly pungent effect, musicians were unable to classify them despite the fact that they were quite simple.... Some believed that a new theory was necessary to explain such chords....[58]

11

Sechter's System at the End of the Century

Capellen's *Streitschrift* was by no means the first criticism directed at Sechter's system, although it was probably the most hostile. By the end of the nineteenth century, Sechter's followers were having an increasingly difficult time accepting his assumption of just intonation and the "intermediate fundamental." And in the domain of chromatic harmony it had become clear that the unconditional prohibition of chromatic fundamentals was impossible to uphold. Two Bruckner students—Josef Schalk and Cyrill Hynais—eventually proposed modifications of Sechter's system of chromatic harmony. The most perceptive criticism of the "intermediate fundamental" was offered by Johannes Evangelist Habert (1833–96), the author of what was probably the last published version of Sechter's system.

Habert and the "Intermediate Fundamental"

Like Bruckner, Habert came from Upper Austria and studied with Dürrnberger in Linz, the provincial capital. But while Bruckner's life changed dramatically when he became acquainted with Wagner's music and later moved to Vienna, Habert remained a provincial organist and liturgical composer throughout his life, eventually gaining considerable prominence as the leader of the Austrian reaction to the "Cecilian Movement."[1]

Moser[2] stresses the close connection between Habert's work and the "historicism" which pervaded the second half of the nineteenth century in Austria, producing most visibly the architectural monuments of Vienna's *Ring*. Indeed, a careful analysis of historical styles characterizes Habert's work both in theory and composition. That is certainly the most important difference between Habert and Sechter—two men who at first glance would appear to be rather similar personalities typical of the organist-theorists. While Sechter was convinced that one theory would account for all of the music he deemed worthwhile, Habert was perfectly willing to accept the differences between the harmonic style and the older contrapuntal styles. Not surprisingly, he believed that a knowledge of Fux was essential to the educated musician;[3] and even his

Harmonielehre[4]—dedicated to Palestrina—contains a section dealing with the church modes, neumatic notation, and chant. In the *Vorrede* he acknowledges his debt to Sechter (whose system forms the basis of most of the book),[5] but he also includes a criticism of the "intermediate fundamental" which results directly from his sensitivity to the contrapuntal styles.

Upon mentioning that stepwise motion is not fundamental motion according to Sechter, Habert gives the following example:

Example 11-1

Of course, Sechter would insert the "intermediate fundamental" A between the C major and D minor chords, to which Habert replies:

> but the C in the second measure of the example is the fundamental of the C major triad, and absolutely no one would have the feeling that this C major triad represents the seventh chord on scale degree VI. What one senses is the harshness which lies in the succession of the C major and D minor triads, since these chords have no common tone. One can say the connective between the two triads is by-passed; the progression is more compact, and consequently more terse and powerful in expression.[6] The restriction [demanding] that C not be viewed as a fundamental and that the connection of the C major and D minor triads not be seen as a fundamental progression would have, as a consequence, a restriction on the use of such progressions. But precisely these progressions play an important role in the antique classical vocal music, in strict composition.[7]

Earlier in this study we found the reverse of the "intermediate fundamental"—the extension of the fundamental through arpeggiation and the passing seventh—to be a more convincing notion. Habert is in agreement:

> That the C major triad here [example 11-2] has a different meaning than above is clear. But to want to generalize this progression because the triad can be the substitute of the seventh chord here, and to demand that under all circumstances the triad be seen as an incomplete seventh chord when the fundamental rises by step—to explain that ascent as an *apparent* ascending stepwise progression—that simply will not do.[8]

Example 11-2

Habert continues with a criticism of Sechter's explanation of the descending stepwise progressions, and rejects Sechter's assumption of just intonation as well.

The criticism of the "intermediate fundamental" is well-founded, to say the least. Although the close connection of "harmony" with the triad and intervals of thirds and fifths would continue to be a useful notion, the idea that all chord-to-chord motion might be explained with these primitives was obviously unacceptable to a musician on intimate terms with both the music and the theory of the older contrapuntal styles.

Further Developments in Chromatic Harmony

Johann Emerich Hasel

Prominently displayed in the subtitle of Johann Emerich Hasel's *Die Grundsätze des Harmoniesystems*[9] are the two main preoccupations of Sechter's disciples: analysis and chromatic harmony. Its length (680 pages) is perhaps a bit shorter than Mayrberger's *Lehrbuch* would have been had he finished it, but Hasel's work suffers from a similar prolixity. The general organization of the book begins to look more like the later Louis and Thuille *Harmonielehre* than Sechter. Hasel devotes more than equal time to chromatic techniques[10] and offers an "Introduction to Analysis of Compositions."[11] Like Habert's *Harmonielehre,* much of the book is illustrated with examples from the musical literature.[12]

Hasel's system follows Sechter almost exactly, albeit with a few curious changes of terminology (e.g., *Scheinaccorde* for "passing chords" and *unterschobenes Fundament* for "intermediate fundamental"). There is no mention of Sechter's "dissonant" fifth of II; and when defining augmented sixth chords Hasel evidently wants to be as complete (or noncontroversial) as possible, calling such a chord an "*amphibolous,* or *mixed,* or a *hybrid* or an *altered* chord."[13] Probably because Sechter's term was already passé, Hasel comes out in favor of "altered" chord.

An apparent inconsistency near the beginning of Hasel's discussion of chromaticism is of interest, for it illustrates an important dilemma facing the proponents of Sechter's system. Like Sechter, Hasel holds by the notion that chromaticism may not be extended to the fundamentals of chords,[14] an idea which was by now quite difficult to defend. He begins his discussion of chromaticism by showing how a common cadence pattern may be embellished through chromaticism (like Bruckner, Hasel starts with the cadence).[15]

Example 11-3

A "bright effect" may be gained by the introduction of sharps (secondary dominants present no problems to Sechter's system); but a "sadder effect" involves the introduction of flats, transforming the example into the following:

Example 11-4

Hasel appears unaware that despite his peculiar analysis of the second and third chords he has already broken the rule which he will state clearly later: as in Sechter, major and minor remain two separate entities in Hasel's book, and therefore we are forced to conclude that the A♭ and D♭ of the first two measures are chromatic alterations of fundamentals. The problem first alluded to in the discussion of Sechter's system of chromatic progression[16] thus continued to plague fundamental bass theorists forty years later.

Cyrill Hynais

Although Bruckner appears never to have met Mayrberger personally, he was familiar with his work,[17] and it was undoubtedly Mayrberger's *Tristan* analysis which inspired Hynais and Schalk to try their hands at the analysis of Wagner's music. Schalk's ideas merit the more extended study we shall devote to them somewhat later. Hynais, on the other hand, did little more than summarize what had already been said by Sechter, Bruckner, Mayrberger, and Schalk. His articles[18] were a last, desperate attempt to regain the authority that Sechter's system once had.

Like Sechter, Hynais was interested in the eternal laws of composition. In noting that these laws should be abstracted from individual works of art,[19] he seems to show the new empiricism that would characterize much of the music theory of the beginning of the twentieth century. But regardless of this admirable attempt at objectivity, his unquestioning faith in Sechter is never really in doubt.

Hynais summarizes the main points of Sechter's system in his first essay; like his teacher, he regards the ninth chord as a "fundamental harmony."[20] In the second essay he deals with progressions by third and fifth, citing Wagnerian *Leitmotive* to illustrate; and, in the third, he discusses the analysis of stepwise progressions by means of Sechter's "intermediate fundamental." It is also here that he discusses Mayrberger's "harmonic ellipsis," quoting Mayrberger's explanation, illustrated by examples of sevenths which remain oblique as consonances upon resolution. But he goes beyond Mayrberger by giving the following example in which the seventh is prolonged by the voice exchange A–F♯/F♯–A (and the passing six-four) before it becomes a consonant member of the F minor triad:[21]

Example 11-5

The six-four in the second measure is, according to Hynais, "easy to explain through the passing motion of the bass (A–G–F♯) and the alto (F♯–G–A), as well as the 'returning passing tone' in the tenor (D–E♭–D); thus [it is] not a true six-four, but artificial."[22] This analysis would later provoke an attack by Capellen, who claimed that Hynais was forced into this interpretation because of Sechter's prohibition of stepwise progressions.[23]

Hynais continues the discussion of the "harmonic ellipsis" in the fourth essay with the notion of the "rising seventh," which he maintains is an important feature of Wagner's style. He offers example 11-6a, from the *Meistersinger* prelude (mm. 128–29) as a demonstration (ex. 11-6b is his harmonic "reduction"):

Example 11-6

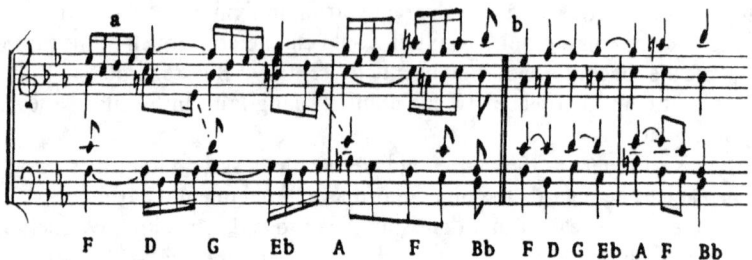

According to Hynais,

> The seventh always ascends in a progression by descending third of two seventh chords, [and] exceptionally, in a progression by descending fifth of two seventh chords so that both may be complete.[24]

There can be little doubt that the melodic nature of the seventh, so respected by earlier composers, became much more harmonic in Wagner's style. Unfortunately, Hynais fails to pursue this idea further.

In the remainder of the essay Hynais illustrates Mayrberger's distinction between harmonic and melodic chromaticism, and agrees with Schalk that chromatic alteration occasionally must be extended to chord fundamentals in Wagner's style.[25] Fittingly, he ends by recommending the works of Mayrberger and Schalk, from whom most of his ideas are derived.

Josef Schalk (1857–1900) and the "Law of Tonality"

Although one recent article deals with Schalk objectively,[26] setting his personality and activities in some perspective, he seems to be remembered at present mainly for his iniquities against Bruckner's symphonies. From the point of view of the music theorist, this is most unfortunate, for Schalk's theoretical ideas are often interesting, and at times, original. Most of them may be found in a series of articles which appeared from 1888-90 under the general title, "Das Gesetz der Tonalität."[27] In addition, there exist unpublished materials, to which we shall turn later.

Proclaimed loudly and widely by Fétis, the term "tonality" was destined to provoke a seemingly unending debate, and to acquire meanings which appeared to change with each of its promulgators. In a recent study of French compositional theory, Renate Groth[28] traces one of Fétis's most important ideas back to Momigny:

> The natural heirarchy of the seven notes placed under the authority of one among them called tonic, being purely metaphysical, is certainly not in the tones, but rather appertains to the mind, which alone may perceive it.[29]

The "metaphysical" nature of tonality would be essential to Fétis's later formulation of the idea. Following Bryan Simms,[30] Groth points out that Choron had used the term to distinguish between strict and free styles; thus he spoke of *tonalité antique*, which he said came from the Greeks but might be observed in plain chant, as opposed to *tonalité moderne ou tonalité vulgaire*, which characterized major-minor music. In his *Dictionnaire de musique moderne* (1821), Castil-Blaze defines the term for the first time, connecting "tonality" to scale structure, as Choron had. But Castil-Blaze also emphasizes the importance of scale degrees I, IV, and V, calling them *cordes essentialles*, as opposed to the *cordes mélodiques* (II, III, and VI), which merely give "color to the tonal force." Moreover, Castil-Blaze claims that if these *cordes mélodiques* become fundamentals, the effect is of a "new mode."[31]

Like Choron, Fétis uses the term "tonality" in a culturally relative sense when he speaks of the "tonality" of the Greeks or the Persians, as opposed to the "tonality" of European music. However, it is certainly the latter "tonality" to which he devotes the lion's share of his energies as a theorist. And here, as Groth points out, Fétis takes over the collected definitions and observations of his predecessors for his "original" notion of tonality.

Fétis too sees the source of tonality in the major and minor scales, claiming that tonality originates in *"the collection of necessary relationships, successive or simultaneous, of the notes of the scale."*[32] Like Castil-Blaze, Fétis attributes varying levels of repose or tension to the scale degrees: I, IV, V, and VI have the character of *repos ou conclusion*, while II, III, and VII are marked by the absence of this quality. In a similar manner, Fétis speaks of intervals which exhibit the character of repose (the fifth and the octave), those which are "attractive" (the "natural dissonance" of the seventh and the *consonances attractives ou appellatives*[33]—the augmented fourth/diminished fifth), and a category of intervals which are neither attractive nor reposeful. Among those in the last category are the sixth and the fourth, which, according to Fétis, are appropriate to accompany the scale degrees which lack repose. Thus sixth chords and other derived forms are best for harmonizing these scale degrees, while root-position triads are appropriate for harmonizing the "reposeful" degrees. To harmonize II, for example, with a fifth amounts to a conflict between "caractère et function": like Castil-Blaze, Fétis maintains that such practice results in a "vague changement de tonalité."[34]

Easily the paradigm of progression in Fétis's system is the motion of a dominant seventh to a triad (demonstrating, as it does, the two states of attraction and repose, as well as the paradigmatic behavior of the "natural dissonance" and the "appellative consonance"). The two states are reflected in Fétis's chord categories as well: all chords are derived from the consonant major and minor triads, or the dominant seventh chord.[35]

A further outgrowth of Fétis's notion of tonality is his well-known theory of the four evolutionary stages of the musical language. According to Fétis, the *ordre unitonique* of *tonalité ancienne* gave way to the *ordre transitonique* of *tonalité moderne* with the discovery of the process of modulation. It is hardly surprising that this rather naive idea did not lead to a profound understanding of the pretonal repertory. But Fétis's notions of the *ordre pluritonique* and *ordre omnitonique* seem to have inspired some very interesting developments in French harmonic theory later in the nineteenth century.[36] Unfortunately, an examination of these is beyond the scope of this study.

Some twenty years after the appearance of Fétis's *Traité*, Helmholtz redefined "tonality" and introduced it into German harmonic theory. Like Fétis, Helmholtz frequently uses the term in a culturally relative sense; but also like Fétis, his primary interest in European tonal music is never in doubt. Helmholtz agrees with Fétis that "tonality" is an aesthetic matter—not a "natural law."[37] But while Fétis rejects acoustical and mathematical explanations of harmony, Helmholtz bases his system upon his investigations in acoustics and the physiology of hearing. Through this work he attempts to provide the empirical-scientific justification for a system of harmony which, on many points, is indebted to Hauptmann. "Tonality," claims Helmholtz, is the "fundamental principle for the development of the European tonal system," and assumes "that the whole mass of tones and the connection of harmonies must stand in a close and always distinctly perceptible relationship to some arbitrarily selected tonic."[38] The "distinctly perceptible relationship" is, in Helmholtz's view, clearly brought about through common overtones. This is the core of Helmholtz's theory of the relationship of both tones and chords: "directly related" chords are those which have at least one note in common; stepwise motion—in both scales and chords—is a "second degree" relation, and is explained harmonically by assuming a tone or chord as an intermediary.[39] Thus, in essence, Helmholtz agrees with Hauptmann and, for that matter, with Sechter.

In Hugo Riemann's use of the term "tonality" there is no longer any cultural relativism: the "tonality" of European tonal music is the only issue. Moreover, Fétis's desire to find tonality in the scale holds little interest for Riemann. Early in his career Riemann had written to Franz Liszt that "the cardinal error of our generally accepted theory of musical structure or harmony is that it takes as its point of departure the scale and not the chord [*Klang*]."[40] As far as Riemann was concerned, the *Stufentheorie* was a mere holdover from the figured bass era. Rather than the scale, Riemann's theory departed from the *Klang*—both *Oberklang* and *Unterklang*—and developed his notion of three functions. It was the mixture of these functions *(Klangmischung)* which determined chordal meaning. The debt to both Hauptmann and Helmholtz is clear,[41] but the difference between Riemann's system and those of his teachers is also clear: "tonality" began to center on the three functions, uninhibited by any diatonic control. The end result was that a progression such as the following was "tonal"[42]:

Example 11-7

In regard to this example, Carl Dahlhaus notes that

> [It is] in the suspension of diatonicism as the basis of tonal chord relationships [that] Riemann sees the distinguishing characteristic of "tonality," as opposed to the "key of the old theory," which was founded upon the diatonic scale.[43]

Despite Riemann's protest that *"our theory of tonal functions of harmony is nothing other than the extension of Fétis's notion of tonality,"*[44] there is little doubt that "tonality" had moved a long way from the "attractions" of certain intervals within the diatonic scale. With the suspension of diatonic control it was a short step to Reger's use of Riemann's theory, or indeed to the more recent ideas of Ernö Lendvai.

With some idea of the interpretations which "tonality" received from French and German theorists, it will be interesting now to see what the term meant to a Viennese theorist steeped in the Sechter/Bruckner system. Schalk's essays do not constitute a "theory" of tonality. Rather, they present suggestions for revision of Sechter's system in light of the holistic approach to musical form and technique which began to emerge towards the end of the nineteenth century. Schalk was doubtlessly as interested as Riemann (or, later on, Schenker) was in viewing the complete work of art and the integration of its parts—in seeing the work of art as an "organism," to use the ever-present metaphor[45]—but the means by which he proposed to do this were quite different.

The earlier works of Riemann[46] may well have had some influence on Schalk, though as we shall see, Schalk's notion of "tonality" has nothing to do with Riemann's mature definition of the term. Schalk was aware of Helmholtz's work and presumably familiar with his use of the term,[47] but this presented no conflict with Sechter's system since Helmholtz and Sechter, despite the radical difference in their points of departure, are largely in agreement here.

Schalk's definition of "tonality" is the noncontroversial one with which most of its many proponents would probably agree: *"A definite main tonality lies at the base of every musical work."*[48] According to Schalk, this principle is equally applicable to the Wagnerian music-drama and to purely instrumental music, though this had not been apparent because of the fascination with modulation:

> Up to now, theory has been satisfied with demonstrating the transition from one key to another. In so doing, the dependence of the second key upon the first is then entirely neglected, and [the second] is viewed and treated just as independently. But [the fact] that this is not so in a work of art is proved by each return to the main tonality, which, like a faint beacon, must guide the composer over even the most remote tonalities.[49]

To a large extent, the problem is due to a definition of "key" which is too limited, as well as to confusion between chromatic progression and modulation:

> The notions of chromatic progression and true change of key (modulation) have become so confused that they are extremely difficult to disentangle. Most importantly, the domain of a key must be thought of in a broader sense than it has been. Then it will not be necessary to find continual modulations where merely chromatically altered chords occur, and actual modulation can be saved for those places where a second key becomes truly independent for one or more periods or sections.[50]

To demonstrate his notion of "tonality," Schalk discusses an excerpt from Wolfram's "Song to the Evening Star" from *Tannhäuser*. His simplified version of the first four bars follows:

Example 11-8

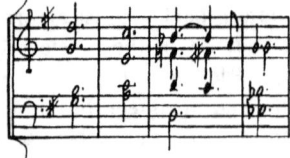

If the harmonic material is viewed in isolation, the first four bars imply the following keys: G major, A minor, B♭ major, G minor and E♭ major. "But if we understand these [chords] in relation to the tonic, they are I and II from G major and then III, V, and VI from G minor."[51] However, Schalk asks, is there any real need to invoke G minor when G major is obviously the prevailing tonality?

> Is the key of G minor really expressed here, or are we dragging it in arbitrarily merely to have an explanation for the fundamental E♭? Would it not be easier to allow the minor sixth as a fundamental in the major key as well?[52]

Although Schalk is obviously in favor of allowing the VI from minor in major, he goes on to say that there is yet another analysis which avoids this difficulty. He explains:

> To this end we return to the third chord of the example. On closer observation, its dependent, passing character is clearly evident. . . . [53]

Thus the argument over whether major or parallel minor is operative is really inconsequential, for the chords borrowed from minor are "nonessential" here anyway. The B♭ triad is a chromatic passing chord—the B♭ a passing tone connecting C and A, and the F a chromatic passing tone to the chordal F♯. In regard to the E♭ triad of measure 4, Schalk continues:

> As is well-known, one also finds returning passing tones, often called (less accurately) neighbor tones. For example, [see ex. 11-9]

Example 11-9

> I should like to designate the apparent root of the fourth bar as such.[54]

In fact, this analysis (without the chromatic fundamentals B♭ and E♭) "may be the truest explanation for the effect of the deceptive cadence, V–♭VI."[55] Some may object to the fact that this "returning passing tone" does not resolve immediately; Schalk replies:

> But why shouldn't the chromatic thirteenth first proceed to its diatonic form and then resolve—all the more so, since this new chord (E, B♭, C♯, G) is clearly perceived only as a delay of the following six-four chord?[56]

After mentioning the one remaining difficulty—the C♯ of m. 5, which is a "neighbor tone introduced by skip"—Schalk presents the following three analyses of the eight-measure passage, expressing his preference for the third:

Example 11-10

108 Sechter's System at End of Century

Schalk's first essay, while obviously not a "theory" of tonality, nevertheless demonstrates an approach to analysis which differs significantly from that of his predecessors, Sechter and Mayberger. First of all, it is clear that Schalk does not exclude all stepwise progressions a priori (see mm. 1 and 2 of ex. 11-10 and see below); nor does he regard major and parallel minor as completely separate entities. Thus he does not resort to an "intermediate fundamental" to explain the deceptive cadence (see mm. 3 and 4), but sees the "truest explanation" of the deceptive cadence in the idea that a "neighbor note" is in the bass. Schalk's use of "nonessential" harmonies also differs from their use by Sechter and Mayrberger. For example, Sechter would most likely have analyzed the diminished seventh chord (m. 5) as an incomplete ninth chord, assigning an A fundamental to it. (This, in turn, would have assumed an E♭ fundamental in the previous chord and an "intermediate fundamental B♭ before that, etc.) Schalk, on the other hand, uses such chords not as a means of avoiding forbidden fundamental progressions, but in order to show that the essential tonality of the excerpt is unaffected by such "nonessential" matters as change of mode and chromatic "passing chords."

Schalk's method combines his notion of tonal unity with the step-by-step interpretation of harmonic progression characteristic of fundamental bass thinking. At some points the results agree with Riemann (as when VI represents I in m. 4); but on other occasions they do not (as in m. 5, where the diminished seventh would have to be a D/D in Riemann's system). In all cases decisions are made through the examination of the particular context at hand. That is to say, the E♭ "neighbor note" (m. 4)—to cite an example which apparently agrees with Riemann's analysis—is not the a priori result of *Klangmischung* (as in Riemann, where it is also a "neighbor note"). Rather, the designation "neighbor note" is dependent upon a particular melodic context.

In the second essay, Schalk deals more specifically with "passing chords." The progression which introduces Wolfram's song is the following:

Example 11-11

```
DM  I  (   )   VI
GM  V  (   )   III    V
```

According to Schalk, the C♯ minor chord was particularly troublesome to musicians of the past. The problem, however, is mainly due to the unprepared soprano C♯, which, in Schalk's estimation, is merely the doubling of the passing C♯ in the bass. Like Mayrberger, he emphasizes that:

> a passing chord—that is, a chord which connects two [more] important harmonies by stepwise motion—by no means loses its dependence through the skip of a single voice.[57]

To be sure, the rest of the analysis is not trouble-free: the G♯ in the middle voice is also passing, according to Schalk, except that it skips first to B before taking its true resolution in the bass of the last chord (see analysis of ex. 11-11). But if that is true, one wonders why Schalk does not consider both the C♯ and B minor chords to be passing, effectively reducing the passage to a motion of G:V–V$_3^4$.[58]

The version of "tonality" proposed by Riemann could never have been compatible with Schalk's ideas. Tonality, in Schalk's view, was ultimately diatonic; and chromaticism, although it might seem harmonic, was of melodic origin. In a later work Schalk would propose a theory of three historical stages of chromaticism: (1.) "melodic chromaticism," in which chromaticism is only applied to nonharmonic tones; (2.) chromatic alteration of chord tones (more or less what is described by Sechter); and (3.) "the use of chromatic tones extends even to the roots (fundamentals) of chords, although in most cases this is merely apparent."[59]

This third stage—the late nineteenth-century harmonic language—may be seen in the greater independence of the Neapolitan chord. Schalk notes that the chord first appears in the literature in first inversion, and gives a number of melodic examples of its usage.

> Thus we are indebted first of all to melodic invention for the use of these tones. Only later were they used also in inversion in the bass voice, whereby they appeared as [root position] triads, and more rarely six-four chords, and acquired greater independence.... [60]

Example 11-12 shows an excerpt from a longer exercise on the use of the Neapolitan. The example proves that, for Schalk, it is more important that fundamental progression be diatonic than that it necessarily be by fifth or third. Thus, in the first four measures, Schalk chooses the fundamental reading G-A-B over the possible G-E♭-A-F-B (which would have been a likely choice for Sechter or Bruckner):

Example 11-12

110   Sechter's System at End of Century

While the third stage of chromaticism can be seen on a local level with the Neapolitan, it is also reflected at a larger level in the choice of secondary key areas in Wagner's works. In the last of his "Law of Tonality" essays, Schalk attempts to discuss a longer span of music: the close of the second act of *Die Meistersinger*.[61] Beckmesser's "contest song" *(Werbelied)* consists of three strophes in G major, and leads into the final scene (Seventh Scene; Piano-Vocal score, p. 318). The chorus imitates Beckmesser (see ex. 11-13), first in G major (p. 325), and then in E major (p. 339):

Example 11-13

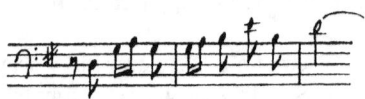

Was gibt's denn da für Zank und Streit?

After a return to G major (p. 344), there is a motion to B♭ major (p. 345). Beckmesser's motive is stated once with augmentation of the second skip of a fourth, and the last expected F is replaced with F♯ (p. 347)—the all-important pitch of the Night Watchman's horn. After discussing the rest of the scene (which continues with a seventeen-measure pedal on this F♯), Schalk returns to this B♭-F♯ motion:

> Finally, we include the derivation of this important transition, [which] comes originally from a succession of chords formed melodically by the returning passing tone [ex. 11-14a]. In [ex. 11-14b] the second chord already gains greater independence through support of the bass voice. Likewise, in [ex. 11-14c this independence] becomes complete through the melodic introduction of the seventh and ninth, making [the chord] the dominant seventh of B major.[62]

Example 11-14

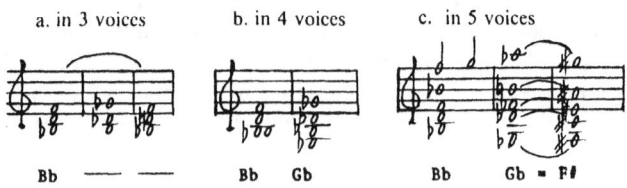

Like "Das Gesetz der Tonalität," Schalk's later essay on chromaticism only begins to address its subject. And thus Schalk takes his place alongside Mayrberger and Hynais: not one of them was able to produce the full-scale study of Wagnerian harmonic technique he had promised.[63] Once again we are left to speculate about what Schalk might have produced had he followed out some of these ideas more thoroughly.

Schalk himself was acutely aware of the impasse. Furthermore, he was not convinced that contemporary music theory was on the right track to its solution. Research in empirical science had furnished the dominant direction to theory in the latter half of the nineteenth century. Understandably, Schalk admits that any theory of chromatic harmony

> is obliged to be in continual contact with the fundamentals of natural science—which, given the present state of this science, is the most difficult thing in the whole undertaking. [If] we admire the ineffable exactitude and thoroughness... with which this science has endeavored to describe the nature of diatonicism, still, in the area of chromaticism we see even a researcher like Helmholtz limited to only a few occasional remarks.[64]

Indeed, Schalk was not convinced that the theory of harmony could ever offer the solution to this dilemma. Harmony was merely concerned with the relationship of two successive chords, the second of which "stands in the most limited relationship of dependency to the first."[65] In Schalk's view, a relationship such as cause and effect was already a larger issue beyond the power of the theory of harmony. Musing over other possible means of explaining the relationship of tones, Schalk contrasts harmonic and contrapuntal thinking:

> Present-day theory prefers the first [harmony]; for it, the chord is of the greatest importance.... However, the second type [of explanation], which is concerned with voice leading (counterpoint), is the much more correct and artistically vital one. The question is whether laws can be abstracted from the leading of voices alone which can be honored in the vertical dimension as well.[66]

The question has lost none of its appositeness in the more than eighty years since it was written; the complete answer is still to be found. Although Schalk himself would have no more to say on the subject, one of his fellow Bruckner students was destined to make considerable headway in the quest for its solution.

Part IV

The Influence of Viennese Fundamental Bass Theory at the Beginning of the Twentieth Century

12

Systems of Harmony at the Beginning of the Century

The first few years of the twentieth century marked an extremely fertile period for the study of harmony. After a half century during which music theory either scaled the heights of Hauptmannian deduction or became a subdiscipline of natural science, theory and pedagogy were once again reunited, and a number of new and interesting harmony books appeared.[1] Certainly Riemann and Sechter were two of the most important influences. But the new books were not mere repetitions of past systems, as one finds in the later nineteenth century. Rather, each was an individual attempt to create a new synthesis from the existing systems, and to bring theory back into touch with practice.

The influence of Hugo Riemann has been addressed, if not somewhat overemphasized.[2] True, among the new books at the beginning of the century we find one which is primarily directed to analysis using Riemann's system almost unaltered (Schreyer), and one which, although rejecting "dualism" for "monism," is essentially an idiosyncratic "modernization" of Riemann (Capellen). However, the systems of harmony which proved to be the most enduring were influenced to a large extent by Viennese fundamental bass theory. Since the fundamental bass was revived and nurtured in Vienna, it is hardly surprising that the works which display its influence most prominently are closely connected with that city, and indeed, with the theory's most influential proponent, Anton Bruckner. Despite the fact that Schoenberg was never formally a student of Bruckner's, the *Harmonielehre* attests to his knowledge of what went on in Bruckner's University lectures. And Schenker, who proposed to remedy the defects of the Viennese theory of harmony in a radically different way, studied harmony and counterpoint for two years with Bruckner at the Conservatory.[3]

It was two of the most important works in nineteenth-century music theory, Hauptmann's *Die Natur der Harmonik* and Sechter's *Grundsätze*, which set the style for the very different harmonic theories which emanated subsequently from Leipzig and Vienna. For the rest of the century German theorists continued to work out Hauptmann's ideas, while the Austrians remained true to Sechter and the fundamental bass. But at the beginning of the twentieth century a system of harmony appeared from another German musical capital: Munich. Just as Catholic Bavaria was originally Austrian and even today retains cultural characteristics which are more Austrian than German, so did the system represent a similar phenomenon in the domain of harmonic theory: it was a synthesis of elements from both German and Austrian harmonic theory—from both the function theory and fundamental bass theory. The system found its first published expression in the *Harmonielehre* by August Halm,[4] a Rheinberger student. It was subsequently treated in much greater detail by Rudolf Louis and Ludwig Thuille.[5] Both Louis and Thuille also had personal ties to the Viennese theory: Louis was a student at the University of Vienna during the period when Bruckner lectured there, and later became his first biographer; Thuille was a Tyrolean who received his first education in music theory at Innsbruck with Josef Pembauer, a Bruckner student, before he studied in Munich with Rheinberger.

The importance of the Schenker and Schoenberg works need not be stressed to American theorists. Schenker's ideas were introduced into this country by his students, and Schoenberg himself educated a generation of American musicians, adapting many ideas from the *Harmonielehre* for American usage in *Structural Functions of Harmony*.[6] A review of subsequent American books on tonal harmony would undoubtedly reveal many debts to Schenker and Schoenberg. The Louis/Thuille *Harmonielehre* has not enjoyed the benefits of personal representation in this country, but it has continued to be an important influence on European pedagogy of harmony. Shortly after its first appearance, Louis wrote the *Grundriss der Harmonielehre* at the behest of the head of the Vienna Conservatory, to facilitate its use there as a text.[7] By the end of the 1920s the *Harmonielehre* had gone through nine editions, and the *Grundriss* at least five.[8] The tenth edition of the *Harmonielehre* was extensively rewritten and heavily "Riemannized," but much of the original character of the book was retained.[9] The book's influence has continued unabated: in his 1966 study, Walter von Forster reported that "among the books which are recommended and used as supplementary reading, the Louis/Thuille *Harmonielehre* stands in first place by a wide margin."[10]

"Speculative" Theory and "Practical" Harmony: Rapprochement at Last

Before discussing the theoretical content of these works, it is important to look briefly at the transformation which "practical" harmony underwent at the beginning of the twentieth century.

During the latter half of the nineteenth century, the methodologies of music theory, according to most authorities, were two: Hauptmannian deduction, or the inductive method of empirical science.[11] Riemann, who was influenced by both methodologies,[12] divided music theory as a whole into two categories: "speculative" theory and "practical" harmony. In Riemann's own works the two were closely connected, the former laying the groundwork for the latter.[13] But with most works of the period the gulf which separated "speculation" and the outmoded "practical" textbooks was simply unbridgable. Neither "practical" harmony nor "speculative" theory—regardless of method—had much to do with musical practice, for analysis, the means by which theoretical precepts could be tested in practice, had all but disappeared from works on harmony. The essays of Mayrberger and Schalk were the last remnants of the eighteenth-century version of empiricism.

The new books of the early twentieth century were attempts to remedy this situation. Indicative of the rapprochement of "speculative" theory and "practical" harmony was the claim by Louis and Thuille that:

> Our harmony book is intended to be a *practical-theoretical* textbook. Thus, it may be distinguished on the one hand from all of the *purely scientific* treatments of this subject which, with no regard for practical aims, have only theoretical interests in view, and on the other hand from all of those methods for whom harmony instruction consists of nothing more than mechanical reinforcement of *purely practical technique*, and who, disdaining any rational explanation and derivation, believe that they can get away without any theory at all in the true sense of the word.[14]

A desire to reconcile theory and practice would lead Schenker to describe similar goals for his *Harmonielehre*:

> In contrast to other books on music theory, conceived, one might say, for their own sake and apart from art, the aim of this book is to build a real and practicable bridge from composition to theory.[15]

Undoubtedly, many would have agreed that those books, "conceived...for their own sake and apart from art," erred either in the direction of irrelevant and outmoded pedantry, or excessive and equally irrelevant speculation. Of the former group, Richter and Jadassohn would receive much-deserved criticism.[16]

But perhaps the most flagrant offense came from "speculation": "dualism," which was not a dead issue in 1906–7. Forced to retreat on the issue of undertones, Riemann had recently returned to the battlefield with a new justification for this basic tenet of his harmonic theory:

> The decisive character of major and minor is attributable to the fact that the *major consonance* has its essence in the *simplest ratios of increasing vibration frequencies*; the *minor consonance*, on the contrary, rests upon the *simplest ratios of increase in vibrating mass* (of wave lengths, string lengths, etc.). In short, the major principle may thus be seen in

growing intensity, the minor principle in *expanding volume*.... Therefore, both are best represented numerically through the same simple series of numbers:

$$\begin{array}{cc} \text{Minor} & \text{Major} \\ 5 \leftarrow 4 \leftarrow 3 \leftarrow 2 \leftarrow 1 \rightarrow 2 \rightarrow 3 \rightarrow 4 \rightarrow 5 \\ \text{(relative string length)} & \text{(relative vibration frequency)}\end{array}$$ [17]

"Dualism" thus had been given a new lease on life, and the authors of practical harmony books were obliged to take a position on the matter. On this they all agreed: the notion that the fifth of a minor triad was actually its root was absurd. Schenker wrote:

> theory has to accept the fact that composers at all times have followed the principle of basing harmonic progression on the roots in the bass voice and that they have proceeded to do so with equal verve in both major and minor modes and without any regard for the occurence of minor triads.[18]

And Louis and Thuille directed their most stinging criticism to the excesses of "speculation":

> to a certain extent the practical musician's aversion to any and all theorizing is understandable, when one considers that up to now harmonic theory has appeared almost exclusively in the form of harmonic *speculation*—that is, as that dogmatic and uncritical type of theorizing whose results, if not completely unusable, are nevertheless only to be employed with the most careful selection, for the "respect for empirical evidence" which prevents the human intellect from setting arbitrary mental constructions in the place of real things and occupying itself with the monstrosities of its excessive imagination—instead of the explanation of reality—is missing.
>
> In contrast to this, we were most zealously intent on assuming a strictly *empirical* point of view, and maintaining it scrupulously.[19]

Admittedly, in this context the word "empirical" could refer once again to the method of natural science—to the rejection of undertones. But Louis and Thuille have more to say about just what they think "theory" should be. Above all, it involves the avoidance of the metaphysical:

> The point of departure for harmony as we see it is the truest and most exhaustive analysis possible of what a musician of our time and culture actually hears in chords and their connections—uninfluenced by any theoretical prejudices. The direct evidence of true musical perception and understanding provides the empirical facts whose simplest and most complete "comprehensive description"... is the true task of a theory of harmony. This "description" achieves a "rational" character—that is, it becomes an "explanation" and acquires "meaning"—in that it is carried out "comprehensively" and thus makes possible the mastery of an inexhaustible abundance of facts through the methodological means of "derivation" or "reduction."[20]

Thus, for Louis and Thuille, theoretical method entailed a return to a type of empiricism reminiscent of the late eighteenth century. This also signaled the return of analysis, and examples from the literature play an important part in their work. And although it can hardly be said that Schenker left German Idealism behind, practical analysis was to play at least as important a role in his "bridge from composition to theory."

The new empiricism brought with it a new understanding of the nature of "rules." Unlike the old absolute laws of the nineteenth-century pedagogues, the "rules" became paradigms, open to possible extensions and exceptions. According to Louis and Thuille, exceptions did not negate the rule, but rather required "the *rationalisation* of the nature of the rule, *in order to be able to maintain the validity of the rule along with the justification of the exception, without contradiction.*"[21] The same notion underlies Schenker's criticism of Bruckner's understanding of "rules":

> Despite his many years of study, Bruckner never realized the way in which countless new [possibilities] can arise from the rule, which, as free as they might appear, are nevertheless based upon the rule.[22]

The dislike of absolute systems (and Riemann's identification of "speculative" theory with aesthetics)[23] would lead Schoenberg to maintain that harmony instruction should not aspire to "theory" or "aesthetics," but merely to a clear and practical system of presentation.[24] Yet the motivation here was clearly personal artistic conviction, for it was one absolute system in particular which Schoenberg wished to depose: tonality. If Schenker's *Harmonielehre* was written to build a "bridge from composition to theory," Schoenberg's was an attempt to build a bridge from Viennese fundamental bass theory to the new music of the early twentieth century.

13

Viennese Fundamental Bass Theory and the German Function Theory: A Synthesis

The Basis of the Tonal System: The Cadence

In their conceptions of the most fundamental aspects of the tonal system, both Halm and Louis/Thuille owe much to the nineteenth-century German theory of harmony. Both trace harmonic phenomena back to the cadence. However, this is no longer Rameau's cadence, or Sechter's "reciprocal effect," but a dynamic notion of cadence probably ultimately derived from Hauptmann. The dialectical tension is apparent in Louis/Thuille's notion of "opposition" vs. "relationship":

> *The elementary harmonic relationships*, which are at the same time the easiest to understand and the most important, arise when the tonic triad is related to harmonics which on the one hand form a decided *opposition* to it, and on the other are bound to it by a close *relationship*.[1]

Louis/Thuille go on to claim, somewhat overconfidently to be sure, that "through the three triads of *tonic, dominant,* and *subdominant,* the key is completely and exhaustively determined,"[2] a process which Schenker later refers to somewhat ironically as the "unfurling" of triads.[3]

For Halm and Louis/Thuille, such words as "force" and "attraction" are essential in describing the effect of the cadence. Like Louis/Thuille, Halm does not give overt dialectical explanations of specific musical techniques, but the dialectical origin of his notion of the "essence" of music is clear:

> Music is, according to its nature, dissonance. That is, life and motion—certainly motion which leads to rest, but not continuous rest! *Unity must be achieved through oppositions* [italics mine]; it must be a result. Constant "unity and rest in itself" is uninteresting.[4]

For Halm the cadence itself embodies this striving for rest, for resolution. Accordingly, he divides it into two parts: question, in which the tonic is dominant of its own subdominant, and answer, in which the true tonality (the higher unity) is revealed. Although Halm does not use dialectical terms, this idea may well be founded on a dialectical explanation taken from Hauptmann. For Hauptmann, the rather abstract notion of "key" arises when the tonic triad is taken to be synthesis, while the subdominant is thesis and the dominant is antithesis.[5] It was Riemann who sought to make the dialectic a practical explanation of progression. In his early work he holds that the motion of I to IV is thesis, the cadential six-four (the "tonic" in conflict with itself) is antithesis, and the concluding V to I is synthesis.[6] Halm may well be thinking of Hauptmann's analysis, but this time applied clearly to the cadence: I–IV is thesis, V–I is antithesis, and the composite is synthesis.[7]

It is interesting that this dialectical analysis is largely in agreement with fundamental bass theory. Halm is no more satisfied with IV–V as an independent progression than Sechter was, maintaining that the only reason that it works is because of the relation of each chord to I on either side. Thus Halm always divides the cadence into two parts—i.e., into two falling fifth progressions. Between every IV and V chord he inserts the sign //, claiming that, "Neither a common tone nor a leading tone offers any sort of drive for further progressions from IV to V; between the two lies an abyss."[8] And Louis/Thuille, while accepting the fundamental progression IV–V, reject its opposite, V–IV. The latter will return, however, in the discussion of passing chords, just as it did in Sechter.

Finally, we should note that if these explanations do not agree with Sechter's "reciprocal effect," in which the tonic turned placidly first to one and then to the other dominant, neither do they agree with Riemann's early dialectical explanation or his completely symmetrical picture—that is, with the "dualistic" interpretation which he propounded in his mature work:

> Just as one tone may be either principal tone (prime) or derived tone..., so also a clang may be either principal clang—in which case it is called *tonic*—or derived clang; and in the latter case it is either nearest related clang on the overtone side or nearest related clang on the undertone side....[9]

Theory of Progression

For both Halm and Louis/Thuille, further progressions are all derived from the cadence. The familiar progressions by third offer no problems in this regard. As Bruckner's "extended cadence" showed, fundamental bass theory and the function theory were largely in agreement on the role of secondary chords in this context. But this method of derivation does mean that independence can never be granted to the "secondary" scale degrees. Practical harmony books, however, did at least have to recognize the existence of fifth progressions involving secondary chords. Regarding the descending fifth progression, Louis/Thuille say:

> The inauthentic dominant relation, in which secondary triads and seventh chords stand at some points in relation to themselves and at others in relation to the primary chords, clearly occurs in *sequences* of triads or seventh chords whose roots fall in fifths (or rise in fourths).[10]

Likewise, sequences of rising fifths express "the inauthentic subdominant relationship." Louis/Thuille continue with the obligatory citation of Fétis as the discoverer of the "true melodic nature" of these progressions—the result of Riemann's castigation of Sechter in his *Geschichte der Musiktheorie*, and the further echoes of this criticism.[11] Obviously, the banishment of Sechter's fifth sequence was necessary for Riemann to prove his theory. But it is curious that he was able to get away with it. In the heat of battle the original cause—the single problematic IV–VII progression—somehow became an excuse to throw out the whole progression. Fundamental bass theory recognized quite clearly that in progressions by fifth the individual chords function autonomously—that they cannot be related back to the "primary chord" model. One bad fifth does not negate this principle: "secondary" scale degrees can act independently—both at local and longer-range levels. As in other phases of the argument between Sechter and Riemann, Riemann's system proves to be an overreaction to certain deficiencies of fundamental bass theory—it is a system equally inadequate, but for the opposite reasons.

Louis/Thuille, in fact, finally decide on a compromise solution. In their view, there are essentially two roles for the secondary chords. In the first, secondary chords substitute for primary chords; but in the second, they are "representatives of primary chords from outside the key" (*Stellvertreter aussertonaler Hauptharmonien*).[12] Thus, in the notion of "implied modulation" (*unausgesprochene Modulation*) (c.f., Fétis, chapter 11 of this study) they managed to preserve Sechter's fifth sequence.

Although the systems of both Halm and Louis/Thuille are cadentially based, their debt to Viennese fundamental bass theory will become clear when we examine the linear derivation of certain chords, as well as the contextual interpretation of "function" which characterizes both systems.

Chord and Context: the Linear Derivation of Chords

In certain musical contexts, figured bass theorists preferred the linear derivation of chords to their explanation through the theory of harmonic inversion.[13] This mode of explanation would later create the "nonessential" harmonies of Kirnberger's system, which in turn would become the "artificial" harmonies and "passing chords" of the system of Sechter and his followers. But as the nineteenth century drew on, the theory of inversion became the only method of chord generation in all systems except Sechter's. Ultimately, Hugo Riemann would develop a harmonic explanation for "passing" and "suspension" chords as well (see below).

As an instance of the eighteenth-century linear interpretation of a six-three chord, Mitchell cites the following example and explanation by Schulz:

> It must be understood that inversion, regardless of the original ground tone, remains answerable to the hearing, for the nature of the progression readily indicates how the chord should be heard. Hence, although the following chord struck as a detail or singly [ex. 13-1a] will sound exactly like the first part of this chord [ex. 13-1b], the latter in its context creates a quite different impression. In the first case, the ear perceives the C chord; in the second, the E chord.[14]

Example 13-1

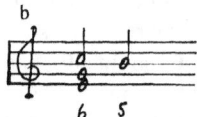

In addition to demonstrating that linear interpretation was on occasion extended to the six-three (the six-four was of course often regarded in this manner), Schulz's statement that "the nature of the progression readily indicates how the chord should be heard" presents in a nutshell the reasoning behind Kirnberger's synthesis of figured bass and fundamental bass thinking. The same kind of thinking would be characteristic of the Louis/Thuille *Harmonielehre* as well.

After the briefest explanation of the theory of inversion, Louis and Thuille continue:

> As we have seen, six chords and six-four chords *can* originate through the inversion of triads. But by no means is *every* six chord or six-four chord to be regarded as the inversion of a triad. Rather, aside from inversion there is a completely *different* mode of origin for these chord formations.[15]

This brings up the first discussion of "nonharmonic" tones, and the authors present the following examples—the same ones Sechter had used to demonstrate similar techniques:

Example 13-2

According to the authors, the first "nonharmonic" tone is the "changing tone" (*Wechselnote*) in "the broadest sense." Indeed, the sense is broad enough that the best English translation might rather be "linear adjacency," under these circumstances. This dissonance appears either on the accented or unaccented portion of the bar, and is thus either a suspension (*Vorhalt*) or "changing tone" in the "narrower sense" of the term. The four examples obviously present single suspensions produced by the delay (*Verzögerung*) of individual voices and with example 13-2d, a double suspension. As in fundamental bass theory, the implicit idea is that the fifth progression is the overriding concern; thus the six-three chord at the beginning of example 13-2c

> would naturally have nothing whatsoever to do with the inversion of the minor triad E–G–B, but on the contrary would be considered as just as much a *suspension formation* as the "*five-four chord*," G–C–D [in ex. 13-2b].[16]

Finally, the six-four chord of example 13-2d "*would not be understood in the sense of the tonic triad* (as its inversion), *but in the sense of the dominant triad* (as a suspension before it).”[17]

Just as the cadential six-four was the first instance of Riemann's *Scheinkonsonanzen*,[18] this same chord served as a model for the definition of Louis/Thuille's notion of the "interpretation-dissonance" (*Auffassungs-dissonanz*):

> Among all of the possible types of suspension formations, those occupy a special place, which consist of *apparently* consonant chords—*sixth* and *six-four* chords which are indistinguishable outwardly from inversions of triads. *Viewed in isolation*, these formations are by all means *consonant*. But the *context* in which they occur imposes an *interpretation* upon our ear, according to which they appear essentially as *dissonant*. We are forced to relate the chords in question to a *fundamental* to which one or more of their components is dissonant.[19]

This is certainly the clearest statement we have seen thus far in regard to the "dissonance" of the passing, neighbor, and suspension chords which were a familiar part of Sechter's system. Such chords are "dissonant"—amenable to melodic analysis, that is—because of the *local context of progression*. "Fundamental," in the previous quote, refers quite clearly to the local fundamental (as examples throughout the book demonstrate), not to the tonic. Furthermore, the authors' own underscorings read like a summary of the important features of fundamental bass theory which we have stressed throughout this study. The *Auffassungsdissonanz* gives us considerable insight into the true nature of Louis/Thuille's synthesis: while adopting the starting point of the German theory, they manage nevertheless to preserve Viennese fundamental bass methodology in the *interpretation* of progression.

"Interpretation-Dissonance" and "Feigning Consonance"

Louis/Thuille were well aware of the name which these chords had recently received:

> Such chords entering under the guise of consonance have been called "feigning consonances," for their consonance is merely apparent. Perhaps the term *interpretation-dissonance* would be more indicative of their individual nature, to the extent that a chord which is always consonant outside of musical context can, under certain circumstances, become dissonant for harmonic *interpretation*.[20]

If any doubt as to the origin of these chords remains, the authors of the tenth edition emphasize: "These can be called *melodic* six and six-four chords"[21] (the tenth edition retained "interpretation-dissonance" rather than adopting Riemann's "feigning consonance"). Curiously, the two terms have subsequently been used in many works as though they were synonymous—a strange state of affairs indeed, since they are based upon opposing assumptions. For Riemann, the source of dissonance was always harmonic, relating not to the context at hand, but back to the inflexible "three pillars":

> It is possible to comprehend two kinds of *Klang*-representation at the same time. However, one *Klang* is always more prominent, and the representation of the other appears as a disturbance of the consonance of the primary *Klang*, as dissonance.... Each of the secondary triads of the key represent [sic] simultaneously two of the three primary harmonies, one primary harmony being comprehended as the main content (consonance), the other, the foreign addition (dissonance).... In addition to the three primary harmonies, all other possible and intelligible chord formations originate through such dissonant formations without abandoning the key.[22]

"Function" and Context

In its most general sense, the term "function" seems to denote the way in which a chord operates in relation to a tonal center. In the usual "step theory," inherited from Weber or Vogler, chords are reduced mechanically to "root position" prototypes, and the resultant roots are assigned Roman numerals in a somewhat primitive attempt to symbolize their "function" in relation to a tonic.

In the "function theory," on the other hand, an attempt is made to reduce functional categories even further. But as we have seen, the assignment of two or more chords to the same "functional" category also took place in fundamental bass theory. The important difference is that in the "function theory" the explanation of function is harmonic, while in fundamental bass theory it is melodic. In fact, there is truth to both explanations.

An investigation of the "function" of III in major will serve as a convenient way to demonstrate the two explanations in practice. According to Riemann, when III "substitutes" for I it is a *leading-tone change* chord—that is, two tones from the tonic are maintained, while the tonic itself moves to the leading-tone. If we call to mind Sechter's model progression, I–III–V, the explanation seems quite acceptable, although it is difficult to see what it adds to Sechter's notion that secondary chords can "mediate" between primary chords. Indeed, such common tone progressions are dealt with in a similar way by Hauptmann as well.[23] But if we think of what is perhaps a more common usage, I–III–IV, it is clear that the origin of III is quite different here. The anticipated leading-tone we can see in I–III–V has absolutely nothing to do with the usage of the same tone in I–III–IV; here it is obviously a passing tone supported by bass arpeggiation, a usage well understood in fundamental bass theory. The effort to see such a tone as the leading-tone of the key is, to use Schenkerian terminology, a *confusion of structural levels*, for it is clear that the "leading-tone" is merely a local melodic *passing tone* in the present *context*. This *confusion of structural levels*—the direct relation of all phenomena to the tonal center and lack of recognition of local context—is endemic to Riemann's system, because of the inflexibility of the "three functions."[24]

A tour through the remaining secondary chords would reveal that the "function" of these chords, to the extent that the term is at all useful, cannot be explained by as simplistic a notion as "feigning consonance."[25] It is ironic indeed that Riemann fell victim to the same dogmatic over-generalization of explanations derived from particular contexts which had plagued Sechter.

"Substitution" in Halm and Louis/Thuille

There is certainly truth to the notion of "substitution," but each individual case must be approached on an ad hoc basis. This is precisely what Louis meant when he wrote that in contrast to Riemann "we indicate much more exactly how the substituting character of the secondary chords does not always remain the same throughout."[26] For secondary chords can act independently ("implied modulation"), or they can act as substitutes, but the latter is somewhat more complex than Riemann's ideas allow. Thus, in explaining the way in which II may substitute for IV, Louis/Thuille say:

> The subdominant meaning of II is most clearly exposed when the chord occurs in first inversion.... The chord acquires a certain similarity to a six chord [functioning as an] *interpretation-dissonance*; the six appears either as *suspension before* or *passing tone after* the fifth of the subdominant.[27]

Examples demonstrate these *particular* contexts. The method of explanation has changed little from fundamental bass theory (there is no mention of II being the *Parallelklang* of IV); only the "model" progression has changed. And even here, the authors admit that "the interpretation-dissonance characteristic of the chord retreats to the background when it is used in root position as a *triad*."[28] The emphasis may be either on II or IV, depending on context. And in the case of II7,

> the other *interpretation* of the II7 [other than the "subdominant" II six-five] will emerge, which is by far the more usual.... Our ear, always ready to seek the fundamental first in the bass, prefers to hear every root position seventh chord such that the bass appears as root, and accordingly, the seventh appears as a dissonance to it.[29]

Example 13-3

Example 13-3 shows one of Halm's voice-leading exercises based upon the cadence. The progression is reminiscent of Bruckner's "characteristic cadence" (see above, p. 76), except that Halm is free to think of II as subsidiary to IV in this context. Having previously discussed an example in which "I7" occurred in place of the "III" in the second half of the first bar, Halm explains:

> Upon playing both examples, no difference can be noticed.... It follows therefore that here the "triad" on III is not an independent consonance, but an incomplete dissonance—that is, the seventh chord on I (with concealed root, which nevertheless does not lose its effect). Further, [it follows] that III as well as I7 are passing formations which owe their existence to the motion from tonic to subdominant.[30]

In addition, the third beat of the penultimate bar shows "III" resulting from displacement of the fifth of the V chord. Halm shows a number of other contexts in which "III" may be found; each receives an individual explanation.

"VII" was of course recognized as a "substitute" of V by Kirnberger (in a particular context) and subsequent fundamental bass theorists. Here Riemann decides to add no new explanation. And the function of VI in the deceptive cadence had been described by Rameau and others. One cannot help wondering what Riemann's rigid formalism adds to the discussion.

Further Developments of the "Interpretation-Dissonance"

Aside from the cadential six-four shown earlier, Louis and Thuille also present clear definitions and examples of passing and auxiliary six-fours. Moreover, their understanding of such dissonant usages allows them to differentiate these clearly from the consonant six-four resulting from arpeggiation.[31]

Other cases include familiar "harmonic" chords in less familiar contexts. For example, the dominant seventh chord may be thought of in its most familiar context: as Kirnberger's "essential" dissonance. But even this chord may occur in another vastly different context:[32]

Example 13-4

a: IV - -

As mentioned repeatedly, progression is the overriding concern; and as with Mayrberger and Schalk, the "passing" function of a chord is unaffected by the skip of a voice:

> The *exclusively* passing interpretation will of course only be used with sixth chords when the inversion interpretation would yield an unnatural progression, as for example, V–IV. Thus, even the sixth chord over A [in ex. 13-5b] would be a passing formation in the broader sense of the term, despite the leaping bass.[33]

Example 13-5

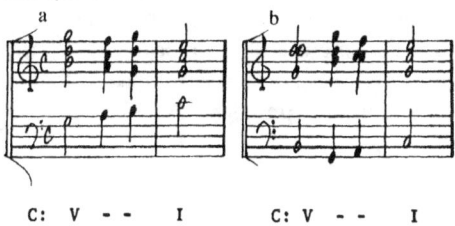

c: V - -   I   c: V - -   I

Earlier, in explaining the nature of the sixth chord as the result of inversion, the authors had emphasized that the bass was a melodic voice and should move only by second or third. But in the next example we see that these rules can be relaxed when a neighbor-note chord is interpolated between.[34]

Example 13-6

One of the most emphasized features of the interpretation-dissonance is the notion that such chords are, in a certain sense, both consonant and dissonant. A direct consequence of this is the fact that "*a suspension of the suspension* is possible if the second suspension enters in the form of a clear *interpretation-dissonance*...."[35] Here Louis/Thuille show an understanding of the possibility of levels of dissonance which makes one think of Schenker.

By and large, Louis and Thuille read no more than two or three passing chords in a row. However, in a long section on "nonessential chordal formations" (*zufällige Harmoniebildungen*), the following appears:

Example 13-7

In such cases, the authors say, it is sometimes doubtful whether one should assume change of fundamental or simply passing motion, but "here it is certainly most natural to view all of the harmonies which appear between the various forms of the tonic triad as *passing*."[36] This idea is developed further in the discussion of the organ-point. The authors approach this device through the notion of passing chords:

Example 13-8

In [ex.13-8] we have a passing chord motion, which acquires meaning through [the fact] that we retain the fundamental of the first chord in our memory unaltered—that is, that we relate all of the chords which result from passing motion to one and the same fundamental (G=CV).[37]

The actual "organ-point" is then explained as the realization of this "ideal organ-point."

As mentioned above, analysis of musical examples from the literature is an important part of the Louis/Thuille *Harmonielehre*. The following shows the application of the "ideal organ-point" in analysis:

Example 13-9

Mozart C minor Phantasie (K. 475)

B:V   [D:V   C:IV   V   Bbm:IV]=B:III V

Chromatic passing motion, which departs from the dominant of B major and again returns to it; thus the entire six measures [represent] an "ideal organ-point" over the F♯ fundamental.[38]

The New Synthesis: A Plea for Reassessment

History has not been kind to the Halm and Louis/Thuille works. Despite their success as pedagogical tools, European opinion seems to have followed Riemann in holding that they are mere paraphrases of his system, while in this country both works are all but unknown. It is true that our discussion of the diatonic aspects of these books tends to point up historical debts owed; but even here, the situation is hardly as simple as Riemann would have it. An assessment of the chromatic section of Louis/Thuille (fully half of the book) is beyond the scope of the present study. Suffice it to say that although this section, too, never leaves its eighteenth-century heritage behind completely, it is considerably more sophisticated than Sechter's *chromatische Fortschreitung*. The authors make many insightful observations on details of chromatic voice-leading, and apply their notion of passing chords here too with interesting results (for example, they show various progressions through equal subdivisions of the octave. In each, a single fundamental is prolonged throughout).[39]

Despite the fact that Louis/Thuille do not formulate any general principle akin to Schenker's "scale-step," the reader has no doubt noticed that their analytical technique often takes them in a direction that is similar to Schenker's. However, in choosing a "middle-of-the-road" position with respect to the theory of harmony, they manage to produce reasonably sophisticated analyses while still maintaining a smooth pedagogical progression from foreground to deeper levels of structure.

Given the excesses of the German theory of harmony, there is little doubt that Schenker's complete separation of harmony and counterpoint was a historical necessity. But the inclusion of voice-leading in recent Schenker-oriented harmony books provides additional evidence that, as desirable as this separation may be in theory, it is not beyond question as a pedagogical method.

14

The Viennese Reaction: Schenker and Schoenberg

The Basis of the Tonal System: Scale and Cadence

Throughout the nineteenth century there was never any doubt that the scale formed the basis of the Viennese theory of harmony, at first in figured bass theory and then in the fundamental bass system. At the beginning of the twentieth century it would form the basis of Schenker's system, albeit in a "purely spiritual universe, a system of ideally moving forces,"[1] instead of the simple fifth sequences of Sechter's system. While other theorists derived the scale from the "primary chords," Schenker generated the scale by rising fifths. Thus the much-debated subdominant—the product of inversion of this progression—is the last tone to enter:

> The system of the tone C, then, represents a community consisting of that root tone and five other root tones whose locations are determined by the rising fifth-relationship. One more root tone, the subdominant fifth, was added to this community and represents, so to speak, its link with the past.[2]

The "procreative urge" of these scale degrees would be fundamental to Schenker's conception of "harmony": indeed, this notion would serve as the basis of his view of modulation, chromaticism, and his new theory of "scale-steps" (*Stufen*), among other ideas. Thus, in much the same way as the diatonic scale was the foundation of Sechter's theories of modulation, "chromatic progression", and incipient "tonicization," a somewhat more abstract diatonic scale forms the foundation of Schenker's theory of harmony.

Moreover, the structural role of the diatonic scale is not only an abstraction, for one of the most common reifications of the "purely spiritual" ascending fifth is the venerable cycle of descending fifths. And here, the "unnatural" diminished fifth, which various theorists had attempted to discredit as a harmonic progression, is essential to Schenker's conception of tonality:

> Whenever the process of inversion is continued below the subdominant, the diminished fifth is inevitable, as schematically indicated here:
> I–IV̰–VII–III–VI–II–V–I
>   diminished fifth

> On such occasions the diminished fifth has the important function of channeling the process of inversion away from the sphere of falling fifths back into the realm of rising fifths; and it is only the fact that the subdominant is followed by the diminished fifth B, and not by the perfect fifth B-flat, which could lure us to continue the process of inversion into yet lower regions of falling fifths, extraneous to our C-system—it is only this fact that makes us fully aware that we are moving in the C-system at all.[3]

In the generation of the "artificial" system (minor) Schenker likewise notes that "this sequence, in the minor mode, is in no way disturbed by the fact that the second fifth in rising order already finds itself in the 'wrong' relationship to the third fifth...."[4]

These views on the fundamental nature of tonality put Schenker squarely at odds with the function theory. Ironically, most of his criticism of that theory is not in *Harmony*, but in *Kontrapunkt* (part 1), perhaps because he felt that the theory of voice leading had suffered most at the hands of the function theorists. In the Introduction to *Kontrapunkt I* Schenker casts Rameau as the ultimate villain, who, "in France, at almost the same time as Fux published his work, came out with the new theory of chordal function, the theory of tonic, dominant and subdominant as primary chords, and of the derivability of all remaining chords from these, etc."[5] More recently, however, Riemann has taken up Rameau's theories once again and drawn the "ultimate consequences" from them. In an obvious reference to Riemann's misguided effort to derive all of the rules of voice leading from his notion of harmonic function (an attempt which Louis/Thuille also reject), Schenker laments that at present "a vast, new and confusing world of 'leading tones' and 'doublings' is fabricated before us—[a world] which can never know the true theory of voice-leading and step progression!"[6]

Citing Louis/Thuille's "unfurling" of triads as the "functional" explanation of the tonal system, Schenker goes on to criticize their rash claim that with the three primary triads, the key is "completely and exhaustively determined" (see chapter 13). How profound can this "system" be when "except for I, IV, and V, one robs the individual scale degrees of their independence, and at the same time of the stimulus (*Reiz*) of their *manifold* function?" (italics mine).[7] Schenker cites a familiar example when he criticizes those who believe in this theory, saying that they do not understand

> how much better it corresponds to the true sense of a composition to understand III, for example, according to its various functions: first, as it confronts the tonic as fourth upper fifth (according to the fifth-principle, *Harmony*, sections 14–19), second, when it is considered antecedent of V, and third, as antecedent of I (according to the third-principle, *Harmony*, section 126).[8]

These ideas will return below. For now it will suffice to point out their obvious correspondence to Sechter's two harmonic roles for III: as mediator between I and V, and as link in the chain of fifths.

Schenker continues by discussing several examples of II–V, in which II is clearly independent and not derived in any sense from IV. Finally he turns his attention to one of the most oft-encountered objections to the cycle of fifths—the notion that it is merely the result of melodic sequence:

> One distances oneself all too much from art and moves decidedly too far into speculation when one believes that such descending fifth progressions as II–V and the like are used by composers mainly as empty sequences and reflex connections (*Rückbeziehungen*).[9]

Schenker proceeds to give a most persuasive example of how important this progression can be: the first eight measures of the Minuet from Bach's D minor French Suite, in which the complete cycle of fifths serves to establish the key, and the voice leading is not sequential. Likewise, his first musical example in minor in *Harmony* (pp. 47–48) is the opening of the Brahms B♭ minor Intermezzo (Op. 117, no. 2), which also establishes B♭ minor with the complete cycle of fifths. He gives similar evidence from the works of Bach in the discussion of fifth progression in *Harmony*, all of which points up the deficiency of the cadential model as an all-encompassing explanation for progression.

As Schenker directed his interest more and more to "scale-steps" of longer duration, he ultimately conceived of such cycles of fifths as a series of "interpolated fifths" before a final V–I motion.[10] But at this early stage in his career there is little doubt that his conception of the basis of the tonal system is a direct lineal descendant of Sechter's. Likewise, the mature Schenker would relegate the subdominant in the IV–V–I cadence (the tonic's "link with the past") to the sphere of counterpoint.[11] However, in *Harmony* he describes it harmonically in a manner which recalls Sechter's "reciprocal effect." Citing the opening of the E♭ minor Prelude from Book I of the *Well-Tempered Clavier*, Schenker says:

> It was almost a rule for [Bach] to anchor his tonic, right at the outset, by quoting, first of all, the subdominant and then the dominant fifth, and only then to proceed with his exposition.[12]

Of course, Bach is no longer obliged to return to the tonic in between the two fifths, as in Sechter. Moreover, the notion of "anchoring" seems compatible with the idea of a tonal "center" which plays such an important role in most *Harmonielehren* at the turn of the century. With respect to their views of the fundamental nature of the tonal system, this idea is probably the only common ground between Schenker and Schoenberg.

As is well known, Schoenberg's opening discussions of such matters as "theory" and "consonance and dissonance" are primarily critiques aimed at dethroning absolute aesthetic standards. Thus we read that tonality is simply one possible type of musical organization, that the categories of consonance and dissonance may well prove to be inadequate for understanding the future evolution of harmonic technique, etc. And at a practical, pedagogical level, Schoenberg criticizes the teaching of harmony through exercises in figured bass and melody harmonization. All of these views are obviously in opposition to both Schenker's and those of the nineteenth-century Viennese theory. Likewise, Schoenberg's view of the fundamental nature of tonality is quite different from the views of Sechter or Schenker.

> If C is taken as the midpoint, then its situation can be described by reference to two forces, one which pulls downward, toward F, the other upward, toward G.[13]

Apparently, C is a true tonal "center" for Schoenberg. As David Lewin has suggested, the organization of the "Chart of Regions" in *Structural Functions of Harmony* gives additional evidence of the extent to which Schoenberg "conceived of a 'tonic' as a fulcrum around which all else balanced...."[14] Although Schoenberg's "inversional balance" is hardly the inflexible inversional symmetry of dualism, it is most certainly opposed to the traditional Viennese view. And just as Schenker's *Stufen* would remain fundamental to his thinking for his whole career, so too would this notion of inversional balance continue to characterize much of Schoenberg's creative work. But as "un-Viennese" as Schoenberg's view of tonality might appear, the influence of Viennese fundamental bass theory would return in his explanation of step progression—the essence of his theory of harmony.

Theory of Progression

After deriving the scale from the "primary chords," Schoenberg discusses chord connection using the diatonic triads. Although he uses the terms "primary" and "secondary" chords,[15] he never bothers to define them. And the content of the discussion makes it clear that his use of the terms is in no way connected with Riemann's usage. The chord connection discussion centers on Sechter's *harmonisches Bindungsmittel,* which Schoenberg calls *harmonisches Band*. The necessity of maintaining this "harmonic link" (Carter's translation) is stressed; the remaining voices are exhorted to follow Bruckner's "law of the shortest way."[16] Because of the importance attributed to the "harmonic link," as in Sechter, the familiar fundamental bass progressions by fifth and third are of primary importance. Sechter's usages of all of the primary and secondary chords except VII are discussed; and when VII finally makes its appearance, it too is treated according to Sechter's demands: its dissonant fifth must be prepared (Schoenberg allows either IV or II as preparatory chords, since the fifth of II is obviously not "dissonant" for him), and it must resolve with a motion to III: "*After VII we shall use for the moment nothing else but III, before VII only IV or II.*"[17] Sechter's fifth sequence is now complete.

Like Bruckner, Schoenberg now spends considerable time practicing these progressions with chords in inversion before finally tackling the stepwise progressions. When these finally arrive, Schoenberg notes the "the older theory" explains the ascending stepwise progression by considering the first chord to be a seventh chord with missing root, and the descending stepwise progression by considering the first chord to be a ninth chord with missing root and third.[18] The equalization of ascending and descending progressions, as well as Schoenberg's examples,[19] show that these ideas come from Bruckner—not from a reading of the *Grundsätze*.

With all progressions in place, Schoenberg now develops his theory of strong ("ascending"), weak ("descending") and super-strong ("over-skipping") progressions. The descending fifth/rising fourth progression is the first of the "ascending" progressions. The apparent paradox results from the fact that the term has nothing to do with direction of root movement. (Schoenberg notes his disagreement with Schenker's very logical "descending.") Rather, it denotes the fact that:

> the bass tone of the second chord is a higher category, a higher power, for it contains the first, the tone that itself was previously the root. In the triad on G the g is sovereign, but in the triad on C the g is subordinate and the c is sovereign.[20]

Progressions by descending third fall into the same category.

One might be tempted, Schoenberg says, to call the progressions by second the strongest, since all notes are "conquered." This would be incorrect, however, for such progressions

> force the connection; and it may be for this reason that the older theory explains them in a unique way: each as the sum of two progressions, of which one, the more important, is a root progression a fourth upward. These sums read: V–VI=V–III–VI... and V–IV=V–I–IV.[21]

The explanation of such progressions as *Doppelschritte*—as sums of fifth and third progressions—again comes from Bruckner. Schoenberg, in fact, is not unconvinced of this explanation, and warns of the overuse of these progressions:

> The conception of the root progressions of a second as sums, as abbreviations, testifies to the reluctance of the older masters to regard them as normal progressions.... Were one of them the strongest progression (which one?), then it would have to play a different role in the...cadence. The cadential progression IV–V is by no means insignificant, but II–V can replace it unobtrusively; and this cannot be said for V–I.[22]

The remaining category of progressions—the descending progressions—consists of the progressions by ascending fifth and third. These have the opposite effect of the ascending progressions; in the progression from C to G, for example, "The fifth, a *parvenu*, is promoted, becomes the root. That is decadence."[23] Schoenberg's debt to the Viennese fundamental bass theory is clear. His opinion of the stepwise progressions is surprisingly similar; only his preference for step progressions or descending fifth and third progressions over the ascending fifth and third progressions is a real departure. In addition, Dika Newlin perceptively notes the influence of Sechter's "intermediate fundamental" on Schoenberg's advice that descending progressions should only be used "in those chord connections where the total effect is still that of ascent."[24] In this regard Schoenberg says "if the progression a fifth upward is followed by that of a second upward, the result is a progression a third downward, thus, an ascent of the harmony."[25] As Newlin points out,[26] the V is, in a sense, an "intermediate fundamental"; Schoenberg has reworked the old Sechter/Bruckner explanation to suit his own needs.

In such matters as the existence of nonharmonic tones, the duration of harmonic steps, and the notion of chords beyond the seventh, Schoenberg and Schenker could not be farther apart; Schoenberg followed Bruckner, while Schenker obviously reacted against his teacher. But in the matter of progression they show a certain affinity due to the common heritage of fundamental bass theory.

The fifth progressions are "natural," according to Schenker, while the step progressions are "artificial."[27] Undoubtedly, Sechter would agree, and he would certainly endorse the examples which Schenker gives to illustrate.

"Progression by thirds may be considered no less natural than progression by fifths."[28] And like the fifth progressions, they may correspond to Schenker's notions of "development" or "inversion"; that is, they may be "rising" or "descending." Here, Schenker clearly describes the most common role of third progressions—what he will later call the third "divider" (*Teiler*):

> If progression by thirds is thus justified by Nature, we must nevertheless remember... that the fifth takes precedence over the third....
>
> The psychological effect of the progression by thirds is quite often that it makes progression by fifths (upward or downward) appear as though it were divided into two phases.[29]

Like Schoenberg, Schenker describes the life cycle of a single pitch as it starts as root, becomes third, and then fifth (in the descending progression by third and then fifth, for example). As with Schoenberg, Sechter's first role for secondary chords—the one in which they mediate between primary chords—is discernible behind the discussion.

The stepwise progressions were described earlier as "artificial"; Schenker continues: "Progression by seconds must thus be considered a secondary derivation from progression by fifths and thirds."[30] Of course, Schenker would later relegate all of the stepwise progressions to the sphere of counterpoint, rendering these youthful (and clearly derivative) ideas obsolete. But here he extends Sechter's method of deriving stepwise progressions by including his ideas of "development" and "inversion." Thus the progression I–II, instead of being interpreted as Sechter's I–(VI)–II, is seen as the sum of two "developing" fifths (I–V–II), or one and a half "inverted" fifths (I–IV–II). Other stepwise progressions are described in a similar manner.[31]

Other Debts to Viennese Fundamental Bass Theory

Both Schenker and Schoenberg remedy one of the major defects of Sechter's theory: the rigid separation of major and minor. Yet neither of their solutions to the problem corresponds exactly with the German theory, which, after Hauptmann, preferred to speak of three modes: major, harmonic minor, and minor-major. Only during Schoenberg's discussion of the region of the minor subdominant do we sense the possible influence of the German theory.[32] Schoenberg's notion of "pivot tones" and his enumeration of scale-degree triads in minor using the variable sixth and seventh steps are most reminiscent of Sechter.[33] But these degrees are also contained in the six "combinations" of Schenker, who is careful to note that his notion of "combination" differs from the mixed modes of both Hauptmann and Riemann.[34] Unlike Sechter, both Schenker and Schoenberg see modal mixture as a source of chromaticism.

With regard to the theory of chords, Schoenberg follows Bruckner in accepting the ninth chord, and enumerating scale-degree ninth chords as well.[35] Few would go this far. Schenker says that the usual category of ninth chords consists only of the one on the dominant, a notion which he rejects forthwith. He goes on to reject any possibility of scale-degree ninths, and the so-called higher chords as well.[36]

Yet with the dominant ninth chord, Schenker and Schoenberg once again partake of their common heritage of fundamental bass theory. Almost immediately after banishing the ninth chord, Schenker nevertheless reads a progression of fifth-related diminished-seventh chords as a cycle of fifths of rootless ninth chords. This interpretation, we are told, is possible when the chords have the status of "scale-steps"; in such cases, only a VII or VII7 may be present, "yet our imminent feeling for the logic of step progression requires us to hear the V7 chord."[37] Apparently, Schenker has less against the ninth chord than he has against the thoughtless chord-labeling and third-stacking which often accompanies its acceptance. Schoenberg complains of the frequent misuse of the diminished seventh chord; its correct usage is determined by the fundamental bass:

> For us [the diminished seventh] is rather, as a ninth chord with omitted root, nothing else but the special form of a degree. Only whenever this degree can also be used otherwise, according

to the standards we have for its use—unaltered, as a secondary dominant, or with other modifications—only in such places shall we write a diminished seventh chord, if it is appropriate. The decisive consideration remains, first and last, the root progression.[38]

With respect to the origin and function of chromaticism, Schenker and Sechter show considerable affinity. We may recall what I have termed Sechter's notion of incipient "tonicization":

> The essence of chromaticism acquires a great extension when, with the exception of the seventh scale-step [*Stufe*], one views each of the remaining [scale-steps] as a *tonic*.[39]

Sechter continues by saying that in such a case, the fundamentals must follow "in such an order that each can be independent".[40] (The prescribed order is passed on in Bruckner's "extended cadence.") The "variations" which follow in Sechter's presentation show that he has relatively short (one-measure) spans in mind for these fundamentals. Like many of Sechter's ideas, this is designed as a practical, compositional technique. Indeed, it is the nineteenth-century, fundamental-bass heir to an extremely practical eighteenth-century technique: the figured bass exercise in "modulation." At the end of Seyfried's essay on Albrechtsberger's figured bass/harmony, he presents several figured basses which "modulate" through the five related keys and return to the opening key within about twelve measures.[41]

Once again, Schenker transports these ideas to the "purely spiritual" realm:

> Not only at the beginning of a composition but also in the midst of it, each scale-step manifests an irresistable urge to attain the value of the tonic for itself as that of the strongest scale-step. If the composer yields to this urge of the scale-step within the diatonic system of which this scale-step forms part, I call this process *tonicalization* and the phenomenon itself *chromatic*.[42]

Jonas cites this as one of many places in which Schenker anticipates his later theory of *Schichten*. The notion of "nested" tonicizations all controlled by *the* tonic is indeed consistent with Schenker's later ideas. Interestingly, it is not consistent with Schoenberg's version of "monotonality," where there is only one tonic, and "secondary dominants" and other nondiatonic chords are conceived of as chromatic alterations of scale-degree chords, rather than applied dominants to structurally superior diatonic triads.[43] As usual, Schenker and Schoenberg are probably speaking at cross-purposes. Schoenberg's idea, as developed more fully in *Structural Functions*, seems particularly well-suited to Austro-Germanic music of the late nineteeth/early twentieth centuries, while Schenker's idea is more at home with the musical language of the eighteenth and early nineteenth centuries.

Schenker's general opinion of chromaticism (which Schoenberg would be unlikely to second) is also well within the Viennese tradition: "chromatic change is an element which does not destroy the diatonic system but which rather emphasizes and confirms it."[44] Indeed, except for the name, Schenker even preserves Sechter's "hybrid-chord" intact: according to him, "tonicalization really is the source of the so-called 'altered chords'." He goes on to describe the seventh chord G B D♭ F as a combination of C:V7 and Fm:II7, just as Sechter would have. Moreover, this particular augmented 6/diminished 3 chord is the prototype for all the others, just as it was in Sechter: "All we have to do now is to transfer this same process, i.e., the new characteristic interval [the diminished third/augmented sixth] to those related chords which may be substituted for the V7 chord."[45] Like Sechter, Schenker attempts to preserve the diatonic fundamental bass in the chromatic domain.

Beyond the Limits of the Received Theory

Although the magnitude of Schenker's debt to Viennese fundamental bass theory has apparently not been general knowledge, the influence of fundamental bass theory on Schoenberg's *Theory of Harmony* has long been recognized.[46] Moreover, fundamental bass theory has been exerting lately a most welcome influence on American thinking about "traditional harmony," certainly because of the influence of Schenker and Schoenberg.[47] But of course the works of Schenker and Schoenberg are far more than accumulations of historical debts; and thus the most fitting conclusion to the present study is to examine briefly the ways in which they transcend their theoretical heritage.

In essence, both Schenker and Schoenberg take extreme positions on certain features of the received theory. Schoenberg manages to write a book which ostensibly teaches tonal harmony, but hardly mentions the existence of "nonharmonic" tones until chapter 17. We recall that the so-called "nonharmonic" tones in the received theory were unrelated to submetrical embellishment, but rather were used to form the various passing and neighbor chords which were an integral part of Sechter's system right from the beginning, enabling him to limit the allowable progression of the fundamental bass. But even the most obvious of these are independent for Schoenberg: "only, the theory of passing harmony, which would impose its accidental harmonies, explains them as dependent."[48] Schoenberg defends the ninth chord and all of its possible inversions, ultimately claiming that any vertical may be explained harmonically, for the "theory that dissonances are the more remote consonances of the overtone series . . . implies that harmonies produced by nonharmonic tones are chords too, just like the others."[49] These ideas, combined with Schoenberg's denunciation of figured bass, produce a system characterized by greater freedom both of voice leading and fundamental succession.[50] (Schenker was able to separate voice leading from harmony because of his vastly different notion of "harmony.") Thus, the movement towards more "harmonic" interpretation initiated by Bruckner was completed by Schoenberg, whose notion of "harmony" essentially reduces to his theory of root progression. Of course, the banishment of the old "accidental" harmonies (Schoenberg uses the unfortunate term as a pretext for his attack) is necessary if he is going to be able to fuse the pre-chapter 17 and post-chapter 17 sections of his book into a unit. Music has evolved to the point exemplified by his music; theory must do likewise.

It was probably inevitable that the notion of "passing harmonies" would cause the greatest controversy between Schenker and Schoenberg: this is precisely the point where their views are completely irreconcilable.[51] Central to Schenker's notion of harmony is his theory of *Stufen*:

> The scale-step is a higher and more abstract unit. At times it may even comprise several harmonies, each of which could be considered individually as an independent triad or seventh chord; in other words: even if, under certain circumstances, a certain number of harmonies look like independent triads or seventh chords, they may nonetheless add up, in their totality, to one single triad....[52]

Schenker is of the opinion that the rules for recognizing "scale-steps" cannot be set down "once and for all"—that they "flow, so to speak, from the spirit and intention of each individual composition."[53] Nevertheless, upon looking at the examples which he gives, one quickly notes the familiar passing and neighbor chords of Viennese fundamental bass theory.[54] Schenker may well have been lead to his notion of *Stufen* through efforts to preserve the "natural" fundamental progression. In any event, it is clear that the method by which these chords are viewed is a descendent of fundamental bass theory, not of Riemann: that is, the chords function melodically and relate directly to a local fundamental (the "scale-step").[55]

But as with "tonicization," which was implicit in Sechter's system, the very naming of the phenomenon is of the greatest significance, for priorities are reversed thereby. Although Louis/Thuille's "interpetation-dissonance" is a more sophisticated notion than the passing chords of fundamental bass theory, it still functions as a means to an end: the avoidance of certain undesirable fundamental progressions. For Schenker, on the other hand, the independence of the scale-steps becomes the main focus in most of his ideas presented in his *Harmonielehre*; and it is this idea which would furnish the main direction for his later work.

While Schenker's *Stufen* would be germinal to an approach to music theory which remains alive and vital, the many prophetic remarks scattered throughout the *Theory of Harmony* remind one of Schoenberg's continuing influence. When, in the chapter entitled "The Chromatic Scale as a Basis for

Tonality," Schoenberg remarks that in modern music "one might reach conclusions concerning the constitution of chords through a procedure similar to figured bass more easily than one could clarify their function by methods of reference to degrees,"[56] we think of recent set-theoretic approaches to twentieth-century music. Earlier attempts to transfer Schenker's ideas to this repertory proved to be naive and premature. Indeed, with this music we are still in the figured bass era.

With such ideas as harmony/counterpoint/free composition, and *Urlinie/ Bassbrechung/ Ursatz*, Schenker was able to elevate the dialectic to a new role in music theory. Unfortunately there is no guarantee that we will be able to find the synthesis of the opposed theories offered to us by Schenker and Schoenberg. Recent interest in "motivic parallelisms" seems to point to such an attempt, at least in the study of tonal music. However, there is no doubt that many of the points upon which Schenker and Schoenberg disagreed continue to be controversial among music theorists today.

Notes

Introduction

1. This is the approach taken by Peter Rummenhöller in his book, *Musiktheoretisches Denken im 19. Jahrhundert* (Regensburg: Bosse Verlag, 1967).
   The relationship of the history of music theory to intellectual history in the nineteenth century is not unproblematic, however. Through Rummenhöller's method, a theorist who is clearly a product of his intellectual environment (for example, Hauptmann) is assured a chapter of his own, regardless of what he actually manages to say about music. Meanwhile, theorists who cannot be pidgeonholed as easily tend to be seen as anachronistic traditionalists. (All of Viennese theory, for example, fits into Rummenhöller's third chapter, "Kompositionslehre und Harmonielehre.")
   For purposes of the present study, it should be remembered that for close to half of a century Vienna stood outside of the currents of intellectual, sociological, and political change which characterized much of nineteenth-century Europe. One need only consider, for example, that while Charles Simon Catel's *Traité d'Harmonie* (Paris: 1802) was chosen for class instruction at the Paris Conservatory by vote of a revolutionary committee, Viennese theorists were writing figured bass books for private instruction.

2. William C. Mickelsen, *Hugo Riemann's Theory of Harmony* and *History of Music Theory, Book III by Hugo Riemann*, trans. and ed. by Mickelsen (Lincoln and London: University of Nebraska Press, 1977). Hereafter cited as "Mickelsen."

3. William J. Mitchell, "Chord and Context in 18th-Century Theory," *JAMS* 16, no. 2 (Summer 1963): 221-39.

4. David Williams Beach, "The Harmonic Theories of Johann Philipp Kirnberger; Their Origins and Influences" (Ph.D. dissertation, Yale University, 1974).

Chapter 1

1. Ulf Thomson, *Voraussetzungen und Artungen der österreichischen Generalbasslehre zwischen Albrechtsberger und Sechter* (Tutzing: Hans Schneider, 1978), p. 26.

2. Manfred Wagner, *Die Harmonielehren der ersten Hälfte des 19. Jahrhunderts* (Regensburg: Gustav Bosse Verlag, 1974), p. 13.

3. In a less conservative environment pedagogy may be considerably more "up to date." Adolf Bernhard Marx's ideas on music theory and pedagogy are an excellent example. See Kurt-Erich Eicke, *Der Streit zwischen Adolf Bernhard Marx und Gottfried Wilhelm Fink um die Kompositionslehre* (Regensburg: Bosse Verlag, 1966).

4. Abbé George Joseph Vogler, *Handbuch zur Harmonielehre und fuer den Generalbaß nach den Grundsaetzen der Mannheimer Tonschule* (Prague: 1802).

5. Vogler's influence was nevertheless considerable. See chapter 2 of the present study.

6. S.v. "Vogler" in: G. Schilling, *Enzyclopädie der gesammten musikalischen Wissenschaften, o. Universal-Lexicon*, 6 (Stuttgart: 1838): 794; quoted after Thomson, *Voraussetzungen*.(Ein Theil staunt ihn an, weil er seinen Geist nicht zu ergründen vermag, der andere schimpft, weil er ihn nicht versteht und sich durch neuere Ansicht vom Monopol des unfehlbaren Contrapunct und Generalbaß-Schlendrians verdrängt sieht.)

7. Ernst Tittel, *Die Wiener Musik Hochschule* (Vienna: Verlag Elisabeth Lafite, 1967), p. 101.

8. Thomson, *Voraussetzungen*, p. 88. (Als zukunftsträchtig muß daher jeder Versuch bezeichnet werden, der das Akkord material funktionell zu deuten versucht, während die statische Akkorderklärung als barock bezeichnet werden muß.) This is the first of many indications of the power of Hugo Riemann's interpretation of the history of harmonic theory.

9. Gottfried von Preyer (1807-1901) was the first head of the Conservatory to have the title "Direktor," serving between 1843 and 1847. A student of Sechter's, he was also the theory instructor at the Conservatory between Salzmann and Sechter. He was the teacher of two theorists who later attempted to use Sechter's theory in the analysis of chromatic harmony (Mayrberger and Hasel; see chap. 10 and 11 of the present work). Judging from the work of these men, he appears to have been a faithful follower of Sechter's teaching. Yet, in his Conservatory classes (1839-48) he is said to have used Reicha's *Vollständiges Lehrbuch der Harmonielehre, des Generalbasses, der Melodie*, trans. by Carl Czerny (Wien: Diabelli, 1833), according to Elfriede Bernhauer, "Gottfried von Preyer, Sein Leben und Wirken (Ph.D. dissertation, University of Vienna, 1951), p. 47.

10. Thomson, *Voraussetzungen*, p. 17. (ihrer genialen Begabung mehr folgten, als der strengen Lehre vom reinen Satz.) Thomson notes that such absurd criticism was directed primarily at Schubert and Beethoven.

11. O.E. Deutsch, *Schubert, die Erinnerungen seiner Freunde* (Leipzig: 1957), p. 246. (ihn Sechter mit der Ledernheit seiner Kompositionen anstecken werde.)

12. O.E. Deutsch, *The Schubert Reader*, trans. Eric Blom (New York: Norton, 1947), p. 819.

13. Friedrich Wilhelm Marpurg, *Abhandlung von der Fuge*, Simon Sechter, ed. (Wien: Anton Diabelli and Co., n.d.). The *Anhang* to this edition is an original analysis by Sechter of the finale of Mozart's "Jupiter Symphony." This section alone was later reissued as: Sechter-Eckstein, *Das Finale von W.A. Mozarts Jupiter-Symphonie* (Vienna: Wiener Philharmonischer Verlag A.G., 1923). Considering that this is Sechter's only published (and known) analysis, it is most disappointing that it is unrelated to his system of harmony.

14. Alfred Mann, "Schubert's Lesson with Sechter," *Nineteenth Century Music* 6, no. 2 (Fall 1982): 59-65. The materials from the lesson with Sechter were originally discovered by Christa Landon ("New Schubert Finds," *Music Review* 31, no. 1 [1970]: 215-31). The manuscript (Ms. V [D.965B]) consists of two pages. The first contains eighteen two-part fugal expositions in Schubert's writing with corrections by Sechter. The other page, entirely in Sechter's handwriting, consists of exercises in double counterpoint, as well as a fugue subject on Schubert's name which was probably an assignment for Sechter's "pupil." On November 28, Diabelli published Sechter's tribute to Schubert: a fugue on this same subject written by Sechter. This piece has recently been reprinted by Schott in Book I of a series entitled *Journal für das Pianoforte* (Franzpeter Goebels, ed. [Schott ED 6874]) together with pieces dedicated to Schubert's memory by Hüttenbrenner and Czerny.

15. *Allg. Wiener Musikzeitung*, I. Jahrgang (Wien: 1841), p. 22; quoted after Thomson, *Voraussetzungen*, p. 20. (seine Compositionen die gute alte Schule bekräftigen, worin richtiger Satz und fehlerlose Durchführung als die Hauptfordernisse galten.)

16. Walter Zeleny, *Die historischen Grundlagen des Theoriesystems von Simon Sechter* (Tutzing: Hans Schneider, 1979), pp. 43-48.

17. The chapters on chorale fugue and canon—both of which are additions to Fux's *Gradus*, which Albrechtsberger otherwise follows—are included in Alfred Mann's *The Study of Fugue* (New York: Norton, 1965), pp. 221-62.

18. J.G. Albrechtsberger, *Kurzgefasste Methode den Generalbass zu erlernen* (Wien: Artaria, n.d. [listed by Thomson as 1793]); *Generalbassschule, Neue vom Verfasser vermehrte Auflage* (Leipzig: Peters, n.d.). According to Thomson's bibliography, a *Neue vermehrte Auflage der kurzgefassten Methode...* (Wien: Artaria, n.d.) also exists; Wagner lists a *General Bass Schule... Neueste, vom Verfasser vermehrte Auflage* (presumably, the same as the above *Generalbassschule*, or at least derived from it) as Wien: Artaria, 1805.

19. *Methods of Harmony, Figured Base, and Composition, adapted for Self-Instruction by J.G. Albrechtsberger*, Seyfried, ed., Merrick, trans. (London: Cocks and Co., n.d. [1834]) is a translation of Choron's French translation: *Méthodes d'harmonie et de composition, à l'aide desquelles on peut apprendre soi-même à accompagner la basse chiffrée et à composer toute espèce de musique; par J.-Georges Albrechtsberger* (Paris: Bachelier, 1830). See Bryan R. Simms, "Alexandre Choron (1771-1834) as a Historian and Theorist of Music," (Ph.D. dissertation, Yale University, 1971), pp. 232-38, for information on Choron's translations of Seyfried's edition of Albrechtsberger and other works of Albrechtsberger. The more generally-available English translation is *J.G. Albrechtsberger's Collected Writings on Thorough-bass, Harmony and Composition, for Self-Instruction*, Seyfried, ed. Novello, trans. (London: Novello, Ewer and Co., 1855).

20. *J.G. Albrechtsberger's Collected Writings* (Novello trans.), p. iii. With respect to the material on figured bass, this translation agrees in substance with the German original and will be used further below.

21. Albrechtsberger, *Kurzgefasste Methode*, pp. 1f. Further locations of cited material from this work will be given in the text.

22. Since Albrechtsberger never mentions possible "inversions" of chords, it is impossible to determine whether he means "root" or "bass tone."

23. (Zu der übermäßigen Sext gehört die verdoppelte große Terz, oder nur eine große Terz, und der Tritonus....)

24. *J.G. Albrechtsberger's Collected Writings* (Novello trans.), pp. 11f. Further locations of cited material from this work will be given in the text.

25. Ignaz von Seyfried, *Ludwig van Beethovens Studien...* (Leipzig/Hamburg/New York: 1853 [2nd ed.]). The ninth, eleventh, and thirteenth chords begin the tenth chapter of the "Lehre vom Generalbass." According to Nottebohm, none of the material on figured bass comes from Beethoven's study with Albrechtsberger (as Seyfried would have us believe), but rather is a collection of quotes from C.P.E. Bach, Türk, Kirnberger, and Albrechtsberger's *Anweisung*, assembled by Beethoven at a later period. Regarding the ninth, eleventh, and thirteenth chords, Nottebohm says that there was no justification for separating them from previous material and making them a chapter unto themselves. "Beethoven only wants to say (with Türk) that besides the first system which was introduced, there is another which differs

148   Notes for Chapter 2

from it in that it explains the ninth, eleventh, and thirteenth chords not as suspension formations, but rather forms [them] through addition of thirds below the root of a seventh chord. (Beethoven will (mit Türk) nichts Anderes sagen, als dass es ausser dem einen, zuerst vorgetragenen System noch eine anderes giebt, welches vom ersten darin abweicht, dass es die Nonen-, Undecimen- und Terzdecimen-Accorde nicht als Vorhaltsbildungen erklärt, sondern durch Terzenzusätze unter den Grundton eines Septimen-Accordes bildet.) G. Nottebohm, *Beethoveniana II* (Leipzig: 1872), pp. 170f.

26. It must be admitted that such evidence *could* exist in the *Neue vermehrte Auflage der kurzgefassten Methode* (note 18, above), which Thomson says is 73 pages in length (Thomson, p. 55). Moreover, *New Grove* (Vol. I, p. 226) lists a manuscript by Albrechtsberger entitled *Generalbass-und Harmonielehre*. Neither of these sources was available to me when this chapter was in preparation.

Chapter 2

1. Thomson, *Voraussetzungen und Artungen der österreichischen Generalbasslehre zwischen Albrechtsberger und Sechter* (Tutzing: Hans Schneider, 1978), pp. 55ff.

2. Manfred Wagner, *Die Harmonielehren der ersten Hälfte des 19. Jahrhunderts*, pp. 45ff. See the first section of Wagner's book ("Der österreichische Kreis," pp. 9–57). Wagner's discussion is arranged topically, and is a useful adjunct to the present discussion (chapters 2 and 3), which is arranged chronologically by treatise.

3. Ernst Tittel, "Wiener Musiktheorie von Fux bis Schönberg," *Beiträge zur Musiktheorie des 19. Jahrhundert*, ed. Martin Vogel (Regensburg: Gustav Bosse Verlag, 1966), p. 176.

4. Wagner, *Harmonielehren*, p. 54.

5. Abbé Georg Joseph Vogler, *Handbuch zur Harmonielehre und fuer den Generalbaß nach den Grundsaetzen der Mannheimer Tonschule* (Prague: 1802) p. 127. The "Abhandlung vom Generalbasse" extends from page 125 to page 142. (man sich einen ganz unrichtigen Begriff vom Generalbasse macht, wenn man ihn fuer eine besondere Wissinschaft ausgibt, weil er nur ein einzelner praktischer Zweig der Harmonielehre...ist.)

6. The development of Vogler's theory of harmony has recently been discussed by Floyd K. Grave in his article, "Abbé Vogler's Theory of Reduction" (*Current Musicology* 29 [1980]: 41–69). Also see Grave's earlier article, "Abbé Vogler and the Study of Fugue" (*Music Theory Spectrum* 1: 41–66 [1979]). In "Reduction" Grave offers a useful summary of Vogler's ideas on harmony, but his effort to see Vogler's system of *Redukzion* as a precursor of the modern notion of "Schenkerian reduction" is strained and misleading.

7. Vogler, *Handbuch*, p. 73. (Es gibt nur eine Harmonie, und diese ist der Dreiklang. Der wesentliche vierte ist schon ein Uibelklang.)

8. Abbé Georg Joseph Vogler, *Choral-System* (Copenhagen: 1800 and Offenbach: n.d.), p. 9. (muß man bei der Redukzion, die alle verschiedene Gestalten in ihre Stamm-Akkorde aufloeset,...sich nicht auf die vollkommenste Harmonie (*l'accord parfait* nach Rameau) einschraenken, sondern auf alle Harmonien, es moegen dabei verminderte oder uebermaeßige Tonverbindungen (Intervalle) vorkommen, zuruekleiten....)

9. Ibid., p. 8.

10. See Robert P. Morgan, "Schenker and the Theoretical Tradition" (*College Music Symposium* 18, no. 1 [Spring 1978]: 88f). Morgan also notes that Vogler was the "first

theorist to speak of a *Reduktionsystem.*" Strictly speaking, this appears to be true. But the process itself would seem to be of greater importance than the terminology. Here and throughout his system Vogler has a habit of putting old wine in new bottles.

11. It is characteristic of Vogler that in the passage previously cited (notes 8 and 9) he refuses to place Rameau's "added sixth" or Kirnberger's "VII7" in the context of progression. While criticizing Kirnberger for considering the "VII7" to be a rootless ninth chord, he neglects to mention that in other contexts Kirnberger sees the "VII7" as a VII7. The mechanical nature of *Redukzion* can only be mollified to an extent by reading a "chord" as a collection of melodic dissonances (like Kirnberger and, later on, Sechter). Vogler is forced to do this with a six-four in order to preserve one of his ten allowable cadence patterns (see Grave, "Vogler's Reduction," p. 53; also see below).

12. Vogler, *Handbuch*, p. 2. Also see Grave, "Vogler's Reduction," p. 46.

13. Vogler, *Handbuch*, p. 2.

14. Thomson, *Voraussetzungen*, p. 87.

15. William C. Mickelsen, *Hugo Riemann's Theory of Harmony and History of Music Theory, Book III by Hugo Riemann* (Lincoln and London: University of Nebraska Press, 1977), p. 209.

16. A clear separation should be made between Vogler and Knecht. As noted above, Vogler's views on dissonance correspond closely to Kirnberger's. Knecht's work is another matter, however. In the *Elementarwerk der Harmonie* (Munich: 1814), Knecht seems to follow Vogler when he calls the ninth, eleventh, and thirteenth "harmonic suspensions," reserving the term "melodic dissonance" for such odd intervals as the diminished octave and augmented unison (*Elementarwerk*, p. 49). He then says that because the suspension is really a "melodic dissonance," *all* of these dissonances, even the "harmonic" ones, must be prepared and resolved. Unfortunately, Knecht does not stop here, but goes on to describe "ninth, eleventh, and thirteenth chords" in a matter which justifies Riemann's accusation. In his *Allgemeiner musikalischer Katechismus* (published in Vienna; see p. 11 of the present study), these chords are generated by third-stacking (not sub-position). Aside from the method of generation, the discussion essentially follows Marpurg: for example, the common figured bass five-two (six-three chord with suspension in bass) is said to be an example of an eleventh chord with the eleventh in the bass (*Katechismus*, p. 98). Three possible inversions of the ninth chord and three inversions of the thirteenth chord are also discussed here. But stacked thirds and the theory of inversion are carried to the most absurd extreme in *Elementarwerk* (p. 194), where Knecht describes the six possible inversions of the "complete thirteenth chord" (a seven-note chord). The figured basses for these inversions follow:

11	9	7	5	10	6
9	7	5	3	7	4
7	5	3	7	6	9
6	6	6	6	5	7
5	4	4	4	4	5
	3	2	2	2	3

Finally, at the end of *Elementarwerk* (pp. 248–62), Knecht gives the ridiculous chord lists which Riemann quotes in part (see Mickelsen, pp. 209 f).

17. Oswald Jonas, "Die Krise der Musiktheorie," *Der Dreiklang Monatsschrift für Musik* 3 (June 1937): 72ff. Indeed, these hybrids—alas, not unlike many later pedagogical efforts—are prime candidates for criticism, showing as they do the "harmonic" mentality of Vogler at work on pieces which were conceived polyphonically.

18. See Thomson, *Voraussetzungen* (p. 84), where Vogler is the *Programmatiker* of romanticism. Kreitz presents a similar view in his dissertation (see note 24). The most important conclusions of both studies are summarized by Wagner, pp. 157–58.

19. Vogler, *Handbuch*, p. 31. (In den drei, zur Schoepfung beider Leitern unentbehrlichen Dreiklaengen sind die urspruenglichen *Schlußfälle* enthalten und die Regeln fuer die Tonfolge werden von der Schlußfallmaeßigkeit hergeleitet.)

20. Ibid., p. 7. (*Schlußfallmaeßig* wird die Harmonie durch die grosse Dritte, ohne sie wird die Harmonie nie entscheidend werden, immer unschlußfallmaeßig bleiben.)

21. Ibid., 44ff. I–V (or V–I) in minor is only allowed if the third of V is raised; similarly, the motion of I–IV–I in minor is forbidden because three minor triads in succession are "not decisive" (*nicht entscheiden*). On the other hand, the motion of VII–I is one of Vogler's ten cadence patterns.

22. Ibid., pp. 57ff.

23. It is fitting that we use the English term coined by the German-American theorist Bernhard Ziehn (1845–1912) for the German *Mehrdeutigkeit*. Ziehn's work is, to a great extent, an outgrowth of Vogler's ideas on modulation and chromatic and enharmonic techniques. See his *Harmonie- und Modulationslehre* (Berlin: 1887), rewritten in English as *Manual of Harmony* (Milwaukee: 1907). Another obvious outgrowth of this approach to modulation is Reger's *Beiträge zur Modulationslehre* (Leipzig: 1903).

24. Helmut Kreitz, "Abbé Georg Joseph Vogler als Musiktheoretiker. Ein Beitrag zur Geschichte der Musiktheorie im 18. Jahrhundert" (Ph.D. dissertation, Saarbrücken, 1957), p. 30.

25. Vogler, *Handbuch*, pp. 101–10.

26. Ibid. A C major chord may be: C:I, a:III, G:IV, F:V, or f:V. Riemann erroneously attributes this innovation to Weber (Mickelsen, p. 211).

27. Vogler, *Handbuch*, pp. 8f. (*Tonleitung* ist das Resultat von einem allmaelig und harmonisch wirkenden Eindruck der Lehre von Schlußfaellen und Mehrdeutigkeit auf das Ohr. Die Tonleitung gibt Aufschluß ueber die Sukzession der Harmonien, und wie das Gefuehl davon affizirt, d.i.: bald überrascht, bald getaeuscht wird. Man macht sich hiedurch einen nicht undeutlichen Begriff von der musikalischen Haltung der Farben.)

28. Ibid., p. 112. (Wir haben in chromatischer Leiter 12 Toene, von jedem Ton kann ich in jeden andern ausweichen; hiedurch entstehen 11 Ausweichungen. Vom harten C z.B. kann ich in 11 harte und 11 weiche Tonarten, und wieder vom weichen C in 11 harte und 11 weiche Tonarten übergehen; da ich den Wechsel vom harten und weichen C keinen Uibergang nennen darf, so bleiben 4mal 11 oder 44 Ausweichungen.)

29. Victor Fell Yellin, "The Omnibus Idea" (unpublished paper: 1976); this is an expanded version of Yellin's paper given at the AMS meeting in Dallas, Nov. 2–5, 1972. Also see Walter Piston, *Harmony*, 4th ed., revised and expanded by DeVoto (New York: Norton, 1978), pp. 440–42. According to Yellin, "the term *omnibus* is of obscure origin."

30. Yellin defines the "classical omnibus" as a motion from a six-five to a root-position dominant seventh, but notes that the progression is reversible. It has been reversed here to facilitate comparison with Vogler's progression.

31. Yellin, "Omnibus," example 7.

32. Ibid., example 4b.

33. Ibid., p. 7.

Chapter 3

1. Emanuel Aloys Förster, *Supplementband* to *Generalbasschule II* (Wien: 1823), p. 19; quoted after Ulf Thomson, *Voraussetzungen und Artungen der österreichischen Generalbasslehre zwischen Albrechtsberger und Sechter* (Tutzing: Hans Schneider, 1978), p. 88. (Ich schicke gegenwärtig ein Verzeichnis von Vorhalten mit der nöthigen Vorbereitung voraus. Uibrigens bin ich der Meinung das diese Accorde in der Einbildungskraft des Componisten auf diese Art, keineswegs aber durch alle nur möglichen Versetzungen des Rameausche Systems entstehen.... Ich bin überzeugt, daß keiner der großen Componisten an das Rameausche System... gedacht hat.)

2. Emanuel Aloys Förster, *Anleitung zum Generalbass* (Wien: Artaria u. Companie, 1823), p. 3. (bey unserer jetzigen Musik gibt es aber weder eine *chromatische*, noch eine *enharmonische* Tonleiter, wohl aber einzelne zufällig erhöhte oder erniedrigte Töne, welche *chromatisch* genannt werden können....) This and all further quotations from Förster are taken from this edition, which is an enlargement of the 1805 edition.

3. Ibid., p. 3. (Auch die Tonleitern von einerley Nahmen, wie C-dur und C-moll... haben eine gewisse Verwandtschaft unter einander, wie solches häufig in Compositionen zu finden ist.)

4. Ibid.

5. Ibid., p. 28. (Ich wiederhole..., daß nach meinen Begriffen nur die siebente Stufe jeder Tonleiter die *empfindsame Note* ist, und diese Auszeichnung verdient: alle übrigen zufällig erhöheten Töne aber blosse chromatische Töne sind, welche die Tonleiter nicht ändern. Das *gis* in A-moll, das *dis* in E-moll u.s.w. ist diatonische, das ist wesentlich zur Tonleiter gehörig....) The reader will notice Kirnberger's *wesentlich* and *zufällig*. In most cases, the latter is translated (somewhat inaccurately, to be sure) as "nonessential," following Beach, "The Harmonic Theories of Johann Philipp Kirnberger; Their Origins and Influences" (Ph.D. dissertation, Yale University, 1974).

6. Förster, *Anleitung*, p. 11. (Alle übrigen Dreyklänge, die bloss desswegen Dreyklänge sind, weil sie aus Terze, Quinte und Octave zusammen gesetzt werden, aber in keiner Tonleiter gegründet sind, übergehe ich, weil sie von keinem Gebrauche sind....)

7. Ibid.

8. Ibid., pp. 14–22. (4. alle übrigen Septimen-Accorde, die keine besondere Aufmerksamkeit verdienen....)

9. Ibid., pp. 25ff. This is consistent with Förster's anti-Rameauian sentiments.

10. Ibid., p. 27. (*Chromatisch* ist also jede Note, welche wegen ihrer zufälligen Erhöhung oder Erniedrigung nicht zur Tonleiter gehört, und für welche man die diatonische Note setzen kann.)

11. Ibid., p. 28; example 121, vol. II.

12. Ibid., p. 28; examples 126 and 127, vol. II.

13. Ibid., p. 28; "Devil's Mill" is example 134, vol. II. (Herr Abt Vogler nennt diesen Gang in seinem Handbuche zur Harmonielehre u.s.w. die chromatische Leiter, von der ich aber als Leiter keinen Begriff habe.)

14. This may have been influenced by Albrechtsberger (or Seyfried's version of Albrechtsberger).

15. August Swoboda, *Harmonielehre* (Wien: 1828), pp. 1f. (Unter *Harmonielehre* (uneigentlich Generalbaß) begreift man die Lehre *aller*, im ganzen Reiche der Musik vorkommenden

Notes for Chapter 3

Tonverbindungen.... Wer auf den Rahmen eines gründlichen Harmonikers Anspruch machen will, muß *jede* Harmonie, ihren *Ursprung*, ihre *Anwendbarkeit* und *Tendenz* (Zweck, Richtung) kennen....)

16. Ibid., p. 6. (in welcher derley Tonverbindungen oder Modulationen ihren Grund haben, und dieß ist die chromatische....)

17. Ibid., pp. 7f. (Die zufaellig erhoehte siebente Stufe der weichen Tonart ist nur ein erborgter Bestandtheil der chromatischen Tonleiter..., denn die weiche Tonart klingt viel weicher, wenn die siebente Stufe nicht erhoeht wird, weil dadurch offenbar eine Haerte entsteht, welche hoechstens am Schluße um eine vollkommene Cadenz zu bewirken, gewissermaßen nothwendig wird.)

18. Ibid., p. 76. (kann also auf jeder Stufe der Tonleiter, wo eine große Sext mit großer Terz steht, einen Sitz haben....)

19. Ibid., p. 82. Unfortunately, his advice was not heeded. Kirnberger's term would last into the twentieth century, at which time Schoenberg would attack the whole notion of "accidental" tones in a theory of harmony (see Schoenberg, *Theory of Harmony*, trans. Roy E. Carter [Berkeley: University of California Press, 1978], chap. 17).

20. Swoboda, p. 89. (schnell und unvermuthet in einen weit entfernten Ton....)

21. Ibid., p. 91. (Man geht auch in entfernte Töne, durch die weitläufige Modulation, wenn man nähmlich von Grad zu Grad fortschreitet.... Allein diese Art Harmoniegang ist längst veraltet und aus unserer Musik neueren Geschmackes gänzlich verbannt....)

22. Ibid. (wenn sie in einen entfernten Ton schließen sollen, und keinen andern Weg wissen, als von Ton zu Ton zu gehen....)

23. Ibid., pp. 97ff. Cf. note 28.

24. Joseph Preindl, *Wiener-Tonschule; oder Anweisung zum Generalbasse, zur Harmonie, zum Contrapuncte und der Fugen-Lehre* (Vienna: T. Haslinger, 1827). This work was "put in order and edited" by Ritter von Seyfried. Tittel notes that it is difficult to find the dividing line between author and editor (See Ernst Tittel, "Wiener Musiktheorie von Fux bis Schönberg," in *Beiträge zur Musiktheorie des 19. Jahrhundert*, ed. by Martin Vogel [Regensburg: Gustave Bosse Verlag, 1966], p. 174.

25. Tittel, "Wiener Musiktheorie," p. 192.

26. Compare, for example, Charles Simon Catel's *Traité D'Harmonie* (Paris: 1802), which was adopted as the text for classes at the Paris Conservatory.

27. Franz Krenn, *Generalbass-(Harmonie-)Lehre zum Selbstunterrichte* (Vienna: Haslinger Witwe u. Sohn, 1845), *Vorrede*.

28. Ibid., p. 28. (ohne Uebergang... gleichsam als ob ein neues Tonstück beginnen würde....) Cf. A.B. Marx, *Die Lehre von der musikalischen Komposition* (Leipzig: 1837), I:198–202, where Marx also says that after a cadence the continuation can "begin in a new key without transition, as though it were completely new. (kann...als wär' er ein neuer, auch ohne Uebergang in einem neuen Tone anheben.) In this section Marx also discusses modulations by pivot on a single tone (cf. Swoboda and note 23).

Notes for Chapter 4

Chapter 4

1. Ernst Tittel, "Wiener Musiktheorie von Fux bis Schönberg," in *Beiträge zur Musiktheorie des 19. Jahrhundert*, ed. by Martin Vogel (Regensburg: Gustav Bosse Verlag, 1966), p. 179. (Wiens berühmtester Musiktheoretiker nach Albrechtsberger's Tod....) American theorists would undoubtedly disagree.

2. Complete biographical details concerning Sechter may be found in Zeleny, *Die historischen Grundlagen des Theoriesystems von Simon Sechter*, Wiener Veröffentlichungen zur Musikwissenschaft, vol. 10 (Tutzing: Hans Schneider, 1979) pp. 5–60. (Essentially this is Zeleny's dissertation—Univ. Vienna, 1938—with some revision. It is especially valuable for the unpublished source material described therein.) Other published biographical sources include: J.C. Markus, *Simon Sechter, ein biographisches Denkmal* (Vienna: Alfred Hölder, 1888); Ernst Tittel, "Simon Sechter, zum 100. Todestag," *Österreichische Musikzeitschrift* 22, no. 9 (September 1967), pp. 550f; the Markus *biographisches Denkmal* forms the basis of Willi Reich's article, "Simon Sechter im eigenen Wort" (*Neue Zeitschrift für Musik* 132, no. 10, 1971, pp. 539–41).

3. Zeleny discusses Sechter's early study in detail, but then concludes, "undoubtedly, the study of the works of Marpurg and Kirnberger had a much greater influence on Sechter than the personal study with Maxandt, Hartmann, and Koželuch" (das Studium der Werke Marpurgs und Kirnbergers hat auf Sechter ohne Zweifel viel grösseren Einfluss ausgeübt als der persönliche Unterricht bei Maxant, Hartmann und Koželůh.), (p. 25).

4. Zeleny, *Grundlagen*, p. 28. Compare Thomson's *Naturalistenstreit* (above, p. 5).

5. *Zwölf Variationen im strengen Style für das Piano-Forte verfasst und dem Herrn I.H. Worzischek gewidmet von Simon Sechter, k.k. Hoforganist*, Op. 7, 1824; *Zwölf Versetten und eine Fuge über das Thema des VIIten Werkes (folgt das Thema in Noten wie vorne angegeben) für die Orgel oder das Pianoforte verfasst und dem Herrn Josef Kerzkowsky gewidmet von Simon Sechter, k.k. Hoforganist*, Op. 12, 1826; *Zwölf neue Variationen im strengen Style mit einer Schlussfuge, über das Thema des 7ten und 12ten Werkes...*, Op. 45, between 1826 and 1828. All dates are according to Zeleny, pp. 67ff. Printed copies of the works may be found in the Austrian National Library and the library of the *Gesellschaft der Musikfreunde* in Vienna.

6. Zeleny, *Grundlagen*, p. 70. (Sowohl das 7te als das 12te Werk sind in dieser Handlung zu haben, und bilden mit Gegenwärtigem ein Ganzes, welches von dem Verfasser in der Absicht geschrieben wurde, um zu zeigen, wie jedes zusammengesetzte Fugenthema ein einfaches Grundthema haben muss. Diese drei Werke bilden also gewissermaßen eine praktische Fugenlehre....) The apparent survival of the Fuxian species is interesting here; Sechter *never* mentions having read Fux.

7. Ibid., p. 30.

8. *Neue Wiener Musikzeitung* (Wien: 1860), p. 58. Quoted after Ulf Thomson, *Voraussetzungen und Artungen der österreichischen Generalbasslehre zwischen Albrechtsberger und Sechter* (Tutzing: Hans Schneider, 1978), p. 25. (Daß ich selbst bemüht war und noch bin, die Grundsätze der Harmonielehre in ein verständliches System zu bringen, glaube ich durch mein Werk "Die richtige Folge der Grundharmonien" bewiesen zu haben, ohne daß es mir nötig geschienen hätte den Generalbaß zu verbannen.)

9. After Salzmann's departure from the Conservatory (1839), Sechter, Preyer, and Seyfried applied for the job. Money may have been the reason why Preyer was chosen over the other two: Sechter wanted twice what Preyer accepted (Elfriede Bernhauer, "Gottfried von Preyer,

Sein Leben und Wirken," Dissertation, University of Vienna, 1951, p. 46). The Conservatory closed during the political and social upheavals of 1848 and remained closed until 1851. When it reopened, Sechter managed to get the appointment as theory instructor, but it appears that he was not nearly as successful in his new classroom teaching position as he had been in his earlier private teaching. In fact, the administration of the Conservatory contemplated giving up the classes in harmony and composition altogether by 1855 (Zeleny, *Grundlagen*, p. 36). The decline in influence of the organist-theorists, as well as the ever increasing historical distance between Sechter and the music that he loved, eventually took their toll.

10. The complete title of Sechter's treatise follows: *Die Grundsätze der musikalischen Komposition: I. Band, Die richtige Folge der Grundharmonien, oder von Fundamentalbass und dessen Umkehrungen und Stellvertretern* (Leipzig: Breitkopf u. Härtel, 1853); *II. Band, Von den Gesetzen des Taktes. Vom einstimmigen Satze. Die Kunst zu einer gegebenen Melodie die Harmonie zu finden* (1854); *III. Band, Vom drei- und zweistimmigen Satze. Rhythmische Entwürfe. Vom strengen Satz mit kurzen Andeutungen des freien Satzes. Vom doppelten Contrapunkte* (1854).

Unless otherwise indicated, all citations from the above in the present work are taken from volume I, hereafter cited as *Grundsätze*. Volume I was well known in America for many years through the edited translation by Carl Christian Müller (1834–1914): *The correct order of fundamental harmonies: a treatise on fundamental basses, and their inversions and substitutes* (New York: W.A. Pond, 1871; 12th ed., 1912). Also see Müller's *Tables for the writing of elementary exercises in the study of harmony. Arranged in conformity with S. Sechter's "Fundamental Harmonies," and adapted for the New York college of music* (New York, W.A. Pond, ca. 1882–86).

11. See Ernst Kurth's *Die Voraussetzungen der theoretischen Harmonik und der tonalen Darstellungssysteme* (Bern: Max Drechsel, 1913) (trans. Lee Allen Rothfarb, *The Requirements for a Theory of Harmony* [Master's thesis, Hartt College of Music, 1979]), and more recently, Carl Dahlhaus, *Untersuchungen über die Entstehung der harmonischen Tonalität* (Kassel: Bärenreiter, 1968).

12. Ernst Tittel, *Harmonielehre* (Vienna: Doblinger, 1965), p. 81.

13. Kurth, *Voraussetzungen*, pp. 7f. (Auf seinem ersten Band der Grundsätze... beruhen fast alle gebräuchlichen Lehrbücher oder Abhandlungen über Harmonik..., soweit sie nicht der im Gegensatz hierzu... Theorie Riemann's sich anschliessen.) Ernst Tittel echoes this opinion in a number of his writings. For example, in "Wiener Musiktheorie" (p. 187) he says: "For all of that [the problems in Sechter's system], almost all commonly used textbooks or treatises on harmony of the second half of the nineteenth century are based upon the first volume of the Grundsätze." (Immerhin beruhen auf dem ersten Band der "Grundsätze" fast alle gebräuchlichen Lehrbücher oder Abhandlungen über Harmonik der zweiten Hälfte des 19. Jahrhunderts.)

14. Tittel, "Wiener Musiktheorie," p. 180. The manuscript is in the library of the *Gesellschaft der Musikfreunde*. It is described by Zeleny, *Grundlagen*, pp. 285–307.

15. Sechter, *Grundsätze*, p. 51. In an appendix, Sechter repeats that only the minor triads III and VI should be regarded as "pure." As evidence for this Sechter includes a very brief description of his tuning system: in C, tune C–G and F–C as pure fifths; tune E, A, and B as pure major thirds from the previous C, F, and G; tune D as a pure fifth from G; the resultant D–A fifth is 1/9 of a whole tone smaller than pure.

16. Ibid., p. 212. (diese wollen also gar nicht mehr das innere Wesen, sondern nur den äusseren Schein beibehalten....)

Notes for Chapter 5   155

17. Manfred Wagner, *Die Harmonielehren der ersten Hälfte des 19. Jahrhunderts* (Regensburg: Gustav Bosse Verlag, 1974), p. 33.
18. Zeleny, *Grundlagen,* p. 425, notes that Rameau's famous statement, "the seventh is... the source of all dissonance" (*Treatise on Harmony,* Gossett, tr. [New York: Dover, 1971], p. 215) never occurs in Sechter. Sechter's conception of dissonance is *not* completely harmonic.
19. Compare Sechter's colleague Franz Krenn: "The complete cadence is a perfectly satisfying close. The chords of which it consists are the dominant chord and tonic triad; the previous chords may be whatever they want." (Die ganze Cadenz ist ein vollkommen befriedigender Schluss. Die Accorde, aus welchen sie besteht, sind: der Dominantaccord und der tonische Dreiklang, die vorhergehenden Akkorde mögen sein, welche sie wollen.) (Quoted after Wagner, *Harmonielehren,* p. 42.)
20. The term was introduced by Allen Forte. See his *Tonal Harmony in Concept and Practice,* 3rd ed. (New York: Holt, Rinehart, and Winston, 1979), p. 103.
21. Sechter, *Grundsätze,* p. 13. (in einer dem Schlussfall ähnlicher Ordnung.)
22. William Earl Caplin has recently discussed progressions which serve as "models" in Sechter's system. See his article "Harmony and Meter in the Theories of Simon Sechter," *Music Theory Spectrum* 2 (1980):74-89. The importance of the circle of fifths to Sechter's system is well known, but, Caplin says, "most historians... have overlooked the presence of a second model within Sechter's system, a model based on the priority of the first, fifth, and fourth degrees of the scale" (p. 77). Caplin goes on to demonstrate the importance which Sechter attributes to the chords on these scale degrees, and to point out that Sechter explicitly distinguishes between primary triads (*Hauptdreiklänge*) and secondary chords (*Nebendreiklänge*) later on in the *Grundsätze* (II:151).

But a word of caution is necessary here: while the rigid dichotomy between Sechter's *Stufentheorie* and Riemann's *Funktionstheorie* which Kurth draws throughout the *Voraussetzungen* is perhaps a bit exaggerated, there is much truth to it. Sechter's system is essentially a theory of *progression* which attempts to derive all progressions from the model progressions by fifth and third. This is quite compatible with the "circle of fifths model," but it means that the "primary chord model" (Caplin's terms) can never occur in its "pure" state. The latter may in fact only appear as progression by fifth (I-V-I-V7-I-IV-I-V7-I), a chain of thirds (e.g., I-VI-IV-II-V-I), or a combination of the two (e.g., I-III-VI-IV-II-V-I). When Sechter eventually uses this model in the discussion of chromaticism (see below, "The Abbreviated Sequence: the Cadence"), he is forced in every case to interpolate a diatonic II between IV and V, often with rather far-fetched results. Here it is his inability to place the "primary chord model" *at the same level* with the "circle of fifths model" which is at the root of the problem.

Chapter 5

1. Matthew Shirlaw, *The Theory of Harmony* (London: Novello, 1917), p. 98.
2. Jean-Philippe Rameau, *Treatise on Harmony,* trans. Philip Gossett (New York: Dover, 1971), pp. 60f.
3. Ibid., p. 215.
4. Initially, the *double emploi* received probably the least support of any of Rameau's ideas. D'Alembert was one of the few to accept the "added sixth" chord (Jean le Rond d'Alembert, *Elémens de la Musique* [Lyon: Durand, 1762], p. 80), and the further development of this idea which may be seen in Johann Friedrich Daube's *Generalbass in drey Accorden* (Leipzig:

Notes for Chapter 5

Breitkopf 1756)—which Riemann cites as a laudable example of the *Funktionstheorie* (see William C. Mickelsen, *Hugo Riemann's Theory of Harmony and History of Music Theory, Book III, by Hugo Riemann* [Lincoln and London: University of Nebraska Press, 1977, pp. 194ff]) is a radical departure from the usual eighteenth-century point of view. Wagner (*Die Harmonielehren der ersten Hälfte des 19. Jahrhunderts* [Regensburg: Gustave Bosse Verlag, 1974, p. 42] attributes the lack of acceptance of Daube's ideas to their attack by Marpurg (*Historisch-kritische Beyträge zur Aufnahme der Musik* [Berlin: 1754–58], II:325ff). The attack would later be renewed by Vogler (see p. 13). It was not until Moritz Hauptmann's *Die Natur der Harmonik und der Metrik* (Leipzig: Breitkopf u. Härtel, 1853) that the function theory movement really began to gather steam, and it never really gained acceptance in Austria.

5. Sechter, *Grundsätze*, p. 18. (Dem Schlussfall müssen auch die Schritte nachgebildet werden, die mit dem Fundamente eine Stufe zu steigen scheinen. Um zum Beispiel den Schritt vom Dreiklang der 1ten zu jenem der 2ten Stufe naturgemäss zu machen, muss dazwischen der Septaccord der 6ten Stufe entweder wirklich gemacht oder hinein gedacht werden. In noten in C dur so: ——oder mit Verschweigung des zweiten Fundamentes so: ——.)

6. Kirnberger, Johann Philipp, *Die wahren Grundsätze zum Gebrauche der Harmonie* (Berlin and Königsberg: Decker and Hartung, 1773), actually written by Kirnberger's student, Johann Abraham Peter Schulz (1747–1800); translated by David Beach and Jurgen Thym, "The True Principles for the Practice of Harmony," *JMT* 23, no. 2 (Fall 1979): 163–224; this example and discussion on pp. 206–7. Although actually written by Schulz, the work is an accurate presentation of Kirnberger's ideas, according to Beach.

7. David W. Beach, "The Harmonic Theories of Johann Philipp Kirnberger; Their Origins and Influence," Ph.D. dissertation, Yale University, 1974, pp. 88f.

8. Ibid., p. 81.

9. Beach, Introduction to Kirnberger's "The True Principles," p. 165; Cecil Power Grant, "The Real Relationship between Kirnberger's and Rameau's Concept of the Fundamental Bass," *JMT* 21, no. 2: 324–38; see p. 331.

10. Grant notes that this interpretation comes from Rameau, but that Kirnberger extended it to include VII7 as a rootless V9 (Grant, "Relationship," p. 329); this was taken over by Sechter.

11. Wilhelm Friedrich Marpurg, *Versuch über die musikalische Temperatur* (Berlin: J.F. Kirn, 1776), p. 223.

12. Grant, "Relationship," pp. 327f.

13. Cf. Robert Morgan, "Schenker and the Theoretical Tradition," in *College Music Symposium* 18, no. 1 (Spring 1978):72–96, where Morgan says (p. 89) that "Sechter adheres to many of Rameau's concepts, such as the fifth as sole fundamental progression and the idea of "implied" harmonies (which he calls *Stellvertreter*, anticipating Riemann)."

14. The discrepancies here between Sechter and Riemann play a role in Capellen's criticism of Sechter. See Georg Capellen, *Ist das System S. Sechters ein geeigneter Ausgangspunkt für die Wagnerforschung?* (Leipzig: C.F. Kahnt, 1902), p. 13. Capellen, whose system is yet another return to the overtone series, cannot accept the idea that II (a minor triad) can assume a more fundamental role than IV (a major triad).

15. While this technique is not to be found in Sechter, it is used by Daniel Gottlob Türk in his *Anweisung zum Generalbassspielen* (Wien: Typo.-Musikalische Ges., 1807; and various other editions). (Beach has commented on the Kirnberger influence in Türk.) The *Anweisung*

was well known to Sechter (see chapter 8) and Bruckner (see chapter 9). The notion of *elision* would later recur as an explanation for certain chromatic progressions in the work of Preyer's student, Karl Mayrberger (see chapter 10).

16. Sechter introduces the ninth chord after the suspension (*Grundsätze*, pp. 30f), for it is always the result of the 9-8 suspension, not third stacking. No chords beyond the ninth are discussed in the *Grundsätze*, although Sechter has a habit of referring to the "suspensions of the eleventh and thirteenth." The 9-8 is shown resolving over a held bass on the dominant, as well as with change of bass to the tonic. "Concealment" of the fundamental enables Sechter to explain such apparent progressions as VII7-I, and delay of the resolution of the ninth beyond the change of bass is used to explain such apparent progressions as VII7-VI6. Sechter also introduces the ninth chord into the sequence.

17. See Türk's *Anweisung*, where precisely this progression (with the voice-leading of example 5-7) is explained through the *elision* of an intervening C-major chord (5th ed., Halle: 1841, p. 28).

18. Sechter, *Grundsätze*, p. 46. (Diese Freiheit... findet nie in der Baßstimme statt und wird auch bei den übrigen Stimmen nur unter folgenden Bedingungen gestattet: daß das Fundament *nicht* gehört wird, also die Sept nicht als solche vernommen werden kann....)

19. Sechter, *Grundsätze*, volume II, p. 363. (Die Zahl der richtigen Fundamentalschritte ist so klein, daß man gerade in solchen Sätzen auch zu den künstlichen Harmonieschritten, wozu besonders die stufenweise Folge von Dreiklängen gehört, Zuflucht nehmen muß, bei welchen erlaubt wird, daß eine Sept, deren Fundament nicht gehört wird, auch steigen, sogar springen darf....) Capellen is quick to see the absurdity of this explanation (*Sechter*, pp. 16f).

20. Sechter, *Grundsätze*, vol. II, pp. 363-67.

21. See chapter 9, p. 74.

22. Ernst Tittel, "Wiener Musiktheorie von Fux bis Schönberg," in *Beiträge zur Musiktheorie des 19. Jahrhundert*, ed. Martin Vogel (Regensburg: Gustav Bosse Verlag), 1966, p. 182. (*das Denken mit nicht existenten Tönen.*)

23. Few musicians would dispute this fact, at least in the relatively short spans which Kirnberger's and Sechter's analyses demand; this is not a question of Schenker's *Fernhören*.

Chapter 6

1. All examples in this chapter are from *Grundsätze*, vol. I. Page locations are given in the text with the example number.

2. Kirnberger uses the term *Tausch* in explaining how the essential seventh may be taken over by another voice and resolved (*Die Kunst, des reinen Satzes in der Musik* [Berlin, Königsberg: Decker and Hartung, 1771-79], p. 83). The discussion and examples may be found in the English translation on pp. 102f (J.P. Kirnberger, *The Art of Strict Composition*, David Beach and Jurgen Thym, trans. [New Haven and London: Yale University Press, 1982]). Kirnberger goes on to note that "free treatment of the seventh also occurs when the seventh is formed over a passing note in the bass that falls between the dominant seventh chord and its first inversion" (*Strict Composition*, p. 107). The example which he describes (5.15, p. 106) is essentially the same as Sechter's example 6-10, except that the "passing chord" falls on the second quarter of the bar. Schulz gives a similar example in "The True Principles" (example 43, p. 193).

158 Notes for Chapter 7

3. Sechter, *Grundsätze*, p. 36. (Während der Dauer eines und desselben Fundamentalaccordes können die Stimmen ihre Antheile vertauschen.)
4. Ibid., p. 39. (gehört nicht zur Wesenheit.)
5. Ibid., p. 42. (Unregelmässig heisst der Durchgang, welches man, statt vor dem Eintritt des neuen Fundamentes, erst bei dem Eintritt desselben erscheinen lässt....)
6. Roger Sessions, *Harmonic Practice* (New York: Harcourt, Brace, and World, Inc., 1951), p. xvii. This is not to imply that the process (or the term) has *precisely* the same meaning to Sechter, Schenker, and Sessions.
7. Sechter, *Grundsätze*, p. 157. "The essence of chromaticism acquires a great extension when, with the exception of the seventh degree, one views each of the remaining degrees of the scale as a *tonic*." (Eine grosse Ausdehnung bekommt das Wesen des Chromatischen dadurch, dass man, ausser der 7ten, jede übrige Stufe als *Tonica* ansieht....)
8. Ibid., p. 160. (Die grossen Buchstaben bedeuten bei allen Veränderungen die Hauptfundamente, die am Anfange und am Ende des Tactes gelten; die dazwischen inneliegenden sind nur Nebenfundamente, die nur den einen Tact auf das erste und letzte Fundament, welches für diesen Tact Tonica ist, bezogen werden. Also sind in diesem Satze Nebentonleitern, die sich alle auf die Haupttonleiter C dur beziehen.)
9. Robert P. Morgan, "Schenker and the Theoretical Tradition," *College Music Symposium* 18, no. 1 (Spring 1978): 89–91. A transcription of the variations may be found on p. 90.
10. Sechter, *Grundsätze*, vol. II, pp. 19–34; discussed by Caplin "Harmony," on pp. 85–88.
11. Caplin, "Harmony," p. 87.
12. See chapter 3, note 21.
13. The *Stellvertreter* can be seen as an abbreviation of both techniques. For example, when VII is the *Stellvertreter* of V7 in the progression VII–I, the actual VII–I may be derived from either VII–(V7)–I or (V7)–VII–I.

Chapter 7

1. *Neue Wiener Musikzeitung* (May 22, 1856) 24:92, quoted after Walter Zeleny, *Die historischen Grundlagen des Theoriesystems von Simon Sechter*, Wiener Veröffentlichungen zur Musikwissenschaft, vol. 10 (Tutzing: Hans Schneider, 1979), p. 400. (Sind jene nicht Heuchler, die eine grosse Verehrung für Bach, Händel, Haydn und Mozart zu haben vorgeben, und doch tadeln, worin alle diese Meister vollkommen einig sind? Jeder von ihnen gebrauchte in der Molltonleiter die 6. und 7. Stufe im Absteigen natürlich und im Aufsteigen erhöht. Seitdem aber Gottfried Weber die 7. Stufe stets erhöht und die 6. stets natürlich gebraucht wissen wollte, achtet man das Ansehen dieser Meister weniger, und bedauert höchstens dass sie zu einer Zeit lebten, wo noch die Vorurtheile herrten. Ja man schmeichelt sich, dass wenn sie jetzt noch leben sollten, sie auch ebenfalls der neuen Ansicht bequemen würden.)
2. Sechter, *Grundsätze*, p. 55. (geht von der 1ten Stufe bis zur 6ten aufwärts, und von da wieder zurück bis zur 1ten, nach welcher der Unterhalbton der Tonleiter folgt und sogleich wieder auf die 1te Stufe zurückgeht.)
3. See William C. Mickelsen, *Hugo Riemann's Theory of Harmony* and *History of Music Theory, Book III*, by Hugo Riemann (Lincoln and London: University of Nebraska Press, 1977), p. 235 and Georg Capellen, *Ist das System S. Sechters ein geeigneter Ausgangspunkt*

Notes for Chapter 7   159

für die Wagnerforschung? (Leipzig: C.F. Kahnt, 1902), p. 6. Like many of Capellen's ideas, this comes from Riemann. The sentiments of both are echoed in Michael Mann's charge that "Sechter would apply Rameau's theories of root progressions to *altered*, as well as pure intervals (augmented and diminished fourths and fifths)" ("Schenker's Contribution to Music Theory," *The Music Review* 10 [1949]:3–26). Although the statement is true, it fails to show the context in which these "alterations" occur. Mann neglects to mention that Sechter maintains diatonic control of the progression through the sequence. Nor does the statement distinguish between the tritone in major or natural minor, and the augmented fifth/diminished fourth in minor (the former is, after all, a fact of life in the diatonic scale). It is interesting that Capellen, in the interest of "nature" and the avoidance of Sechter's "altered" root progressions, proposes a sequence of secondary dominants as the "model" from which Sechter's diatonic sequence is derived (*Sechter*, p. 12).

4. Emanuel Aloys Förster, *Anleitung zum Generalbass* (Vienna: A Steiner, 1805, Vienna Artaria, 1823) p. 13. (Bey 7-2a zeige ich die natürliche *Sexte d* zur sechsten Stufe *f* von A-moll. Bey 7-2b ist die *Sexte d* in *dis* chromatisch erhöht, und dadurch in die übermässige Sexte verwandelt worden... lässt sie sich sogar in die *Dur*-Tonleiter hinüber ziehen....) The examples are 154, 155, and 156 of the *160 Noten Beispiele*.

5. Sechter, *Grundsätze*, p. 121. (Der Gebrauch der *leiterfremden* Töne darf nicht auf die Fundamente ausgedehnt werden, daher bleiben auch in der chromatischen D dur Tonleiter alle Fundamente so wie in der diatonischen....)

6. See chapter 3, example 3-2, p. 23. Like many nineteenth-century systems of harmony (and many newer books as well), Sechter sees the source of all chromaticism in tonicization. Förster's view of chromaticism, although limited, does explain a perfectly legitimate traditional origin of chromaticism: the chromatic passing or neighbor chord which is not the result of tonicization. Thus Förster's example 3–3 (above) is difficult to explain in Sechter's system.

7. Sechter, *Grundsätze*, p. 120. (den meisten Stoff zu chromatischen Fortschreitungen liefern....)

8. Ibid., p. 130. (Die Harmonie der 5ten Stufe der C dur Tonleiter kann durch Veränderung der Non zu jener der 5ten Stufe in C moll gemacht werden, wonach jedoch wieder die Tonica der C dur Tonleiter folgt.)

9. Ibid., pp. 129–32.

10. Ibid., p. 146. (Macht man nun die Terz zur grossen, ohne die falsche Quint zu verändern, so hat ein solcher Accord eine *Zwitternatur*, dessen grosse Terz in einer andern Tonleiter gefunden wird, als die falsche Quint... er ist deshalb ein eigentlicher *chromatischer* Accord, der in keiner diatonischen Tonleiter gefunden werden kann.)

11. Ibid., p. 150. (Um diesen chromatischen Septnonaccorden das Herbe zu benehmen....)

12. Ernst Kurth's criticism of the "hybrid-chord" seems particularly relevant here: "One sees how it [the theory of the "hybrid-chord"] wants desperately to hold together that which by its very nature flows apart, and how it struggles blindly against the recognition of the living, sweeping processes which here represent not a combination of chords, but rather their dissolution." (Man sieht, wie diese mit ängstlicher Gewaltsamkeit zusammenhalten will, was seiner Natur nach auseinanderflutet, und wie blind sie sich gegen die Erkenntnis der lebensvoll durchgreifenden Vorgänge sträubt, die hier nicht eine Klangkombination, sondern im Gegenteil Klangzersetzung darstellen.) (*Romantische Harmonik und ihre Krise in Wagner's "Tristan"* [Berlin: 1923], p. 49.) This is not to say that Kurth had the final answer on chromatic

harmony either; he, in fact, preserved the fundamental bass in his own analysis of chromatic chords. But Kurth shifted the emphasis: "chromatic alteration" (*Alterationstechnik*) became the focal point, not diatonic chord roots.

13. See above, chapter 4, note 22.
14. Here Sechter refers to the "suspensions of the ninth, eleventh, and thirteenth."
15. Sechter, *Generalbassschule* (Vienna: 1830), p. 44. See Zeleny, *Grundlagen*, p. 100.
16. Ibid., p. 38. See Zeleny, *Grundlagen*, p. 95.
17. Sechter, *Grundsätze*, p. 217. (Um die Begründung durch eine Fundamentfolge kümmert man sich nicht und lässt es durch die Mehrdeutigkeit entschuldigen.)
18. Ibid., p. 218. (Die enharmonischen Verwechslungen in der weitesten Ausdehnung sind die natürlichen Feinde der gesunden Melodie, dafür ist ihre Wirkung geheimnissvoll und überraschend. Sie sind das Bild der grossen Welt, worin das Familienleben untergeht und wo die Täuschungen häufig vorkommen, und auch das Unwichtige in einem gewissen Glanze erscheint; dafür aber kann man dabei nicht erkennen was Hauptsache oder Nebensache ist.)
19. Here, Sechter does *not* follow Kirnberger, who discusses such modulations as C–D_b and C–F# by pivot on a single tone (the bass). See Kirnberger, *Die Kunst des reinen Satzes in der Musik* (Berlin, Königsberg: Decker & Hartung, 1771–79), p. 128.
20. The job left to the next generation of Austrian theorists who accepted Sechter's system was to make the necessary adjustments such that the system would fit the music of the time. Analysis became of prime importance.

Chapter 8

1. To be sure, the title of the third volume of Sechter's *Grundsätze* runs in part *Vom strengen Satz, mit kurzen Andeutungen des freien Satzes* (Of Strict Composition, with Brief Allusions to Free Composition). The "allusions" are brief indeed, comprising a mere six pages ("Etwas Weniges vom freien Satzes," pp. 151–56). There are no examples from the actual musical literature—merely a few primitive attempts to copy techniques of "free composition." If comparison is made to Schenker's later notion of "free composition" (cf., Robert P. Morgan, "Schenker and the Theoretical Tradition," *College Music Symposium* 18, no. 1 [Spring 1978], p. 91), Kirnberger probably deserves higher marks: Sechter's treatment of the subject can hardly be considered an improvement on Kirnberger's *Kunst*, upon which Sechter modeled his treatise. Moreover, Morgan's statement that "like Schenker, Sechter conceives of strict composition as species counterpoint confined to the major and minor scales" is incorrect. The fundamental bass is everywhere in Sechter's theory- as we saw in the discussion of the "intermediate fundamental" in "strict composition." And the evidence seems conclusive that Sechter did not know Fux's *Gradus* (see, in addition to Sechter's testimony, Habert's statements in chapter 11).
2. The average German *Kompositionslehre* of the first half of the century was a very practical book. See Rummenhöller, "Kompositionslehre und Harmonielehre," *Musiktheoretisches Denken im 19. Jahrhundert* (Regensburg: Bosse Verlag, 1967), pp. 27–38. Also see Franz Wirth, *Untersuchungen zur Entstehung der deutschen Praktischen Harmonielehre* (Munich: 1966).
3. Sechter's naive philosophical stance did not fail to arouse criticism from his contemporaries: "Herr Sechter wanted so persistently to hold to the purely practical side of the most comprehensive and detailed instruction possible that he disdained the elucidation of his

theories by means of even a moderate philosophical standpoint—a curious contrast to M. Hauptmann's theory which appeared at about the same time and which develops all musical rules from Hegelian categories. In the formation of concepts Sechter's efforts fall quite short, as the extremely inadequate definitions on the first pages of both works demonstrate." (Herr Sechter wollte die rein praktische Seite einer im Detail möglichst ausführlichen Instruktion so konsequent festhalten, dass er es verschmähte, seine Theorien aus einem auch nur mittleren philosophischen Standpunkt zu beleuchten. Ein merkwürdiger Kontrast zu der etwa gleichzeitig erschienenen Theorie M. Hauptmanns, die alle musikalischen Regeln dialektisch aus Hegel'schen Kategorien entwickelt. In der Begriffsbestimmung bleiben uns die Sechter'schen Arbeiten viel schuldig, wie schon die sehr mangelhaften Definitionen auf der ersten Seite der beiden Werke darthun. (*Wiener Zeitung*, Aug. 8, 1854, quoted after Rummenhöller, p. 32.) Sechter's use of such terms as "natural" and "artificial" also leads Rummenhöller to accuse him of the "absolutizing of theoretical principles which thereby acquire the appearance of axioms which are no longer reducible." (Die Verabsolutierung der theoretischen Prinzipien, die dadurch den Anschein von nicht mehr reduzierbaren Axiomen bekommen....) (p. 32).

4. *Wiener Allgemeine Musikzeitung* (1846), p. 448; quoted after Zeleny, *Grundlagen*, p. 56. (Voltaire habe ich nur insoweit kennen gelernt, dass ich fand, er würde mich unzufrieden machen und habe mir nichts mehr von ihm verlangt. In meiner Jugend habe ich zwar auch viele Romane gelesen, ich habe aber nicht gefunden, dass sie viel zu meiner Zufriedenheit beigetragen hätten, im Gegenteil waren sie es, die mir die ernsteren Bücher nötig machten.)

5. *Neue Wiener Musikzeitung* 1/53 (Dec. 30, 1852); quoted after Zeleny, *Grundlagen*, p. 56. (Auch von dem, was der Mensch Gutes zu schaffen im Stande ist, ist Gott der Urheber, denn von ihm haben wir alles. Deine schönsten Ideen, o Künstler, hast du dir nicht selbst gegeben, dann sie stammen von ihm....)

6. Zeleny, *Grundlagen*, p. 386. (Lehrbücher, die ich studierte, sind: Marpurgs Abhandlung von der Fuge, dessen Harmonielehre und dessen Temperatur; Kirnbergers Kunst des reinen Satzes, dessen wahren Grundsätze der Harmonie; Emanuel Bachs Lehre vom Accompagnement; Albrechtsbergers Generalbass- und Compositionslehre; Mathissons vollkommener Capellmeister; Türks Generalbasslehre. In neuerer Zeit las ich auch: Gottfried Webers Theorie, die Compositionslehre von Reicha, auch ein paar Theile vom System des Herrn Marx aus Berlin und noch einige andere kleine Lehrbücher. Dass ich auch Riepels Werke gelesen, hätte ich bald vergessen.)

7. Ibid. (Bei diesem Verzeichnisse der studierten Lehrbücher fällt sogleich die beherrschende Rolle Marpurgs und Kirnbergers auf, die an erster Stelle und mit mehreren Werken genannt sind. Diese beiden Theoretiker sind es auch tatsächlich, welche Sechter am meisten gegeben haben. Sechter, der Logiker, hat also schon mit der Reihenfolge der Nennung ein Urteil über die Werke gefällt, wenigstens in der Hinsicht, wie sie eben gerade für ihn von Bedeutung geworden waren.)

8. An exception to this statement may be found in Zeleny's discussion of the possible influence which Mattheson may have had upon Sechter (Zeleny, *Grundlagen*, p. 416). Zeleny quotes examples (from *Der Vollkommene Capellmeister* [Hamburg: 1739], "Von gebrochenen Akkorden") which show Mattheson explaining the multipart implications of single melodic lines and examples of two part counterpoint. These may well have influenced Sechter in his discussion "Vom einstimmigen Satze" (*Grundsätze* II). (See also Kirnberger, *Kunst*, §9, "von den harmonischen und unharmonischen Fortschreitungen in der Melodie," where similar ideas occur.)

9. It was undoubtedly due to Sechter that Kirnberger's distinction between melodic and chordal dissonance survived into the twentieth century.

10. Beach, "Harmonic Theories of Kirnberger," p. 70.
11. Tittel, "Wiener Musiktheorie," p. 181, to cite one of the latest sources where this may be found.
12. Zeleny, *Grundlagen,* (p. 442) sums up the relationship between Marpurg, Kirnberger, and Sechter by saying that the "fundamental conceptions" (*grundsätzliche Auffassungen*) common to Marpurg and Kirnberger may be found in Sechter. Of course, these are essentially the noncontroversial features of Rameauian theory which may be found in any number of neo-Rameauian systems of harmony.

Chapter 9

1. Ernst Decsey, *Bruckner, Versuch eines Lebens* (Berlin: Schuster and Loeffler, 1919), p. 65.
2. See Friedrich Eckstein, *Erinnerungen an Anton Bruckner* (Vienna, New York: Universal Edition, 1923), who claims that the influence does exist: "I have often seen that while he worked on his own scores he not only numbered the bars of the periods, but also notated the fundamental tones underneath in black note heads or with the aid of letters" (ich habe sogar des öfteren gesehen, dass er selbst in seinen eigenen Partituren, während er an diesen arbeitete, nicht allein die Takte der Perioden numerierte, sondern mitunter auch die Fundamentaltöne, sei es in solchen schwarzen Notenköpfen, sei es mit Hilfe von Buchstaben, notierte.) (p. 30).
3. Ernst Tittel, "Bruckner's musikalischer Ausbildungsgang" in *Bruckner-Studien,* ed. Franz Grasberger (Wien: Musikwissenschaftlicher Verlag, 1964), pp. 105–11.
4. Tittel's dates do not agree with Thomson, who lists the "neue verbesserte Ausgabe" as "Wien: S.A. Steiner, 1822"; another edition of the *Anweisung* is listed as "Wien: Haslinger, 1828" (Thomson, p. 61). Wagner (p. 49) agrees with Thomson. A *zweyte, verbesserte und sehr vermehrte Auflage* was published in Halle and Leipzig in 1800.
5. Elisabeth Maier and Franz Zamazal, *Anton Bruckner und Leopold von Zenetti* (Graz: Akademische Druck- u. Verlagsanstalt, 1980). Maier describes the notebook on pp. 110–14.
6. The present discussion of Bruckner's system of harmony draws upon sources which may be grouped into three general categories:
    1. Manuscript sources in Bruckner's own hand. The following two are discussed: Austrian National Library, Mus. Hs. 6072 A/Bruckner 197; New York Public Library, *MNZ—Toscanini Memorial Collection.
    2. Reminiscences by Bruckner students; student notes from Bruckner lectures (in chronological order of publication):
        Decsey, Ernst. *Bruckner* (see note 1). Studied with Bruckner at the Conservatory.
        Eckstein, Friedrich. *Erinnerungen* (see note 2). Defense of Sechter's system; mistakenly attributes *Zwischenfundament* to Marpurg (p. 31); class and private study with Bruckner.
        Klose, Friedrich. *Meine Lehrjahre bei Bruckner.* Regensburg: Bosse Verlag, 1927. Sympathy for Bruckner the composer, criticism of Bruckner the teacher, violent polemic against Sechter; studied privately with Bruckner from 1886–89.
        Orel, Alfred. *Ein Harmonielehrekolleg bei Anton Bruckner.* Berlin-Wien-Zürich: Verlag für Wirtschaft und Kultur, Payer & Co., 1940. Discussion of Carl Speiser's notes from Bruckner's University of Vienna lectures (Winter 1889–90).
        Bruckner, Anton. *Vorlesungen über Harmonielehre und Kontrapunkt an der Universität Wien.* Edited by Ernst Schwanzara. Wien: Oesterreichische Bundesverlag für

Notes for Chapter 9   163

Unterricht, Wissenschaft und Kunst, 1950. The most extensive source in category two, Schwanzara's notes are a compilation of notes taken from three cycles of lectures, 1891–94.

Schenk, Erich and Gruber, Gernot. "'Die Ganzen Studien' zu Josef Vockners Theorieunterricht bei Anton Bruckner." In *Bruckner-Studien,* edited by Othmar Wessely. Wien: Verlag der Oesterreichischen Akademie der Wissenschaften, 1975. Discussion of the notes of Volkner, the only student known to have taken Bruckner's complete private theory course.

Flotzinger, Rudolf. "Rafael Loidols Theorie Kolleg bei Bruckner 1879/80" in *Bruckner-Studien* (1975). Discussion of notes from an earlier cycle of University lectures.

The following unpublished materials by Friedrich Eckstein (now in the Austrian National Library) were also consulted: "6 Notenhefte zum Theorieunterricht bei Anton Bruckner" (Mus. Hs. 28.447 A/Bruckner 208f).

"Anton Bruckner System der Musiktheorie"(Mus. Hs. 29.333/1–3 A/Bruckner 208d); Eckstein's fullest *(three* volume) account of Bruckner's system of music theory.

"Universitäts Vorlesungen und Nachträge zur Harmonielehre/Notizen zum doppelten Kontrapunkt" (Mus. Hs. 28.444 A/Bruckner 208e).

"Studien über Harmonielehre, gemacht bei Anton Bruckner. 5 Notenhefte" (Mus. Hs. 28.446 A/Bruckner 208g).

"Anton Bruckners Universitäts Vorlesungen über Harmonielehre, gehalten 1884–86 zu Wien" (Mus. Hs. 28.445 A/Bruckner 208b).

3. Secondary articles—*non*-eyewitness accounts—(alphabetical):

Flotzinger, Rudolf. "Bruckner als Theorielehrer an der Universität." *Anton Bruckner in Lehre und Forschung.* Regensburg: Bosse Verlag, 1976.

Sulz, Josef. "Anton Bruckner als Didaktiker." *Anton Bruckner in Lehre und Forschung.*

Tittel, Ernst. "Wiener Musiktheorie."

Waldstein, Wilhelm. "Bruckner als Lehrer" in *Bruckner-Studien* (1964).

7. "Anton Bruckners Universitäts-Vorlesung... 1884–85."

8. Decsey, *Bruckner,* p. 66.

9. Eckstein, *Erinnerungen,* p. 34.

10. Bruckner, *Vorlesungen,* p. 54. (bei meinen Vorträgen mich an keines der jetzt aufliegenden Werke zu binden, sondern *frei* meine Vorträge zu halten....)

11. Ibid., p. 57. (Das Ganze wird hier vorgetragen nach Sechter, 1. Buch.)

12. Cf., Tittel, "Wiener Musiktheorie," pp. 190f. Klose, however, says that in "simple counterpoint," Bruckner followed Cherubini (*Lehrjahre,* p. 80). Also, see the closing section of Bruckner, *Vorlesungen,* pp. 284f.

13. Decsey, *Bruckner,* p. 66.

14. Klose, *Meine Lehrjahre,* p. 73 and pp. 53f.

15. Orel, *Harmonielehrekolleg,* pp. 6f. Orel was the first to point out the Dürrnberger influence. Eckstein's notes ("Universitäts Vorlesungen und Nachträge") furnish additional evidence.

16. Arnold Schoenberg, *Theory of Harmony* (Berkeley: University of California Press, 1978), p. 39. Carter uses Schoenberg's translation of the phrase ("law of the shortest way"), which originally appeared in his *Structural Functions of Harmony* (New York: Norton, 1969), p. 4.

17. The "Gesetz des nächsten Weges" enters relatively early (Bruckner, *Vorlesungen*, p. 129), but stepwise progressions enter later than they do in Sechter (*Vorlesungen*, p. 177). See "intermediate fundamental," below.

18. It is Schwanzara's opinion that Sechter's theory formed the basis of both Bruckner's creative work and his system of instruction (Bruckner, *Vorlesungen*, p. 8). Thus he echoes the opinion of Eckstein. Looking back from a later period, Waldstein maintains that "the oft-repeated legend [that] he [Bruckner] passed on Sechter's theory exclusively, is long refuted..." (Die oft wiederholte Legende, er habe ausschliesslich die Theorie Sechters weitergegeben, ist längst widerlegt....) ("Bruckner als Lehrer," p. 118). But insofar as Bruckner can be said to have taught a "theory" of harmony, that theory was essentially Sechter's; all other influences are superficial by comparison.

19. It is clear that Dürrnberger's influence upon Bruckner was not superceded by Sechter once Bruckner became acquainted with the latter's system; rather, the two continued to coexist as "authorities." Bruckner's copy of Dürrnberger's *Elementarbuch* (Austrian National Library, S.m. 28.246 A/Bruckner 217) was still used after his study with Sechter: on the second page of the *Vorerinnerung* of the *Praktischer Teil* Bruckner writes "Sechter:...," and notates a progression of descending six-three chords to which he applies a fundamental bass analysis using Sechter's "intermediate fundamental."

20. Sechter, *Grundsätze*, p. 30. (man der hier als willkürlich angebrachten Non, die eigentlich nur das Eintreten der Octav verzögert, eine, zwar uneigentliche, Selbständigkeit beilegen kann, indem man den Zusammenklang von Grundton, Terz, Quint, Sept und Non einen Septnonaccord nennt.)

21. Bruckner, *Vorlesungen*, p. 128. (Dreiklang, Vierklang und Fünfklang sind die drei Stammakkorde der Musik. Sechs- und Siebenklänge kommen nur nebenbei vor.)

22. Ibid., p. 178. Given the thoroughly "harmonic" nature of Bruckner's system, it is hardly surprising when Schwanzara says that passing tones and suspensions were "only occasionally" mentioned and used (p. 58).

23. Ibid., p. 58.

24. Eckstein, "6 Notenhefte," number 2.

25. Flotzinger, "Rafael Loidols Theorie Kolleg," p. 405. (Sonderbar! / dass man es nicht / tut, *Bruckner* will es tun und *Wagner* hat es.) The phrase "sounding root" is meant to distinguish the "complete" dominant ninth from VII7, which Sechter, under certain circumstances, considered to be an incomplete dominant ninth.

26. Schoenberg, *Theory of Harmony*, pp. 345ff. According to Schoenberg, it was this "last-inversion" ninth chord which lead a Viennese concert society to deny *Verklärte Nacht* a performance!

27. Bruckner, *Vorlesungen*, pp. 253f.

28. Eckstein, "6 Notenhefte," number 2. (Unterschied zur *Undez* u. *Tredez* gegenüber der *Sept* u. *Non:* Die Undez u. Tredez müssen sich immer auf demselben Fundament auflösen, während die 7 u. 9 auch auf *anderen Fundamenten* aufgelöst werden können, folglich sind die Undez u. Tredez keine selbständige Dissonanzen.) The explanation is obviously derived from the distinction between "essential" and "nonessential" dissonance as defined by Schulz/Kirnberger in "The True Principles" (see p. 171, paragraph 6), except that the ninth has become an "essential" dissonance for Bruckner.

Notes for Chapter 9   165

29. This passage received quite a bit of discussion at the beginning of this century. Cf. August Halm, *Harmonielehre* (Leipzig: G.J. Göschen'sche Verlagshandlung, 1902; Neudruck, 1905), pp. 122f., ex. 100; Heinrich Schenker, *Harmonielehre* (Vienna: Universal Edition, 1906), pp. 274ff (example and discussion not included in *Harmony*, trans. Borgese, ed. Jonas [Chicago and London: 1954]); and Kurth, *Voraussetzungen*, pp. 30ff.

30. Austrian National Library, Mus. Hs. 6072 A/Bruckner 197.

31. Bruckner, *Vorlesungen*, p. 169. (In der IX. Symphonie verwende ich Siebenklänge mit Auslassung von Terz und Quint und vollständiger Auflösung.)

32. Schenk and Gruber, "Die Ganzen Studien," p. 367 and *Abbildung 3*.

33. Ibid., pp. 364f.

34. Flotzinger, "Rafael Loidols Theorie Kolleg," p. 404.

35. Ernst Tittel, who was probably the first to emphasize the importance of Kirnberger as an influence upon Sechter, nevertheless repeats Riemann's accusation, saying in regard to Sechter's system that "the formation and explanation of dissonance is carried out constructively, since the schematicism of stacked thirds advances mechanically throughout and leads to an almost inexhaustible abundance of seventh, ninth, eleventh and thirteenth chords" (die Dissonanzbildung und -erklärung erfolgt konstruktiv, weil der schematische Terzenbau durchaus mechanisch vor sich geht und in einer schier unerschöpflichen Fülle zu Sept- , Non- , Undezim- und Tredezimakkorden führt.) ("Bruckners Ausbildungsgang," p. 109).

36. It is important to note that Bruckner's notion of chords beyond the seventh on the dominant, while obviously descended from Marpurg, is quite different from the eighteenth-century version of the idea. Upon adding the thirteenth chord to Rameau's chords constructed by *supposition*, Marpurg used them to account for common suspension chords of figured bass practice. For example, he chooses to call a G♯ diminished seventh over an A bass a "chord" of the "seventh, ninth, eleventh, and thirteenth" (*Handbuch bey dem Generalbasse und der Composition*, p. 186), although these tones subsequently resolve to an A minor triad over the *same* bass. In Bruckner's eleventh and thirteenth chords on the dominant, the dissonant tones do not resolve over the same bass; they move by step or remain oblique only with the change of bass. This idea became quite common in the nineteenth century and may be seen in any number of sources from Marx onward.

37. Bruckner, *Vorlesungen*, p. 177, ex. 74a and 74b.

38. Symmetrical constructs play an increasingly important role in nineteenth-century systems of harmony from Hauptmann onward. This may be yet another symptom of Bruckner's "modernity."

39. Bruckner, *Vorlesungen*, p. 180. (Das G...wird...unhörbare Sept genannt. Weil sie also nicht wirkliche Sept ist, kann sie oft unter Umständen auch steigen, geradeso auch eine unhörbare verminderte oder unreine Quint.)

40. Ibid., p. 187. (Weil aber das G als Non nicht springen soll, so mache ich einen Durchgang. Das G löst sich dabei abwärts in F auf und das folgende E is durchgehende Sept, die sich richtig ins D auflöst.... Der Stufenfall von der *Quint*lage aus ist sehr interessant und selten in den Lehrbüchern zu finden.... Die unhörbare Non G ist im Sopran, und damit sie nicht wie in 9-4a springt, mache ich einen Durchgang, diesmal nach aufwärts.)

41. Ibid., p. 179.

166 Notes for Chapter 9

42. Ibid., p. 179 and p. 191. Because the stepwise progressions are further reducible to progressions by fifth and third, they are also called "apparent steps" (*sheinbare Schritte*).

43. Decsey, *Bruckner*, p. 66.

44. Bruckner, *Vorlesungen*, p. 59.

45. Eckstein, "Anton Bruckners Universitäts-Vorlesungen... 1884–85...." In regard to VII7 Eckstein has written that it "can enter freely, for it is the substitute of the dominant Zenetti (Marpurg)!" (kann frei eintreten, denn er ist der Stellvertreter der Dominante Zenetti (Marpurg)!) Is Bruckner attributing the idea to Zenetti (and Marpurg)?

46. Bruckner, *Vorlesungen*, p. 133.

47. Ibid., p. 114.

48. Sechter, *Grundsätze*, pp. 154ff.

49. As Orel (p. 18), among others, has pointed out, Sechter too saw I, IV, and V as "primary chords"; this point of view is not necessarily dependent upon complete acceptance of Riemannian functionalism. Still, Bruckner clearly went farther in this direction than Sechter had; in Eckstein's notes ("6 Notenhefte"), for example, there is an analysis of the following progression in A minor: I–N6–V–I. Eckstein notes: "explanation of the B_b: free neighbor of A, thus actually D fundamental." (Erklärung des B: Frei[e] Wechselnote vor A, also eigentl[ich] D-Fund.) The explanation is consistent with Sechter's reading of the Neapolitan, but with this particular progression a stepwise fundamental motion would have to follow. Did Bruckner read stepwise fundamental motion on some occasions (in spite of Sechter)? Although we cannot answer this question, there is no doubt that his student Josef Schalk did (see chapter 11).

50. Bruckner, *Vorlesungen*, p. 171 (first mention); later examples include examples 116 and 120 (text pages 192ff).

51. Ibid., pp. 150–51. (Die Quart für sich ist eine Konsonanz. Ebenso ist die Sext für sich allein eine Konsonanz. Wenn aber Quart und Sext *zusammen* erklingen, so klingt die Quart nicht mehr konsonant. Der Quartsextakkord hat also eine Doppelnatur.)

52. Klose, *Meine Lehrjahre*, pp. 45–46.

53. Bruckner, *Vorlesungen*, p. 155. (Dem *Wesen* nach sind aber die Septakkorde nicht vom Dreiklang *abgeleitet*, sondern selbständig....)

54. Ibid., p. 211. In Eckstein's notes ("6 Notenhefte") the following example is also given among the "zufällige, künstliche, Accordbildungen":

Eckstein writes: "The seventh *ascends* when a *sixth chord* follows or when the seventh goes *up by step* in passing tone [motion]." (Die Sept *steigt*, wenn ein *Sextaccord* folgt, oder wenn die Sept im Durchgange [*sic*] *stufenweise aufwärts* geht.)

55. Bruckner, *Vorlesungen*, p. 61.
56. Decsey, p. 66.
57. Bruckner, *Vorlesungen*, ex. 106; text, p. 193.
58. Flotzinger, "Rafael Loidols Theorie Kolleg," p. 386.
59. Eckstein, "6 Notenhefte," number 3.
60. Bruckner, *Vorlesungen*, p. 276. (Bei der chromatischen Tonwechslung macht man den Uebergang mit leiter*fremden* Akkorden.)
61. Ibid.
62. Eckstein, "System" (vol. III: "Anton Bruckners Theorie der diatonischen Modulation, der Chromatik und der Enharmonic"), p. 79: "With his students Bruckner insisted that every chromatic chord connection be justified logically through an underlying diatonic structure." (Bruckner hat bei seinen Schülern streng darauf gedrungen, dass jede chromatische Akkordverbindung durch einen ihr zum Grunde liegenden diatonischen Satz logisch gerechtfertigt werde.) It may be added that in the few surviving chromatic examples in Loidol's and Vockner's notes there is nothing to contradict this. "Simple" and "compound" progressions are discussed by Eckstein on p. 101.
63. Ibid., pp. 44f. According to Eckstein, Bruckner handled these modulations in the discussion of chromaticism, not along with diatonic modulation. Eckstein also assures us that Bruckner had no knowledge of Hauptmann's *Moll-Dur* (*Erinnerungen*, p. 46).
64. Schenk and Gruber: In the discussion of chromaticism "Bruckner went directly back to Sechter, ... while [his teaching] of the enharmonic is not derivable from any model." (greift Bruckner unmittelbar auf Sechter zurück ... während die [Lehre] der Enharmonic von keinem Vorbild ableitbar ist.) ("Die ganzen Studien," p. 352.) Eckstein: "On the whole, Bruckner followed Sechter's procedures in the treatment of enharmonic changes, even more than in [his treatment of] chromaticism." ("ist Bruckner, ehr noch als bei der Chromatik, auch bei der Behandlung der enharmonischen Veränderungen im Grossen und Ganzen den Ausführungen Sechters gefolgt. ...") ("System" vol. III, pp. 143f.)
65. Eckstein, "6 Notenhefte," number 3.
66. Rudolf Louis and Ludwig Thuille, *Harmonielehre* (Stuttgart: Carl Grüninger, 1907), p. 214.
67. Eckstein, "System" (III), pp. 81ff.
68. New York Public Library Music Division, *MNZ-Toscanini Memorial Collection.
69. Carl Dahlhaus, "Schoenberg and Schenker," *PRMA*, vol. 100 (1973-74), pp. 209-15.
70. Heinrich Schenker, *Harmony*, ed. O. Jonas, trans. E.B. Mann (Chicago and London: University of Chicago Press, 1955), p. 177. For more on Schenker's understanding of "rules" vs. Bruckner's understanding of them, see chapter 12.

Chapter 10

1. Mayrberger apparently studied with Preyer in Vienna, eventually following the traditional vocation of the Viennese theorists: in 1864 he became *Kapellmeister* at the cathedral of Pressburg (which during the days of the Empire was in Hungary; today it is Bratislava, Czechoslovakia). He also taught at the teacher training school in Pressburg (for which he undoubtedly wrote his *Lehrbuch*) and was a composer.

2. The first part of Mayrberger's study *Die Harmonik Richard Wagner's an den Leitmotiven aus 'Tristan und Isolde' erläuert* appeared in *Bayreuther Blätter* 4, 1881. The second section was in preparation for the next issue at the time of the author's death. Both parts were subsequently issued as a separate publication (Bayreuth: 1882). According to Hans von Wolzogen, Wagner "believed ... with pleasure to have found the long-awaited theorist for our *Blätter* in this man from far-off Hungary who was previously unknown to us." (glaubte ... mit Freude in dem bisher uns fremdgebliebenen Manne aus dem fernen Ungarn den längst erwarteten Theoretiker unserer "Blätter" gefunden zu haben.) (Introduction to 1882 publication.)

3. *Drei Wandtafeln über das diatonische und enharmonische Modulationsverfahren mittelst der verminderten Septimenharmonien (der sogenannten enharmonischen Akkorde)* (Pressburg and Leipzig: Carl Stempel, 1880). Mayrberger manages to explain the modulatory properties of the diminished seventh, while at the same time retaining Sechter's fundamental bass. However, in both the *Wandtafeln* and the *Tristan* monograph Mayrberger departs from Sechter's practice by reading the lowest note of a root-position diminished seventh chord as the fundamental of the chord; he then interpolates the sub-posed third (Sechter's fundamental) as an "intermediate fundamental" before resolution to the next chord.

4. *Lehrbuch der musikalischen Harmonik* (Pressburg and Leipzig: Gustav Heckenast, 1878).

5. Ibid., p. 110.

6. Ibid., pp. 12f. *(auf eine Stufe bezogen, zu derselben eine reine Octav, eine reine Quint, eine grosse oder kleine Terz oder einen reinen Einklang bilden....)*

7. See Hauptmann, *Die Natur der Harmonik und der Metrik*, p. 21, where the three *direct verständliche Intervalle* are the octave, perfect fifth, and major third. Also see Matthew Shirlaw, *The Theory of Harmony* (London: Novello, 1917), pp. 354ff.

8. Mayrberger, *Lehrbuch*, p. 143. *(sich ... auf dem ihr zugehörigen Fundamente auflösen kann, zum Unterschiede von den bis jetzt kennen gelernten Dissonanzen d.i. der verminderten Quint und der Sept, welche sich nie auf ihrem Fundamente auflösen können, sondern zu ihrer Auflösung eines neuen Fundamentes bedürfen, und desswegen auch die eigentlichen Accord-Dissonanzen genannt werden.)* Cf. Kirnberger/Schulz, "The True Principles," p. 171, Section 6, and p. 72 above.

9. Mayrberger, *Lehrbuch*, p. 143. *(Es zeigt sich ... deutlich, dass die Accord-Dissonanzen wesentliche Bestandtheile ihres Accordes sind, welche von demselben nicht getrennt werden können—die Vorhaltsdissonanz hingegen eine zufällige Erscheinung ist, deren Vorhandensein die Wesenheit des Accordes, zu dem sie in Beziehung steht, nicht im mindesten alterirt.)*

10. Ibid., p. 144. *(Ist aber ein Vorhalt kein wesentlicher Accordton, so ist es in unserem Beispiele auch nicht die Non, mithin kann von einem Nonenaccord als Stammaccord, wie ihn so manche Lehrbücher irrthümlich bezeichnen [Marx, 168] auch nicht die Rede sein.)*

11. "*Since our eleventh can resolve over the same fundamental just as the previously discussed ninth can, it cannot be counted among the chordal dissonances either.... Thus there is just as little chance of an eleventh chord as there is of a ninth chord.*" *(Da sich unsere Undecim gleichfalls wie die bereits gekannte Non auf ihrem Fundamente auflösen kann, so zählt auch sie nicht unter die Accord-Dissonanzen... es kann daher so wenig einen Undecimen-Accord geben, als einen Nonen-Accord gibt.)* Ibid., p. 162f. The same of course goes for the "thirteenth chord." Mayrberger's typesetter evidently had as much trouble here as some later commentators have had: among the *Druckfehler* are two instances where *Tredecimen-Vorhalt* is to be substituted for the incorrect *Tredecimen-Accord*.

12. Ibid., p. 147. (Aus diesen beiden... geht deutlich hervor, dass nur, wenn der Accordton gleichzeitig mit dem Vorhalte erklingt, die Vorhaltgestaltung unzweifelhaft zur Erscheinung gebracht wird, während, wenn dies... nicht der Fall ist, es wenigstens sehr zweifelhaft ist, ob auf dem ersten und zweiten Viertel nicht der Septaccord der sechsten Stufe wirklich gemeint sei.) This is consistent with Sechter's explanation of suspensions (see *Grundsätze*, pp. 27ff).

13. While these "suspensions" require preparation in *strenger Satz*, they may enter unprepared in *freier Satz* (ibid., p. 223).

14. See Marx, *Kompositionslehre*, vol. I, pp. 137–48, for a very complete discussion of *harmonische Figurirung*. Kurt-Erich Eicke points out the influence of Logier on Marx (*Der Streit zwischen Adolf Bernard Marx und Gottfried Wilhelm Fink um die Kompositionslehre* [Regensburg: Bosse Verlag, 1966], p. 77). *Harmonische Figurirung* may be descended from Logier's "diversification of the common chord," as it appears in his book, *A System of the Science of Music and Practical Composition* (London: 1827), p. 23.

15. Mayrberger, *Lehrbuch*, pp. 118ff. (was mit einer Stimme geschehen kann, kann auch mit zwei oder mehreren Stimmen gleichzeitig geschehen.)

16. Ibid., p. 120. *(Hier sei Erwähnung gethan, dass, wenn ein und derselbe Accord harmonisch figurirt wird, ein gleichzeitiger neuer Quartenanschlag zum Basse erlaubt ist.)*

17. Ibid., p. 124. (Zu den Durchgängen kann gleichzeitig in einer andern Stimme die harmonische Figurirung angebracht werden.)

18. See above, p. 45, example 6-1.

19. Mayrberger, *Lehrbuch*, p. 124.

20. Ibid., p. 127. The x's and °'s, indicating passing and changing tone motion respectively, are Mayrberger's.

21. Ibid., p. 130. (Bis jetzt haben wir zwei Accorde dadurch gebildet, dass jeder Accord auf seinem ihm zugehörigen Fundamente gestanden ist.
    Jetzt wollen wir eine andere Art Accordbildung kennen lernen, welche darin besteht, dass zwei Accorde und zwar verschiedener Klangstufen auf einem und demselben Fundamente gebildet werden, wodurch natürlicher Weise der folgende Accord immer auf dem Fundamente des vorhergegangenen Accordes zu stehen kommt.
    Zu dieser Accordverbindung benöthigen wir aber die bereits abgehandelte Lehre von der harmonischen Figurirung, den Durchgangs- und den Wechselnoten.
    Wir werden diese drei Hilfsmittel je nach Bedarf einzeln oder vereint, anwenden, und die dadurch entstandenen Accorde *Durchgangs-Accorde*... heissen.)

22. Ibid., pp. 253ff.

23. Mayrberger does, however, reject Sechter's assumption of just intonation (Ibid., p. 59).

24. See Max Arend, "Harmonische Analyse des Tristanvorspiels," *Bayreuther Blätter* 24 (1901):160–69, and Emil Ergo, "Über Wagner's Harmonik und Melodik," *Bayreuther Blätter* 35 (1912):34–41, 138–49, 293–308.

25. Georg Capellen, *Ist das System S. Sechters ein geeigneter Ausgangspunkt für die theoretische Wagnerforschung?* Also see Capellen's "Harmonik und Melodik bei Richard Wagner," *Bayreuther Blätter* 25 (1902):3–10.

26. Kurth, *Romantische Harmonik.*

27. See Martin Vogel, *Der Tristan-Akkord und die Krise der modernen Harmonielehre* (Düsseldorf: Verlag der Gesellschaft zur Förderung der systematischen Musikwissenschaft, e.V., 1962). The first part of Vogel's study contains an excellent history of the theoretical discussions of *Tristan*. Also see William J. Mitchell, "The Tristan Prelude: Techniques and Structure," *The Music Forum*, I (New York and London: Columbia University Press, 1967), pp. 162–203.

28. Cyrill Kistler (1848–1907) was a school teacher from 1867–76, at which point he gave up teaching to go to Munich and study with Rheinberger. It appears that a personal meeting with Wagner during the late 1870s had an important effect on his career. From the early 1880s until his death he composed a considerable amount of Wagnerian music and wrote several pedagogical works.

29. Cyrill Kistler, *Harmonielehre für Lehrer und Lernende* (Munich: 1879); second edition, *Harmonielehre für Lehrende, Lernende und zum wirklichen Selbstunterrichte* (Bad Kissingen: 1898). The second edition was also published in English.

30. Hauptmann, *Die Natur der Harmonik*, pp. 46f.

31. Ibid., p. 152.

32. Kistler, *Harmonielehre* (second edition), pp. 81f.

33. Mayrberger, *Die Harmonik Richard Wagner's*, pp. 8f.

34. Alfred Lorenz, *Der musikalische Aufbau von Richard Wagners "Tristan und Isolde"* (Berlin: 1926), p. 194; quoted after Vogel, *Der Tristan Akkord*, p. 18.

35. Mitchell, "The Tristan Prelude."

36. See Vogel, *Der Tristan Akkord*, p. 36.

37. Mitchell, "The Tristan Prelude," p. 177.

38. Mayrberger, *Die Harmonik Richard Wagner's*, p. 10. (d ist der freie Vorhalt der Undezime, der, um hinaufgehen zu können, den melodisch chromatischen Durchgang nach dis macht.
    gis ist Vorhalt der hinaufgehenden Septime, der auf dem im Geist gedachten Fundamente fis zur None wird und auch später in die Dominant-Septime des Fundamentes H auflöst.
    f ist der Vorhalt der Tredezime, der sich regelrecht auflöst. eis der Oberstimme ist die melodisch chromatische untere Wechselnote von fis.)

39. Mayrberger discusses the "suspension of the ascending seventh"(*Vorhalt der hinaufgehenden Sept*) in the *Lehrbuch*, p. 197.

40. Mayrberger restates his limitations on chords in the *Anhang* to *Die Harmonik Richard Wagner's (Musikalische Aphorismen*, X).

41. Vogel, *Der Tristan Akkord*, p. 20. (Den Zusammenklang c–f–gis–d deutete er als Zwitterakkord aus der I. Stufe von a-Moll und der IV. Stufe von e-Moll.)

42. Arend (see note 24), p. 163. "F^1 is a suspension to E^1, $G\sharp^1$ [an alteration] of G^1 striving for A^1; D^2 and $D\sharp^2$ are suspensions to E^2 from below.... Bar 73 proves that the harmony must be understood unconditionally in this sense."(F^1 ist Vorhalt zu e^1; gis^1 ein nach a^1 strebendes g^1; d^2 und dis^2 Vorhalte von unten vor e^2.... Dass die Harmonie unbedingt in dem dargelegten Sinne verstanden werden muss, beweist der 73. Takt.) Measure 73 does in fact offer additional support for this analysis; perhaps this bar influenced Mayrberger as well.

43. "Taken out of context, the third harmonization of the motive (measures 10 and 11) is based not upon a dominant cadential motion, but upon a *subdominant* cadential motion: E7–B7. The E from the chord E–G♯–B–D appears with a free, suspensionlike chromatic neighbor note (F) which presses downward linearly. Moreover, in place of the B the chromatic neighbor C [appears], which only progresses further with the chord of resolution."(Die dritte Motivharmonisierung (10. und 11. Takt) beruht, für sich allein herausgehoben, nicht mehr auf dominantischer, sondern auf *unterdominantischer* Kadenzierung: E7–H7, vom Klange: e–gis–h–d erscheint das e mit einer freien, vorhaltsartigen chromatischen Nebentoneinstellung (f), im linearen Zug abwärts weiterdrängend, ferner an Stelle des h die chromatische Nebentoneinstellung c, die erst mit dem Lösungsakkord zum h weiterschreitet.) (*Romantische Harmonik*, p. 51.) Both Kurth and Mayrberger are forced to call upon the notion of an unprepared nonchord tone lasting for the complete duration of the first chord. It is simply a matter of which note of the augmented triad on the last beat of the bar one chooses to displace.

44. Mitchell, "The Tristan Prelude," p. 177. Even Mitchell cannot completely escape the history of conflicts over this passage. His example 7 suggests that the "Tristan Chord" here is a diminished seventh functioning as an appoggiatura chord to the B7. In fact, that analysis was first stated by Lorenz (*Der musikalische Aufbau von "Tristan,"* p. 196; see Vogel, *Der Tristan Akkord*, p. 37).

45. But he does not cover it all. Arend was the first to discuss the whole piece, maintaining that there were no modulations, and pointing out the important enharmonic reappearance of F–B–D♯–G♯ as F–C♭–E♭–A♭ in m. 83.

46. Mayrberger, *Die Harmonik Richard Wagner's*, p. 12. Mitchell agrees with this interpretation (p. 180).

47. Ibid., p. 16.

48. Ibid., p. 5.

49. Ibid., p. 23.

50. Ibid., p. 20. (Cf., Peters orchestral score [Dover], p. 38.)

51. Ernst Kurth complains that Mayrberger reads seven modulations within eight bars in his analysis of the *Liebestod* (*Romantische Harmonik*, p. 281). And in this case, the resultant keys are almost completely isolated from one another.

52. While the distinction between the two types of chordal chromaticism is implicit in Mayrberger's analyses, it is never explicitly defined. Harmonic and melodic (embellishing) chromaticism, on the other hand, are clearly distinguished from one another throughout.

53. Salomon Jadassohn, *Melodik und Harmonik bei Richard Wagner* (Berlin: Verlagsgesellschaft für Literatur und Kunst, n.d. [1899, according to Kurth]).

54. Salomon Jadassohn, *Lehrbuch der Harmonie* (Leipzig: Breitkopf und Härtel, 1883; many subsequent editions); trans. Theodore Baker, *A Manual of Harmony* (New York: G. Schirmer, 1893).

55. Jadassohn, *Melodik und Harmonik bei R. Wagner*, p. 26.
56. Ibid., p. 27. (Man kann... hier nicht von frei eintretenden, sich vom unteren zum oberen Tone auflösenden Vorhalten sprechen und ebensowenig von durchgehenden Noten; denn das Charakteristische der Vorhalts- wie der Durchgangs-Noten besteht darin, dass sie nicht Bestandteile eines Akkordes bilden, sondern gegen einen solchen dissonieren.)
57. Vogel claims that both the *Stufentheorie* and *Funktionstheorie* make too much use of suspension chords and alteration. While these ideas were useful in earlier styles, he is not convinced of their usefulness in the Wagnerian style. (*Der Tristan Akkord*, p. 127).
58. Heinrich Schenker, "Fortsetzung der Urlinie-Betrachtungen," *Das Meisterwerk in der Musik II* (Munich, Vienna, Berlin: Drei Masken Verlag, 1926), p. 29. Trans. Sylvan Kalib, "Thirteen Essays from the Three Yearbooks 'Das Meisterwerk in der Musik'..." (Ph.D. Dissertation, Northwestern University, 1973) 2:197.

Chapter 11

1. The "Cecilian Movement" of the nineteenth century was descended from the various *Caecilien-Bündnisse* of the late eighteenth century which attempted to preserve *a capella* singing and stem the tide of liturgical instrumental music. The "Allgemeine Cäcilien-Verein" was founded by F.X. Witt (1834–88) in Germany in 1869 and became the model for similar organizations in other areas, all of which were dedicated to the promotion of vocal music. A reaction against the movement erupted in Austria in 1875 under Habert's leadership. Although Habert would not tolerate the liturgical music of Liszt, Bruckner, or even the Viennese Classicists—or of those who composed in this manner in Germany (Rheinberger) and France (Gounod)—neither would he accept the *Cäcilien-Verein's* demand for a return to Palestrina (despite his profound knowledge of this literature). Rather, Habert fought for instrumental music, claiming that this genre provided a "path which lead from J.J. Fux through the Viennese Classic to the present." (einen Weg, der von J.J. Fux über die Wiener Klassiker zur Gegenwärt führte.) (*MGG*, 5: col. 1197–99, s.v., Habert.)
2. J.N. Moser, *Johannes Evangelist Habert 1833–1896; Ein oberösterreichischer Komponist und Musiktheoretiker* (Graz: published by the author, 1976).
3. Speaking of his student Josef Labor (1842–1924), who had studied earlier with Sechter, Habert complains that "he had not learned simple counterpoint in the church modes according to *Fux* with Sechter. I lent him Fux, since he was unfamiliar with the work. The church modes were completely foreign to him." (Den einfachen Contrapunkt nach *Fux* in den Kirchentonarten hat er bei Sechter nicht gelernt, ich habe ihm Fux geliehen, da er das Werk nicht kannte. Die Kirchentonarten waren ihm ganz fremd.) (Moser, *Habert*, p. 65) The same Labor, incidentally, has been mentioned as a "teacher" of Schoenberg; the connection is, however, on the order of Sechter's relationship to Schubert (see Willi Reich, *Schoenberg; a Critical Biography* [New York: Praeger, 1971], p. 5). Habert's *Harmonielehre* (see note 4) was the first of four volumes entitled "Beiträge zur Lehre von der musikalischen Komposition"; the remaining three are all concerned with counterpoint.
4. Johannes Ev. Habert, *Beiträge zur Lehre von der musikalischen Komposition; erstes Buch. Harmonielehre* (Leipzig: Breitkopf u. Härtel, 1899). Interestingly enough, the *Harmonielehre* is the product of Busoni's study with Habert. As a ten-year old boy Busoni had already had some dozen lessons in harmony with Nottebohm (also a Sechter student) in Vienna when he was brought to Habert in 1876. But after barely beginning study, the family moved to Vienna and Habert was asked to continue to teach Busoni by mail. The resulting *Unterrichtsbriefe* formed the basis of the *Harmonielehre*. (Moser, *Habert*, pp. 69f; also see Habert, *Harmonielehre*, p. XIV.)

5. The book is also evidence of the wide acceptance Sechter's system achieved in Austria, for there is no evidence that Habert had studied in Vienna.
6. Cf. Schoenberg's explanation of the "superstrong" (stepwise) progressions (*Theory of Harmony*, p. 119).
7. Habert, *Harmonielehre*, pp. Xf. (Nun ist aber... C im zweiten Takte Fundament des C-dur-Dreiklanges und es wird wohl niemand die Empfindung haben, dass dieser C-dur-Dreiklange den Septakkord der VI. Stufe vertritt. Was man empfindet, das ist die Härte, die in der Folge des C-dur- und des D-moll-Dreiklanges liegt, weil diese Akkorde keinen gemeinschaftlichen Ton haben. Man kann sagen, hier ist das Bindeglied zwischen den zwei Dreiklängen übersprungen, der Satz ist knapper, und weil knapper, prägnanter und kräftiger im Ausdruck. Die Beschränkung, C nicht als Fundamentton und die Verbindung von dem C-dur- und D-moll-Dreiklange nicht als Fundamentalschritte anzusehen, müsste eine Beschränkung im Gebrauche solcher Schritte zur Folge haben. Nun aber spielen gerade diese Schritte in der alten klassischen Vokalmusik, im strengen Satze eine grosse Rolle.)
8. Ibid., p. XI. (Das hier der C-dur-Dreiklang eine andere Bedeutung hat, wie oben, ist klar. Deshalb aber, weil er hier Stellvertreter des Septakkordes sein kann, diesen Schritt generalisieren zu wollen und unter allen Umständen verlangen, man müsse den ersten Dreiklang als unvollständigen Septakkord ansehen, wenn das Fundament eine Stufe steigt, und diese Steigen als *scheinbares* stufenweises Steigen erklären, das geht doch nicht an.)
9. Johann Emerich Hasel, *Die Grundsätze des Harmoniesystems. Ein vollständig umfassendes Lehrbuch über den Bau, die Verbindung und die chromatische Umgestaltung aller Accorde auf ihren unveränderlichen diatonischen Fundamenten nebst einer Anleitung zur Analyse der vorhandenen Harmonie-Complicationen* (Vienna: V. Kratochwill, 1892). Like Mayrberger, Hasel claims to have been a student of Preyer's.
10. Diatonic harmony: pp. 18–251; chromatic harmony: pp. 259–561.
11. "Anleitung zur Analyse der Compositionen," pp. 583–628.
12. The harmony books by Mayrberger, Hasel, and Habert are the only works from the latter half of the nineteenth century clearly based upon Sechter (cf., Kurth, chapter 4, p. 33f. above). A purely analytical work dates from the turn of the century: Ernst von Stockhausen, *Die harmonische Grundlage von 12 Fugen aus Joh. Seb. Bach Wohltemperirtem Klavier sowie der As moll-Orgelfugue von J. Brahms nach den Grundsätzen von S. Sechter dargestellt und erläutert* (Leipzig: Breitkopf und Härtel [ca. 1901, according to New York Public Library]). And some forty years later an extremely curious American publication appeared: *Modern Harmony... by S. Sechter*, ed. Samuel Spivak (New York: Clef music, 1943).
13. Hasel, *Grundsätze des Harmoniesystems*, p. 366. (ein *doppeldeutiger-*, oder ein *Misch-*, oder ein *Zwitter-*, oder ein *alterirter* Accord.)
14. See the full title of Hasel's book and the following tautology on p. 281: "The *root* of these diatonic triads may *never be chromatically altered*, because their *fundamentals* may not be subjected to chromatic alteration." (Der *Grundton* dieser diatonischen Dreiklänge darf *nie chromatisch verändert* werden, weil auch ihr *Fundament* keiner chromatischen Veränderung unterzogen werden darf.)
15. Hasel, *Grundsätze des Harmoniesystems*, p. 263.
16. See above, p. 57.
17. Eckstein, *Erinnerungen an Anton Bruckner*, p. 52.

18. Hynais, "Die Harmonik R. Wagner's in Bezug auf die Fundamentaltheorie Sechter's," *Neue Musikalische Presse* X (1901), 4:50–52, 5:67–69, 6:81–82, 7:97–100.
19. Ibid., p. 50.
20. Ibid., p. 51.
21. Ibid., p. 82.
22. Ibid. (Der Quartsextaccord im 2. Tacte des letzten Beispieles ist durch die durchgehende Bewegung des Basses a–g–fis und der oberen Mittelstimme fis–g–a, so wie durch den zurückkehrenden Durchgang der unteren Mittelstimme d–es–d leicht zu erklären, also kein wirklicher, sondern künstlicher oder zufälliger Quartsextaccord.)
23. Capellan, *Sechter*, p. 19.
24. Hynais, "Die Harmonik R. Wagner's," p. 97. (Die Sept steigt stets bei zwei aufeinanderfolgenden Septaccorden bei Terzfall; ausnahmsweise auch bei zwei aufeinanderfolgenden Septaccorden bei Quintfall, um sie vollständig zu haben.)
25. Ibid.
26. Thomas Leibnitz, "Josef Schalk; Ein Wagnerianer zwischen Anton Bruckner und Hugo Wolf," *Bruckner Jahrbuch 1980* (Linz: 1980). Schalk started studying music theory with Bruckner in 1877. Thus began an uneasy association, which deteriorated markedly in the early 1890s, although Schalk did visit Bruckner in 1895 and 1896, shortly before the latter's death. Essential to Leibnitz's portrayal is the notion of Schalk the true "Wagnerian," with interests which were both literary and musical. Such a personality could hardly have avoided eventual conflict with Bruckner. The idea proves to be a convincing explanation for Schalk's developing friendship with Wolf (of whom Bruckner was clearly jealous), as well as Schalk's controversial "programs" for Bruckner's symphonies. Leibnitz also considers the changes in Bruckner's symphonies, and presents a list of Schalk's published works.
27. Josef Schalk, "Das Gesetz der Tonalität," *Bayreuther Blätter* 11 (1888):192–97, 381–87; 12(1889):191–98; 13(1890):65–70.
28. Renate Groth, *Die französische Kompositionslehre des 19. Jahrhunderts* (Wiesbaden: Franz Steiner, 1983). The present discussion of "tonality" as understood by French theorists is heavily indebted to Groth's excellent work (see pp. 58–68).
29. (La hiérarchie naturelle des sept notes rangées sous l'autorité de l'une d'entre elles, qu'on nomme tonique, étant purement métaphysique, n'est point du ressort des sons, mais appartient à l'esprit qui seul peut en connaître.) *Encyclopédie méthodique, ou par ordre de matières. Musique*. N.E. Framéry, P.L., Ginguené and J.-J. de Momigny, ed. (Paris: 1791, 1818), vol. 2, p. 179. Quoted after Groth, p. 58.
30. Bryan Simms, "Choron, Fétis, and the Theory of Tonality," *JMT* 19/1 (Spring 1975): 112–38.
31. Groth, *Die französische Kompositionslehre*, p. 59.
32. F.J. Fétis, *Traité complet de la Théorie et de la Practique de l'Harmonie* (Paris: Braudus et Cie, 1844), p. 22. (*La tonalité se forme de la collection des rapports nécessaires, successifs ou simultanés, des sons de la gamme.*)
33. Ibid., p. 9. According to Simms, this idea is also derived from Choron. See his "Alexandre Choron (1771–1834) As a Historian and Theorist of Music" (Ph.D. dissertation: Yale University, 1971), pp. 205f.

34. Fétis, p. 3 and pp. 19f. Quoted after Groth, p. 60.

35. The concentration on melodic attraction and the "two-state" notion of harmony are typical traits of other systems of harmony from the first half of the nineteenth century. The importance of melodic attraction in Vogler's system has already been noted (chapter 2). The *Theoretisch-praktische Harmonielehre* (Berlin: Thomes, 1840) by S.W. Dehn, which appeared shortly before Fétis's book, is another system based upon Rameau's "major and minor leading tones" and their resolution. But unlike Fétis, who follows Kirnberger in the melodic derivation of other chords from the dominant seventh, Dehn's category of dissonant chords starts with VII°, deriving the remaining chords by both superimposing and subposing thirds. This system was later taken over by Dehn's student C.F. Weitzmann and mixed with ideas taken from Hauptmann, with whom Weitzmann had also studied. Its most complete exposition may be found in Weitzmann's *Harmoniesystem* (Leipzig: C.F. Kahnt, 1860).

36. See Groth, *Die französische Kompositionslehre*, pp. 63–68.

37. Hermann von Helmholtz, *Die Lehre von den Tonempfindungen* (Brunswick: F. Vieweg, 1863), trans. and rev. John Alexander Ellis as *On the Sensations of Tone* (London: Longmans, Green and Co., 1875), reprinted with a new introduction by H. Margenau (New York: Dover, 1954), p. 249.

38. Ibid., p. 249.

39. Ibid., p. 296.

40. La Mara, ed., *Briefe hervorragender Zeitgenossen an Franz Liszt*, 3 vol. (Leipzig: Breitkopf u. Härtel, 1895-1904), vol. 3, no. 259, p. 342. Letter dated Oct. 6, 1879. (*Der Cardinalfehler unserer noch immer allgemein üblichen Lehre des musikalischen Satzes, der Harmonielehre, ist, daß sie ihren Ausgang von der Scale und nicht vom Klange nimmt.*)

41. See Rummenhöller, "Der Syntheseversuch Hugo Riemanns," *Musiktheoretisches Denken*, pp. 95ff.

42. Quoted after Carl Dahlhaus, *Untersuchungen über die Entstehung der harmonischen Tonalität*, p. 12. The example is taken from Riemann's *Musik-Lexikon* (Leipzig: 1909), s.v. *Tonalität*. The five chords are analyzed by Riemann as tonic, contra-third chord (*Gegenterzklang*), tonic, plain-third chord (*schlichter Terzklang*) and tonic.

43. Ibid., p. 12. (in der Suspendierung der Diatonik als Grundlage tonaler Akkordzusammenhänge sieht Riemann das Unterscheidungsmerkmal der "Tonalität" gegenüber der "Tonart älterer Lehre," die durch die diatonische Skale fundiert wurde.)

44. Hugo Riemann, *Handbuch der Harmonielehre* (Leipzig: Breitkopf u. Härtel, 1906), p. 214. (*Unsere Lehre von den tonalen Funktionen der Harmonie ist nichts anderes als der Ausbau des Fétis'schen Begriffes der Tonalität.*)

45. See Ruth A. Solie, "The Living Work: Organicism and Musical Analysis," *Nineteenth Century Music* 4, no. 2 (Fall 1980): 147–56.

46. Possible influences may have been *Musikalische Syntaxis* (Leipzig: Breitkopf u. Härtel, 1877); "Die Natur der Harmonik," in *Sammlung musikalischer Vorträge*, ed. Paul Graf von Waldersee (Leipzig: Breitkopf u. Härtel, 1882), pp. 157–90; or "Ueber Tonalität," *Neue Zeitschrift für Musik* (1872), No. 45–46.

47. See note 64.

48. Schalk, "Tonalität" (I), p. 194. (*Jedem Tonwerke liegt eine bestimmte Haupttonart zu Grunde.*...(Cf., Helmholtz, above.)

49. Ibid., p. 195. (Die Theorie begnügte sich bisher den Uebergang von einer Tonart in die andere aufzuzeigen, wobei dann die Abhängigkeit der zweiten Tonart von der ersten ganz ausser Acht gelassen und sie als ebenso selbständig betrachtet und behandelt wurde. Dass aber im Kunstwerk dem nicht so ist, beweist die jedesmalige Rückkehr zur Haupttonart, welche also als leises Grundgefühl den Komponisten auch über die fernsten Tonarten begleiten musste.)

50. Ibid., p. 195. (Ueberhaupt sind die Begriffe von chromatischer Fortschreitung und wirklichem Tonwechsel (Modulation) so durcheinander geworfen worden, dass sie nur sehr schwer zu entwirren sind. Vor allem ist das Gebiet einer Tonart im weiteren Sinne zu fassen als bisher. Man wird dann nicht nöthig haben fortwährend Uebergänge zu konstatiren, wo nur chromatisch alterirte Akkorde auftreten, und wird die eigentliche Modulation für jene Stellen aufsparen, wo sich eine zweite Tonart wirklich selbständig für eine oder mehre Perioden oder Abschnitte geltend macht.)

51. Ibid., p. 196. (Fassen wir sie aber in Beziehung zur Tonika auf, so sind es die Akkorde der I. and II. Stufe von G-dur, dann der III. V. und VI. Stufe von g-moll.)

52. Ibid. (kommt denn die Tonart g-moll hier wirklich zum Ausdruck oder zerren wir sie nicht blos willkürlich herbei um für den Fundamentston es eine Erklärung zu haben? Wäre es nicht einfacher die kleine Sext auch in der Durtonart als Fundamentston zuzulassen?

53. Ibid. (Wir greifen zu diesem Zwecke auf den dritten Akkord des Beispieles zurück. Bei genauer Prüfung zeigt sich deutlich sein unselbständiger, durchgehender Charakter....)

54. Ibid. (Wie bekannt gibt es auch zurückkehrende Durchgänge, oft weniger richtig als Wechselnoten bezeichnet z. B. [musical example]. Als eine Solche möchte ich den scheinbaren Grundton des vierten Taktes bezeichnen.)

55. Ibid. (dürfte aber doch die wahrste Erklärung der Trugschlusswirkung V–bVI sein.)

56. Ibid., p. 197. (Warum soll aber nicht die chromatische Tredezime in die diatonische gehen und erst dann sich auflösen, umsomehr als dieser neue Akkord (e,b,cis, g) deutlich nur als eine Verzögerung des folgenden Quartsextakkordes empfunden wird?)

57. Schalk, "Tonalität" (II), p. 381. (*ein durchgehender d.i. zwei Hauptharmonien durch stufenweise Tonfolge verbindender Akkord durch den Sprung einer einzelnen Stimme seine Unselbstandigkeit keineswegs verliert....*)

58. The discussion of the "passing chord" leads, logically enough, to the "suspension chord." The most important among Schalk's numerous examples is the *Todesverkungigung* motive from *Die Walküre* which was cited previously in the Bruckner discussion (see above, p. 79). The analytical interpretation is precisely the same as it was in both Eckstein's notes and Hynais's essay: the opening D-minor chord is "nonessential."

59. Josef Schalk, "Aufsatz über die Chromatik," Austrian National Library, F 18 Schalk 410, p. 2. (In der dritten erstreckt sich der Gebrauch chromatischer Töne, (wenn auch meist nur scheinbar) sogar die Grundtöne (Fundamente) der Akkorde....)

60. Josef Schalk, "Ubungsheft (Harmonielehre); mit handschr. Notizen," Austrian National Library, F 18 Schalk 409. The material on the Neapolitan comes from an insert in the front of the book. The book is undated, but it contains sketches for the *Bayreuther Blätter* articles of 1888–90. (Die Anwendung dieser chromatischen Töne verdanken wir daher zunächst der melodischen Erfindung. Erst später würden sie auch in der Umkehrung als Baßstimme gebraucht, worauf sie als Dreiklänge oder seltener als Quartsextakkorden erschienen u. größere Selbständigkeit...gewannen.)

61. Schalk, "Tonalität" (IV), p. 69.

62. Ibid., p. 70. (Wir geben schliesslich noch die Ableitung des Hauptüberganges, entstanden aus einer ursprünglich im zurückkehrenden Durchgange melodisch gebildeten Akkordfolge a). Bei b) erhält der zweite Akkord durch die Unterstützung seitens der Bassstimme schon grössere Selbständigkeit, welche bei c) durch ebenfalls melodische Einführung der Septime und Non vollkommen wird und ihn als Dominantseptnonakkord von H-dur geltend macht.)

63. Despite the obvious limitations on their work, both Mayrberger and Schalk would have an influence on one of the most important harmony books written at the beginning of the twentieth century: the *Harmonielehre* by Rudolf Louis and Ludwig Thuille (Stuttgart: Carl Grüninger, 1907). In his book on Bruckner, Louis notes the obvious faults with Sechter's system, but concludes: "in any case it is testimony to the usefulness of Sechter's system... that men like Karl Mayrberger and Josef Schalk believed that they were able to account for even the modern and complex harmonic technique of Wagner with Sechter's method, and indeed, they achieved more than many modern theorists," Louis, *Anton Bruckner* (Berlin: Gose u. Tetzlaft Verlagsbuchhandlung, 1904), p. 15. (Immerhin zeugt es auf alle Fälle für die Brauchbarkeit der Sechterschen Harmonielehre..., daß Leute wie Karl Mayrberger und Josef Schalk selbst der modernen und komplizierten Harmonik Richard Wagners gegenüber mit Sechter vollkommen glaubten ausreichen zu können, und in der Tat damit auch weiter kamen, als manch kühner harmonic-theoretischer Neuerer.) See chapter 13, below.

64. Schalk, "Aufsatz über die Chromatik," p. 11. (ist nur genöthigt sich in fortwährender Begegnung auf die naturwissenschaftliche Grundlage zu verhalten, was freilich bei dem heutigen Stande dieser Wissenschaft das Schwierigste aus dem ganzen Unternehmen ist. Bewundern wir die unsägliche Genauigkeit und Gründlichkeit... mit der diese Wissenschaft bemüht war, das Wesen der Diatonik festzustellen, so sehen wir noch im Gebiete der Chromatik selbst bei einem Forscher wie Helmholtz nur auf wenige gelegentliche Fingerzeige beschränkt.)

65. Ibid., p. 17. (stehe hiebei nur in wenigstem Abhängigkeitsverhältnisse von Eins.)

66. Ibid., p. 16. (Die heutige Theorie bevorzugt die erster, der Akkord hat für sie die Hauptbedeutung (Harmonielehre). Die zweiter Art, welche sich mit der Stimmführung (Contrapunkt) beschäftigt ist aber der weit richtigere und künstlerisch lebensvollere. Es fragt sich, ob aus der Führung der Stimmen allein Gesetze genommen werden können, welche auch für den Zusammenklang verbürgend sind?)

Chapter 12

1. The most important of these works are (in chronological order): August Halm, *Harmonielehre* (Leipzig: G.J. Göschen'sche Verlagshandlung, 1902); Johannes Schreyer, *Von Bach bis Wagner* (Dresden: Holze und Pahl, 1903), later rewritten and published as *Lehrbuch der Harmonie*...; Heinrich Schenker, *Neue musikalische Theorien und Phantasien*, vol. 1, *Harmonielehre* (Vienna: Universal, 1906); Rudolf Louis and Ludwig Thuille, *Harmonielehre* (Stuttgart: Carl Grüninger, 1907); Georg Capellen, *Fortschrittliche Harmonie- und Melodielehre* (Leipzig: C.F. Kahnt Nachfolger, 1908); Heinrich Schenker, *Neue musikalische Theorien und Phantasien*, vol. 2/1, *Kontrapunkt* (Vienna: Universal, 1910) (despite the title, Schenker has much to say about harmony in this work); Arnold Schoenberg, *Harmonielehre* (Vienna: Universal, 1911).

2. See Elmar Seidel, "Die Harmonielehre Hugo Riemanns" in *Beiträge zur Musiktheorie des 19. Jahrhundert*, and more recently, see Mickelsen. Mickelsen's assessment of Riemann's

Notes for Chapter 12

influence upon Schenker is most certainly overstated (see William C. Mickelsen, *Hugo Riemann's Theory of Harmony...and History of Music Theory, Book III, by Hugo Riemann* (Lincoln and London: University of Nebraska Press, 1977), pp. 95–97, and see chapter 14, below).

3. Schenker studied for three years (fall, 1887 through spring, 1890) at the Vienna Conservatory (the present-day *Hochschule für Musik*). He studied harmony with Bruckner during the first year, and counterpoint during the second. He left during the third year, after having completed requirements for the Dr. jur. at the University (Nov. 20, 1889). See Hellmut Federhofer, "Heinrich Schenkers Bruckner-Verständnis," *Archiv für Musikwissenschaft*, XXXIX Jahrgang, Heft 3 (1982), 3. Quartal, p. 198.

4. See note 1 for publication data. August Halm (1869–1929) studied theology at Tübingen before going to Munich to study with Rheinberger. Subsequently, he devoted himself mainly to music pedagogy, and became important in the "youth music" movement of the twenties. It was in this capacity that he came into contact with Ernst Kurth; certain of Halm's theoretical ideas seem to have found their way into Kurth's work (see Rothfarb's translation of Kurth's *Voraussetzungen*, pp. 19ff). Judging from the number of citations of Halm's *Harmonielehre* in other works of the period (Schoenberg, for example), the work's influence was considerably greater than its brevity might seem to indicate.

5. See note 1 for publication data. Rudolf Louis (1870–1914), although a composer, was primarily active as a critic and writer on music. Ludwig Thuille (1861–1907) was a composer, and succeeded Rheinberger as professor of harmony and composition at the Conservatory in Munich. A common opinion holds that the theoretical aspects of the *Harmonielehre* stem from Louis, while the practical exercises and analyses are by Thuille (this is Oskar Kaul's opinion; *MGG* vol. 8, col. 1232, s.v. "Louis, Rudolf"). But Thuille's student, Friedrich Munter, claims that the theoretical explanations are just as much the "intellectual property" of Thuille as they are of Louis; and that both the theoretical ideas and their order of presentation accurately represent Thuille's teaching method (Friedrich Munter, *Ludwig Thuille, Ein erster Versuch* [Munich: Drei Masken Verlag, 1923], p. 110). According to Munter, only the philosophical and music-historical excurses are definitely by Louis.

This is especially interesting with respect to the polemic with Riemann in which Louis eventually became involved. Louis announced the publication of the *Harmonielehre* with an attack on "dualism" and the excesses of "speculation" ("Unsere Harmonielehre," *Süddeutsche Monatshefte* [1906] 10:430–37). The passages quoted below from the Introduction to the *Harmonielehre* offer a sample of Louis's ideas. Riemann was assigned to review the book, and after calling it one of the most interesting theory books of the previous ten years, he proceeded to accuse the authors of plagiarizing his system—undoubtedly in response to the tone of Louis's announcement ("Eine neue Harmonielehre: Harmonielehre von Rudolf Louis u. Ludwig Thuille," *Süddeutsche Monatshefte* 4 [1907]:500–504). Louis immediately leapt to the defense of his recently deceased colleague (Thuille had died just before the book appeared), claiming that: "he [Thuille] did not know Riemann's works. That in spite of this he used to explain the nature of secondary chords through their derivation from the primary chords (even in regard to III and VI) in his harmony teaching, offers new evidence for the oft-proved fact that *agreement* and *dependence* in any question are two very different things." (er Riemanns Arbeiten nicht kannte. Daß er trotzdem in seinem eigenen Harmonieunterricht das Wesen der Nebenharmonien (und zwar auch bezüglich der III. und VI. Stufe) durch deren Zurückführung auf die tonalen Hauptharmonien zu erklären pflegte, ist ein neuer Beleg für die oft erwiesene Tatsache, daß *Uebereinstimmung* und *Abhängigkeit* in irgend einer Frage zwei sehr verschiedene Dinge sind.) Louis, "Zu Hugo Riemanns Besprechung der Louis-Thuilleschen Harmonielehre," *Süddeutsche Monatshefte* 5 [1907]:615.

Munter also agrees that Thuille knew no Riemann (p. 109). Although Louis knew Riemann's works ("Zu Riemann's Besprechung," p. 615), the book is at least as closely related to Viennese fundamental bass theory as it is to Riemann's system (see chapter 13, below).

6. Arnold Schoenberg, *Structural Functions of Harmony* (New York: Norton, 1969).

7. Rudolf Louis, *Grundriss der Harmonielehre*, 5th ed. (Stuttgart: Klett, 1914). This information is taken from the *Vorwort*. The first edition appeared in 1908.

8. Related publications by Louis include: *Aufgaben zur Harmonielehre*, 5th ed. (Stuttgart: Klett, 1914); *Schlüssel zur Harmonielehre*, 4th ed. (Stuttgart: Klett, 1914).

9. *Harmonielehre von Rudolf Louis und Ludwig Thuille* (10th ed.), *Neubearbeitung* by Dr. Walter Courvoisier, Dr. Richard G'schrey, Gustav Geierhass, Dr. Karl Blessinger (Stuttgart: Klett, 1933). Riemann's T, S, and D replace the Roman numerals of the first edition, but many features of that edition are retained (for example, the "interpretation-dissonance"; see chapter 13, below).

10. Walter von Forster, "Heutige Praktiken in Harmonielehreunterricht an Musikhochschulen und Konservatorien," in *Beiträge zur Musiktheorie des 19. Jahrhnderts*, ed. Martin Vogel (Regensburg: Bosse Verlag, 1966). (Unter den Büchern, die als Lehrbehelfe empfohlen und verwendet werden, steht mit Abstand an erster Stelle die Harmonielehre von Louis-Thuille.)

11. See Peter Rummenhöller, *Musiktheoretisches Denken im 19. Jahrhundert*. Regensburg: Bosse Verlag, 1967, pp. 53ff.

12. Perhaps to differentiate his work from Helmholtz and Stumpf, Riemann calls his method "deductive" in one of his later works ("Ideen zu einer 'Lehre von den Tonvorstellungen,'" in *Jahrbuch der Musikbibliothek Peters für 1914/15* [Leipzig: C.F. Peters, 1916], p. 1). But for Rummenhöller, Riemann's notion of "deduction" is rather "induction at a higher level" (Rummenhöller, *Musiktheoretisches Denken*, p. 104).

13. For example, Seidel notes that one of Riemann's most famous theories—the three tonal functions—was developed in a "practical" book: *Vereinfachte Harmonielehre* (Seidel, "Harmonielehre," p. 40). The "practicality" of this book is not beyond question, however.

14. Louis/Thuille, *Harmonielehre*, p. V. (Unsere Harmonielehre will ein *praktisch-theoretisches* Lehrbuch sein. Dadurch unterscheidet sie sich einerseits von allen *rein wissenschaftlichen* Bearbeitungen des Gegenstandes, die ohne Rücksicht auf praktische Zwecke das theoretische Interesse allein im Auge haben, anderseits aber auch von allen jenen Methoden, für die der Harmonieunterricht in nichts anderem besteht als im mechanischen Eintrichtern einer *rein handwerksmässigen Technik* und die, alle rationale Begründung und Herleitung verschmähend, überhaupt ohne jegliche Theorie im eigentlichen Sinne des Wortes glauben auskommen zu können.)

15. Schenker, *Harmony*, p. xxv.

16. Like all of the "pre-Wagner" books, Richter is outmoded in Louis's estimation ("Unsere Harmonielehre," p. 431). Cf. Schenker's "Critique of Current Methods of Teaching" (*Harmony*, pp. 175ff), and Schoenberg's criticism of Richter's modulations (*Theory of Harmony*, p. 15).

17. Hugo Riemann, *Das Problem des harmonischen Dualismus* (Leipzig: Verlag von C.F. Kahnt Nachfolger, 1905), pp. 21f. (die *Durkonsonanz* in den *einfachsten Verhältnissen der Steigerung der Schwingungsgeschwindigkeit* ihr Wesen hat, die *Mollkonsonanz* dagegen auf den *einfachsten Verhältnissen der Vergrösserung der schwingenden Masse* (der Schallwellenlänge, Saitenlänge, etc.) beruht, so dass man kurzweg das Durprinzip in der

Notes for Chapter 12

wachsenden *Intensität* und das Mollprinzip in dem *zunehmenden Volumen* sehen kann.... Daher sind beide zahlenmässig am besten durch dieselbe einfache Zahlenreihe auszudrücken.)

18. Schenker, *Harmony*, p. xxvi. Cf. Rudolf Louis: "A harmonic theory which wishes to do justice to that which we actually hear can only accept as the basic or fundamental form of a chord that form in which the most important harmonic tone lies in the *bass*, or in Riemannian terms: the *minor-interpretation* is a phantasy-formation which absolutely never exists in reality, since it is never actually *heard*." (eine harmonische Theorie, die dem, was wir faktisch hören, gerecht werden will, kann nur diejenige Gestalt eines Zusammenklangs als seine Grund- oder Stammform annehmen, bei der der harmonisch wichtigste Ton im *Basse* liegt, oder Riemannisch gesprochen: die "*Mollauffassung*" von Zusammenklängen ist ein Phantasiegebilde, das in Wirklichkeit gar nicht existiert, weil es niemals faktisch *gehört* wird.) "Unsere Harmonielehre," p. 435.

19. Louis and Thuille, *Harmonielehre*, p. VI. (Anderseits begreift man aber auch bis zu einem gewissen Grade die Abneigung der Praktiker gegen alles und jedes Theoretisieren, wenn man bedenkt, dass harmonische Theorie bisher fast einzig und allein unter der Form harmonischer *Spekulation* aufgetreten war, d.h. als jene dogmatisch unkritische Art des Theoretisierens, deren Resultate schon deshalb für die Praxis, wenn nicht ganz unbrauchbar, so doch nur mit allervorsichtigster Auswahl zu benutzen sind, weil ihr jene "Erhfurcht vor den Tatsachen" mangelt, die es verhindert, dass der menschliche Geist willkürliche Gedankenkonstruktionen an die Stelle der realen Dinge setze und statt diese zu erklären mit den Ausgeburten siner eigenen ausschweifenden Phantasie sich beschäftige.

Demgegenüber waren wir mit ganz besonderem Eifer darauf bedacht, einen streng *empirischen* Standpunkt einzunehmen und aufs ängstlichste zu wahren.)

20. Ibid., pp. VIf. (Für die Harmonik, wie wir sie fassen, ist der Ausgangspunkt die möglichst treue und erschöpfende, durch keinerlei theoretisches Vorurteil beeinflusste Analyse dessen, was der Musiker unserer Zeit und unserer Kultur bei den musikalischen Zusammenklängen und ihren Verbindungen tatsächlich hört. Die unmittelbaren Aussagen des wirklichen musikalischen Empfindens und Auffassens liefern das Tatsachenmaterial, dessen vollständigste und einfachste "zusammenfassende Beschreibung" (...) die eigentliche Aufgabe der theoretischen Harmonielehre ist. Diese "Beschreibung" bekommt nun einen "rationalen" Charakter, d.h. sie wird zur "Erklärung" und "Deutung" eben dadurch, dass sie "zusammenfassend" verfährt und so eine Bewältigung der unerschöpflichen Fülle des Tatsächlichen durch das methodische Mittel der "Herleitung" bezw. "Zurückführung" ermöglicht.) The ellipsis in this quote is a reference to *Psychologie als Erfahrungswissenschaft* by Hans Cornelius (Leipzig: B.G. Teubner, 1897). The *Vorwort* to Cornelius's book states that the aim of the work is "the establishment of a *purely empirical* theory of psychic data under the *exclusion of all metaphysical assumptions*" (die Begründung einer *rein empirischen* Theorie der psychischen Thatsachen unter *Ausschluss aller metaphysischen Voraussetzungen*). The author goes on to note the agreement of certain of his ideas with such diverse authorities as William James and Ernst Mach. The rest of the description of empirical method in Louis's introduction is very much a paraphrase of Cornelius's ideas, which begin to sound like logical positivism.

21. Ibid., p.VIII.(... der *Rationalisierung* des Regelwesens..., um die *Gültigkeit der Regel und die Berechtigung der Ausnahme widerspruchlos nebeneinander behaupten zu können*.)

22. "Heinrich Schenker: Über Anton Bruckner" (a collection of various writings of Schenker on Bruckner put together by Jonas), *Der Dreiklang Monatsschrift für Musik*, vol. 7 (Vienna: Krystall-Verlag, Oct. 7, 1937), p. 168. (Wie sich aus dem Sinn der Regal zahllos Neues

ergeben kann, das, so frei es scheint, doch innerhalb der Regel ruht, hat Bruckner trotz seiner vielen Lehrjahre nicht erkannt.)

23. The investigation of *musikalisches Hören* forms the technical basis for any system of aesthetics (see Seidel, "Harmonielehre," p. 40). "Tonality" is thus a necessary condition of aesthetic value.

24. Schoenberg, *Theory of Harmony*, p. 12. "And I would be proud if, to adapt a familiar saying, I could say: 'I have *taken* from composition pupils a bad *aesthetics* and have *given* them in return a good *course in handicraft*.'"

Chapter 13

1. Rudolf Louis and Ludwig Thuille, *Harmonielehre*, (Stuttgart: Carl Grüninger, 1907), p. 2. (Die am leichtesten verständlichen und zugleich wichtigsten harmonischen *Elementarverhältnisse* ergeben sich dadurch, dass der Tonika-Dreiklang mit solchen Harmonien in Beziehung tritt, die einerseits einen deutlich ausgesprochenen *Gegensatz* zu ihm selbst bilden, anderseits aber auch wieder durch enge *Verwandtschaft* mit ihm verbunden sind.)

2. Ibid., p. 3. (Durch die drei Dreiklänge der *Tonika, Dominante* und *Unterdominante* ist die Tonart vollständig und erschöpfend bestimmt.)

3. Heinrich Schenker, *Kontrapunkt I*, in 2nd. vol. of *Neue Musikalische Theorien und Phantasien* (Vienna: Universal, 1910), pp. 35f.

4. August Halm, *Harmonielehre* (Leipzig: G.J. Göschen'sche Verlagshandlung, 1902), p. 14. (Die Musik ist ihrem Wesen nach Dissonanz, nämlich Leben und Bewegung, freilich Bewegung, die zur Ruhe führt, nicht aber das Verharren in der Ruhe! Die Einheit muß durch Gegensätze gewonnen werden, sie muß Resultat sein; die unveränderliche "Einheit und Ruhe in sich selbst" interessiert nicht.) It is interesting that this point of view, which may have its origin in Hauptmann, was to influence Kurth significantly.

5. Moritz Hauptmann, *Die Natur der Harmonik und der Metrik* (Leipzig: Breitkopf u. Härtel, 1853), p. 27.

6. See Elmar Seidel, "Die Harmonielehre Hugo Riemanns," in *Beiträge zur Musiktheorie des 19. Jahrhunderts*, ed. Vogel (Regensburg: Gustav Bosse Verlag, 1966), pp. 48f.

7. David Lewin brought this possibility to my attention. Seigfried Schmalzriedt cites other evidence of the influence of the dialectic on Halm's thinking in his introduction to a collection of Halm's essays (*Von Form und Sinn der Musik*, Schmalzriedt, ed. [Wiesbaden: Breitkopf u. Härtel, 1978]). In describing the sonata, for example, Halm says: "We may understand the return of the main theme group after the development best through the image of a spiral, which returns us again to the locale of earlier events, but not at the earlier level." (Das Wiederkehren der Hauptgruppen nach dem Durchführungsteil verstehen wir am besten unter dem Bild einer Spirale, die uns in die Nähe des früheren Ereignisses wieder zurückführt, aber nicht auf dem früheren Niveau.) (*Von Form und Sinn der Musik*, p. 7.) Schmalzriedt cites numerous correspondences of Halm's thought with Hegelian philosophy, which, according to Schmalzriedt, Halm first became acquainted with through his friendship with Gustav Wyneken, the author of a dissertation entitled *Hegels Kritik Kants* (1898). Whether Halm's music-theoretical use of the dialectic stems from his friendship with Wyneken or a knowledge of Hauptmann (or Riemann) is unclear. But whatever their origin, Halm's music-theoretical ideas are perfectly consistent with his other musical and philosophical views.

8. Halm, *Harmonielehre*, p. 32. (Weder ein gemeinschaftlicher Ton, noch ein Leitton bietet irgend eine von IV zu V weiterführende Potenz: zwischen beiden Akkorden ist eine Kluft.)

Notes for Chapter 13

9. Hugo Riemann, *Harmony Simplified* (London: Augener and Co., 1896), p. 7.

10. Louis/Thuille, *Harmonielehre*, p. 107. (Die uneigentliche Dominantbeziehung, in der die Nebendreiklänge und Nebenseptakkorde teils untereinander teils zu Hauptharmonien der Tonart stehen, tritt namentlich deutlich hervor in den Sequenzen von Dreiklängen oder Septakkorden mit quintweise fallendem (bezw. quartweise steigendem) Grundton.)

11. "Simon Sechter...sees in the progression of the subdominant triad to the leading-tone diminished triad a normal and typical harmonic movement!" (William C. Mickelsen, *Hugo Riemann's Theory of Harmony and History of Music Theory, Book III, by Hugo Riemann* (Lincoln and London: University of Nebraska Press, 1977, p. 235). Undoubtedly, this was the inspiration for Capellen's Sechter essay.

12. Louis/Thuille, *Harmonielehre*, p. 111.

13. See William Mitchell, "Chord and Context in 18th-Century Theory," *JAMS* (Summer 1963) 116, no. 2, 221-39.

14. Ibid., p. 227.

15. Louis/Thuille, *Harmonielehre*, p. 27. (Sextakkorde und Quartsextakkorde *können*, wie wir gesehen haben, durch Umkehrung von Dreiklängen entstehen. Darum ist aber doch noch keineswegs ein *jeder* Sextakkord oder Quartsextakkord als Dreiklangsumkehrung anzusehen. Vielmehr gibt es ausser der Umkehrung noch eine ganz *andere* Entstehungsweise dieser Akkordgebilde.)

16. Ibid., p. 29. (natürlicherweise mit der Umkehrung des Molldreiklangs c–g–h ganz und gar nichts zu tun hätte, sondern genau ebenso als eine *Vorhaltsbildung* anzusehen wäre wie in Beispiel 13-2b der *"Quartquintakkord"* g–c–d.)

17. Ibid. (*nicht im Sinne des Tonikadreiklangs* (als dessen Umkehrung) *aufzufassen wäre, sondern im Sinne des Dominantdreiklangs* (als Vorhalt vor diesem).)

18. Riemann, *Harmony Simplified*, trans. H. Bewerung (London: Augener and Co., 1896), p. 22.

19. Louis/Thuille, *Harmonielehre*, p. 29f. (Unter allen möglichen Arten von Vorhaltsbildungen nehmen diejenigen eine ganz besondere Stellung ein, bei denen auf solche Weise *scheinbar* konsonierende Akkorde, also namentlich *Sextakkorde* und *Quartsextakkorde* entstehen, die sich ihrem Aussehen nach in nichts von Umkehrungen konsonierender Dreiklänge unterscheiden. Diese Gebilde sind, *isoliert betrachtet*, durchaus *konsonant*. Aber der Zusammenhang, in dem sie auftreten, zwingt unserm Ohr eine *Auffassung* auf, in der sie tatsächlich als *dissonant* erscheinen. Wir müssen die betreffenden Zusammenklänge auf ein *Fundament* beziehen, zu dem jeweils einer oder auch mehrere ihrer Bestandteile dissonieren.)

20. Ibid., p. 30. (Man hat solche unter der äusseren Gestalt von konsonierenden Akkorden auftretende dissonierende Harmonien *Scheinkonsonanzen* genannt: denn ihre Konsonanz ist nur scheinbar. Noch bezeichnender für ihre Eigenart wäre vielleicht der Ausdruck: *Auffassungsdissonanz*, insofern nämlich ein solcher ausserhalb des musikalischen Zusammenhangs jederzeit konsonierender Akkord unter gewissen Umständen für die harmonische *Auffassung* dissonant werden kann.) The first sentence was changed to include Riemann's name in the third edition.

21. Louis/Thuille, *Harmonielehre*, 10th edition, p. 66. (Man kann sie *melodische* Sext- und Quartsextakkorde nennen.)

22. Mickelsen, *Hugo Riemann*, p. 219.

23. Hauptmann, *Die Natur der Harmonik*, pp. 64ff.

24. Although his explanation is somewhat different, Hellmut Federhofer also points out the inappropriateness of the term "leading-tone" in the present context. See his *Beiträge zur musikalischen Gestaltanalyse* (Graz, Innsbruck, Vienna: Akademischen Druck- u. Verlagsanstalt, 1950), pp. 11f. Also see chapter 1 of his *Akkord und Stimmführung in den Musiktheoretischen Systemen von Hugo Riemann, Ernst Kurth und Heinrich Schenker* (Vienna: Verlag der Oesterreichischen Akademie der Wissenschaften, 1981). Needless to say, the function theory excludes a priori the independent role of III as a link in the cycle of fifths. This defect is the basis for Ernst Kurth's criticism (*Musikpsychologie* [Berlin: Max Hesses Verlag, 1931], p. 220). Also see Heinrich Schenker's similar criticism (chapter 14, below).

25. Cf., Carl Dahlhaus: "The notion of 'feigning consonance' embraces phenomena which are so various that one doubts whether it is sensible that they be subsumed by the same category." *Untersuchungen über die Entstehung der harmonischen Tonalität*, p. 47. (Der Begriff der "Scheinkonsonanz" faßt Phänomene zusammen, die so verschieden sind, daß man zweifeln kann, ob es sinnvoll ist, sie der gleichen Kategorie zu subsumieren.)

26. Louis, "Zur Riemanns Besprechung," p. 615. (wir weit schärfer darauf hinweisen, wie der stellvertretende Charakter der Nebenharmonien sich durchaus nicht immer gleich bleibt....)

27. Louis/Thuille, *Harmonielehre*, p. 82. (Am klarsten offenbart sich die Unterdominantbedeutung des Dreiklangs der II. Stufe, wenn er in der ersten Umkehrung als Sextakkord auftritt.... Der Akkord bekommt dann eine gewisse Ähnlichkeit mit einem *auffassungsdissonanten* Sextakkord; die Sext erscheint als *Vorhalt* vor oder als *Durchgang nach* der Unterdominantquint.)

28. Ibid., p. 83. (Ganz in den Hintergrund tritt dagegen der auffassungsdissonante Charakter des Akkords, wenn er in der Grundstellung als *Dreiklang* angewendet wird.)

29. Ibid., p. 85 (wird ... jene andere *Auffassung* der Septharmonie der II. Stufe sich aufdrängen, die überhaupt weitaus die häufiger ist.... Unser Ohr, stets bereit, den Fundamentston zunächst im Bass zu suchen, wird jeden Septakkord in der Grundstellung gern so hören, dass der Basston als Grundton der Harmonie und demgemäss die Sept als Dissonanz zu diesem Grundton erscheint.)

30. Halm, *Harmonielehre*, pp. 59f. (Beim Spielen der beiden Beispiele wird ein harmonischer Unterschied nicht zu bemerken sein.... Daraus geht hervor, daß hier der "Dreiklang" III keine vollwertige Konsonanz, sondern unvollständige Dissonanz, nämlich Septharmonie der I. Stufe ist (mit verschwiegenem Grundton, der aber seine Macht doch nicht verliert); ferner, daß sowohl III als I7 Durchgangsbildungen sind, welche dem Fluß der Tonikaharmonie zu den Unterdominant ihr Dasein verdanken.)

31. Louis/Thuille *Harmonielehre*, pp. 39f (for consonant six-four). Perhaps as a result of the radical position the authors had taken with respect to the linear generation of chords, the order of presentation was changed in the third and subsequent editions, where the *consonant* six-four is discussed *before* dissonant usages. In regard to both, the discussion is one of the earliest, yet one of the most cogent. Although Schenker takes the authors to task for not recognizing his notion of the "boundary interval" *(Grenzintervall)*, his review of their efforts to discuss the dissonance of the fourth and sixth is largely complimentary (see *Kontrapunkt I*, pp. 167f).

32. Louis/Thuille, *Harmonielehre*, p. 58.

33. Ibid., p. 54. (Ja, *exklusive* Durchgangsauffassung wird beim Sextakkord überhaupt nur dann Platz greifen, wenn die Umkehrungsauffassung eine widernatürliche Fortschreitung wie z. B. V–IV ergeben würde. So hätte denn auch der Sextakkord über a bei 13-5b als Durchgangsbildung im weiteren Sinne des Wortes zu gelten trotz des abspringenden Basses.)

184 Notes for Chapter 14

34. Ibid., p. 55.
35. Ibid., p. 162. (Ein *Vorhalt vor dem Vorhalt* ist namentlich dann möglich, wenn der zweite Vorhalt unter der Form einer blossen *Auffassungsdissonanz* auftritt....)
36. Ibid., p. 171. (Hier ist es gewiss am natürlichsten, alle zwischen den verschiedenen Gestalten des Tonikadreiklangs auftretenden Harmonien als *durchgehend* anzusehen.)
37. Ibid., pp. 282f. (In Beispiel 13-8 haben wir eine durchgehende Akkordbewegung, die ihre harmonische Deutung dadurch erhält, dass wir in Gedanken das Fundament des Anfangsakkords unverändert beibehalten, d.h. dass wir alle durch die Durchgangsbewegung sich ergebenden Zusammenklänge auf ein und dasselbe Fundament (G = CV) beziehen.) Compare the section of Halm's *Harmonielehre* entitled "The Capacity to Persist. The Organpoint." (Das Beharrungsvermögen. Der Orgelpunkt) (pp. 102-6; see in particular example 82, pp. xxiv-v.)
38. Ibid., 3rd and later editions, p. 361. The analysis was added to the third edition by Louis. (Chromatische Durchgangsbewegung, die von der Dominante von H ausgeht und zu derselben Harmonie auch wieder zurückkehrt, also gewissermaßen die 6 Tacte hindurch "ideeller Orgelpunct" über Fis-Fundament.)
39. Ibid., pp. 329ff.

Chapter 14

1. Heinrich Schenker, *Harmony* (Chicago and London: University of Chicago Press, 1954), p. xxv.
2. Ibid., p. 39.
3. Ibid., p. 42.
4. Ibid., p. 46.
5. Schenker, *Neue Musikalische Theorien und Phantasien; Zweiter Band: Kontrapunkt* (Part I) (Vienna: Universal, 1910); (hereafter cited as *Kontrapunkt I*), p. XXIX. (Fast um dieselbe Zeit, da Fux sein Werk erscheinen ließ, trat nämlich in Frankreich Rameau mit der neuen Lehre von den Klangfunktionen auf, mit der Lehre von der Tonika, Dominante, Subdominante als Hauptklängen, von der Zurückführbarkeit aller übrigen klänge eben auf diese letzteren u.s.w.)
6. Ibid., p. XXXII. (eine neue, wirre große Welt von 'Leitetönen,' 'Verdopplungen' wird uns vorgetäuscht, von denen die wahre Stimmführungs- und die wahre Stufenlehre nichts wissen kann!)
7. Ibid., p. 36. (wenn man dessen einzelnen Stufen, ausgenommen die I., IV., und V., ihre eigene Selbständigkeit, gerade damit aber zugleich auch den Reiz ihrer vielfältigen Funktion raubt?)
8. Ibid., pp. 36-37. (wieviel besser es dem wahren Sinne der Komposition entspricht, z. B. die III. Stufe just in ihren verschiedenen Funktionen zu verstehen: wie sie erstens bald als vierte Oberquint (gemäß dem Quintenprinzip, Bd. I,§14–19) der Tonika gegenübertritt, zweitens bald aber auch (gemäß dem Terzenprincip- vgl. Bd. I. §126) als Vorläufer der I. oder drittens der V. Stufe zu gelten hat....)
9. Ibid., p. 40. (Man entfernt sich eben allzusehr von der Kunst und geht entschieden zu weit im Spekulieren, wenn man solche und ähnliche Quintfälle, wie z. B. eben II–V oder dergleichen von den Komponisten meist nur in leeren Sequenzen und Rückbeziehungen angewendet glaubt.)

10. Schenker, *Free Composition (Der freie Satz)*, trans. and ed., Ernst Oster (New York and London: Longman Inc. and AMS, 1979); see §283, "Additional fifth-interpolations as harmonic degrees," pp. 116–17.
11. Ibid., p. 31.
12. Schenker, *Harmony*, p. 38.
13. Schoenberg, *Theory of Harmony*, p. 23.
14. David Lewin, "Inversional Balance as an Organizing Force in Schoenberg's Music and Thought," *PNM* 6. no. 1 (1967):3. Schoenberg's chart of regions may be found on p. 20 of *Structural Functions of Harmony*.
15. Schoenberg, *Theory of Harmony*, p. 38. Of course, the terms were common currency before Riemann's "formalization" of substitution.
16. Ibid., p. 39.
17. Ibid., p. 52.
18. Ibid., p. 113.
19. Ibid.; see the examples on p. 113, but especially example 73b on p. 117, which shows V–IV.
20. Ibid., p. 116.
21. Ibid., p. 117.
22. Ibid., p. 118.
23. Ibid., p. 119. One wonders what Schenker might have thought of this assessment of his "developmental" fifth.
24. Ibid., p. 120.
25. Ibid.
26. Dika Newlin, *Bruckner-Mahler-Schoenberg*, revised edition (New York: Norton, 1978), p. 244. Also see pp. 47–53.
27. Schenker, *Harmony*, p. 232. Jonas notes that, "In characterizing step progression by seconds as 'artificial,' Schenker anticipates his later theory, according to which this kind of step progression is relegated to the field of voice leading." In this sense, Viennese fundamental bass theory anticipated Schenker's later theory.
28. Ibid., p. 235.
29. Ibid.
30. Ibid., p. 236.
31. Ibid., pp. 237ff.
32. Schoenberg, *Theory of Harmony*, pp. 222ff.
33. Ibid., pp. 98ff.
34. Schenker, *Harmony*, p. 86.
35. Schoenberg, *Theory of Harmony*, pp. 345ff.; *Structural Functions of Harmony*, p. 4.
36. Schenker, *Harmony*, pp. 190ff and pp. 203ff.

Notes for Chapter 14

37. Ibid., p. 192.
38. Schoenberg, *Theory of Harmony*, p. 196.
39. Sechter, *Grundsätze I*, p. 157. Cf. chapter 6, above, note 7. The term "Stufen" was obviously common long before Schenker's redefinition.
40. Ibid. ("in einer solchen Ordnung folgen, damit jeder selbständig sein könne.")
41. *Albrechtsberger's Collected Writings* (Novello translation), pp. 58f.
42. Schenker, *Harmony*, p. 256. "Tonicalization" and "Tonicization" are of course synonomous; we have chosen to use Sessions's more generally accepted translation.
43. See Schoenberg's footnote which compares the two views; *Theory of Harmony*, pp. 427ff.
44. Schenker, *Harmony*, p. 288.
45. Ibid., pp. 279f.
46. Riemann characterized Schoenberg's book as "a peculiar hodgepodge of reactionary compositional rules derived from S. Sechter's method, and the radical negation of all norms!" in *Handbuch der Musikgeschichte* (Leipzig:1913), vol. II:254. (ein seltsames Gemengsel rückständiger, aus S. Sechters Methode stammernder Satzregeln und radikaler Negation alles Normativen!). Ironically, Schenker's reaction to this (diary entry of May 17, 1913) was: "In the *Handbuch der Musikgeschichte* Riemann excluded me, but not Schoenberg, who derived his work [the *Harmonielehre*] from me! This foolishness will yet be avenged!" Quoted after H. Federhofer, "Heinrich Schenkers Verhältnis zu Arnold Schönberg" (Vienna:1981), pp. 381f. (Riemann verschweigt im Handbuch der Musikgeschichte just mich, nicht aber Schönberg, der sein Werk von mir abgeleitet! Die Frivolität soll noch geahndet werden.)
47. The recent Schenker-oriented harmony books come to mind immediately; we also note that all augmented-sixth chords are now derived from II in the latest edition of the Piston harmony book (Piston/De Voto, *Harmony*, 4th ed.). The book still contains errors in fundamental bass reading, however (see example 23-20, p. 355).
48. Schoenberg, *Theory of Harmony*, p. 337. Among the examples are Sechter's "artificial" (passing) six-four and passing "III."
49. Ibid., p. 329.
50. For example, in the summary of harmony given in *Structural Functions* (chapter 2), the first rule for treatment of the chordal seventh is that it "usually descends one step to become the third or fifth of the following harmony, or is held over to become its octave" (p. 5). II7 moving to II6 illustrates the latter alternative.
51. Schenker criticized Schoenberg's isolation of "dissonant chords" from tonal compositions (*Theory of Harmony*, pp. 322ff) in his essay "Fortsetzung der Urlinie-Betrachtungen" in *Das Meisterwerk in der Musik* (2:199ff in Kalib's translation). The secondary literature describing this polemic includes: C. Dahlhaus, "Schoenberg and Schenker"; J. Dunsby, "Schoenberg and the Writings of Schenker, *Journal of the Arnold Schoenberg Institute* (2[1977]:26-33); B. Simms, "New Documents in the Schoenberg-Schenker Polemic," *PNM* (16, no. 1 [1977]:110-24); and Federhofer (see note 46).
52. Schenker, *Harmony*, p. 139.
53. Ibid., p. 141.

54. Ibid., pp. 141–53. August Halm expresses a similar opinion in his rather belated review of Schenker's *Neue Musikalische Theorien und Phantasien:* "Perhaps the main theory is Schenker's notion of 'scale-step.' Now, that there are chords which are more or less important, deliberate, and incidental (I mean harmonically, not artistically incidental), [and] likewise that there are apparent and real, inauthentic, and genuine modulations; certainly, this was known before Schenker. In spite of that, I believe that he illuminates harmonic events more effectively with his ideas...." (*Der Merker,* xi (1920):417.) (Nun, daß es mehr oder weniger ernstgemeinte, daß es gewollte und zufällige (ich meine harmonisch, nicht künstlerisch zufällige) Akkorde, desgleichen, daß es scheinbare und wirkliche, uneigentliche und echte Modulationen gibt: gewiß, das wußte man auch schon vor Schenker. Trotzdem glaube ich, daß er mit seinen Begriffen die harmonischen Geschehnisse noch wirksamer erhellt....)

55. Mickelsen's idea that Schenker's *Stufen* might come from Riemann is doubtful (see Mickelsen, *Hugo Riemann,* p. 96).

56. Schoenberg, *Theory of Harmony,* p. 389.

Bibliography

Books

Albrechtsberger, J. G. *Anweisung zur Komposition*, Leipzig: Breitkopf, 1790. Sections translated in Alfred Mann's *The Study of Fugue*. New York: Norton, 1965.
_____. *Generalbassschule, Neue vom Verfasser vermehrte Auflage*. Leipzig: Peters, n.d. This is presumably the same edition which was reprinted by Artaria, Vienna: 1805.
_____. *Kurzgefasste Methode den Generalbass zu erlernen*. Vienna: Artaria, n.d. (listed by Thomson as 1793).
_____. *Sämtliche Schriften über Generalbass, Harmonielehre und Tonsetzkunst*. Seyfried, ed. Vienna: Anton Strauss, n.d. Second edition, Vienna: 1837. Translated as *Methods of Harmony, Figured Base, and Composition*. Seyfried, ed., Merrick, trans. London: Cocks and Co., n.d. (1834); and *J.G. Albrechtsberger's Collected Writings on Thorough-bass, Harmony and Composition, for Self-Instruction*. Seyfried, ed., Novello, trans. London: Novello, Ewer, and Co., 1855.
Alembert, Jean le Rond d'. *Elémens de la musique*. Paris: Durand, 1752. 2nd expanded edition, Lyon: 1762. First edition translated and enlarged by Marpurg as *Systematische Einleitung in die musikalische Setzkunst*. Leipzig: 1757.
Bruckner, Anton. *Vorlesungen über Harmonie und Kontrapunkt an der Universität Wien*. Edited by Ernst Schwanzara. Vienna: Oesterreichische Bundesverlag für Unterricht, Wissenschaft und Kunst, 1950.
Capellen, Georg. *Fortschrittliche Harmonie- und Melodielehre*. Leipzig: C. F. Kahnt Nachfolger, 1908.
_____. *Ist das System S. Sechters ein geeigneter Ausgangspunkt für die Wagnerforschung?* Leipzig: C. F. Kahnt, 1902.
Catel, Charles Simon. *Traité D'Harmonie*. Paris: 1802.
Dahlhaus, Carl. *Untersuchungen über die Entstehung der harmonischen Tonalität*. Kassel: Bärenreiter, 1968.
Daube, Johann Friedrich. *Anleitung zum Selbstunterricht in der musikalischen Composition*. Vienna: Schaumburg, 1797. *Zweiter Teil*. Vienna: Tauvelt/J. Funk, 1798.
_____. *Generalbass in drey Accorden*. Leipzig: Breitkopf, 1756.
Decsey, Ernst. *Bruckner, Versuch eines Lebens*. Berlin: Schuster and Loeffler, 1919.
Dehn, S.W. *Theoretisch-praktische Harmonielehre mit angefügten Generalbassbeispielen*. Berlin: Thomes, 1840.
Deutsch, O.E. *Schubert, die Erinnerungen seiner Freunde*. Leipzig: Breitkopf u. Härtel, 1957.
_____. *The Schubert Reader*. Translated by Eric Blom. New York: Norton, 1947.
Drechsler, Joseph. *Harmonie- und Generalbass-Lehre*. Vienna: 1816.
Dürrnberger, Johann August. *Elementar-Lehrbuch der Harmonie-und Generalbass-Lehre*. Linz: 1841.

Bibliography

Eckstein, Friedrich. *Erinnerungen an Anton Bruckner.* Vienna, N.Y.: Universal, 1923.
Eicke, Kurt-Erich. *Der Streit zwischen Adolf Bernhard Marx und Gottfried Wilhelm Fink um die Kompositionslehre.* Regensburg: Bosse Verlag, 1966.
Federhofer, Hellmut. *Akkord u. Stimmführung in den Musiktheoretischen Systemen von Hugo Riemann, Ernst Kurth u. Heinrich Schenker.* Vienna: Verlag der Osterreichischen Akademie der Wissenschaften, 1981.
_____. *Beiträge zur musikalischen Gestaltanalyse.* Graz, Innsbruck, Vienna: Akademische Druck- und Verlagsanstalt, 1950.
Fétis, F.J. *Traité complet de la Théorie et de la Practique de l'Harmonie.* Paris: Braudus et Cie, 1844.
Förster, Emanuel Aloys. *Anleitung zum Generalbass.* Vienna: A. Steiner, 1805. 2nd expanded edition. Vienna: Artaria, 1823.
Forte, Allen. *Tonal Harmony in Concept and Practice.* 3rd edition. New York: Holt, Rinehart, and Winston, 1979.
Güldenstein, Gustav. *Theorie der Tonart.* Basel, Stuttgart: Schwabe u. Co. Verlag, 1973.
Groth, Renate. *Die französische Kompositionslehre des 19. Jahrhunderts.* Wiesbaden: Franz Steiner, 1983
Habert, Johannes Ev. *Beiträge zur Lehre von der musikalischen Komposition; erstes Buch. Harmonielehre.* Leipzig: Breitkopf u. Härtel, 1899.
Halm, August. *Harmonielehre.* Leipzig: G.J. Göschen'sche Verlagshandlung, 1902. Neudruck, 1905.
_____. *Von Form und Sinn der Musik.* Seigfried Schmalzriedt ed. Wiesbaden: Breitkopf u. Härtel, 1978.
_____. *Von Grenzen und Ländern der Musik. Gesammelte Aufsätze.* Munich: Georg Müller, 1916.
Hasel, Johann Emerich. *Die Grundsätze des Harmoniesystems. Ein vollständig umfassendes Lehrbuch über den Bau, die Verbindung und die chromatische Umgestaltung aller Accorde auf ihren unveränderlich diatonischen Fundamenten nebst einer Anleitung zur Analyse der vorhandenen Harmonie-Complicationen.* Vienna: V. Kratochwill, 1892.
Hauptmann, Moritz. *Die Natur der Harmonik und der Metrik,* Leipzig: Breitkopf u. Härtel, 1853.
Helmholtz, Hermann von. *Die Lehre von den Tonempfindungen.* Brunswick: F. Vieweg, 1863. Translated and revised by John Alexander Ellis as *On the Sensations on Tone.* London: Longmans, Green, and Co., 1875. Reprinted with a new introduction by H.Margenau. New York: Dover, 1954.
Hoffman, Joachim. *Harmonie (Generalbass-) Lehre.* Vienna: 1846.
Jadassohn, Salomon. *Lehrbuch der Harmonie.* Leipzig: Breitkopf u. Härtel, 1883, and many subsequent editions. Translated by Theodore Baker as *A Manual of Harmony.* New York: G. Schirmer, 1893.
_____. *Melodik und Harmonik bei Richard Wagner.* Berlin: Verlagsgesellschaft für Literatur und Kunst, n.d. (1899 according to Kurth.)
Kirnberger, Johann Philipp. *Gedanken über die verschiedenen Lehrarten in der Composition.* Berlin: 1782. Also Vienna: 1793.
_____. *Grundsätze des Generalbasses.* Berlin: J. J. Hummel, probably 1781. Vienna: Musicalisch-typographische Gesellschaft, ca. 1793.
_____. *Die Kunst des reinen Satzes in der Musik.* 2 vol. Berlin, Königsberg: Decker and Hartung, 1771–79. Vienna: Musicalisch-typographische Gesellschaft, 1793. *The Art of Strict Composition,* David Beach and Jurgen Thym, trans. New Haven and London: Yale University Press, 1982.
_____. *Die wahren Grundsätze zum Gebrauche der Harmonie.* Actually written by J.A.P. Schulz. Berlin and Königsberg: Decker & Hartung, 1773. Also Vienna: chem. Drukerey, 1793. "The True Principles for the Practice of Harmony," trans. David Beach and Jurgen Thym. *JMT* 23, no. 2 (Fall 1979): 163–225.

Kistler, Cyrill. *Harmonielehre für Lehrer und Lernende.* Munich: 1879. 2nd edition published as *Harmonielehre für Lehrende, Lernende und zum wirklichen Selbstunterrichte.* Bad Kissingen: 1898. The 2nd edition was also published in English.
Klose, Friedrich. *Meine Lehrjahre bei Bruckner.* Regensburg: Bosse Verlag, 1927.
Knecht, Justin Heinrich. *Allgemeiner Katechismus. Oder kurzer Inbegriff der allgemeinen Musiklehre.* Vienna: Haslinger, n.d. *Neueste, verbesserte und vermehrte Ausgabe.* Vienna: Steiner & Co., 1822.
———. *Elementarwerk der Harmonie.* Munich: 1814.
———. *Theoretisch, praktische Generalbassschule.* 2nd edition. Bozen: 1838.
Krenn, Franz. *Generalbass-(Harmonie-) Lehre zum Selbstunterrichte.* Vienna: Haslinger Witwe u. Sohn, 1845.
Kurth, Ernst. *Musikpsychologie.* Berlin: Max Hesses Verlag, 1931.
———. *Romantische Harmonik und ihre Krise in Wagner's "Tristan."* Berlin: 1923.
———. *Die Voraussetzungen der theoretischen Harmonik und der tonalen Darstellungssysteme.* Bern: Max Drechsel, 1913. See "Rothfarb" for translation.
La Mara, editor. *Briefe hervorragender Zeitgenossen an Franz Liszt.* 3 vol. Leipzig: Breitkopf u. Härtel, 1895–1904.
Lobe, Johann Christian. *Lehrbuch der musikalischen Komposition.* 4 vol. Leipzig: Breitkopf u. Härtel, 1855–67.
Logier, J.B. *A system of the Science of Music and Practical Composition.* London: 1827.
Louis, Rudolf. *Anton Bruckner.* Berlin: Gose u. Tetzlaft Verlagsbuchhandlung, 1904.
———. *Grundriss der Harmonielehre.* 5th edition. Stuttgart: Klett, 1914.
———. *Schlüssel zur Harmonielehre.* 4th ed. Stuttgart: Klett, n.d.
———, and Thuille, Ludwig. *Harmonielehre.* Stuttgart: Carl Grüninger, 1907. 7th ed. Stuttgart: 1920. 10th ed., Neubearbeitung von Courvoisier, G'schrey, Geirerhaas, und Blessinger. Stuttgart: Ernst Klett Verlag, 1933.
Maier, Elisabeth and Zamazal, Franz. *Anton Bruckner und Leopold von Zenetti.* Graz: Akademische Druck- u. Verlagsanstalt, 1980.
Mann, Alfred. *The Study of Fugue.* New York: Norton, 1965.
Markus, J.C. *Simon Sechter, ein biographisches Denkmal.* Vienna: Alfred Hölder, 1888.
Marpurg, Friedrich Wilhelm. *Abhandlung von der Fuge.* Berlin: 1753–54. Edited by Simon Sechter. Vienna: Anton Diabelli and Co., n.d.
———. *Handbuch bey dem Generalbasse und der Composition.* 4 vol. Berlin: 1755–60.
———. *Historisch-kritische Beyträge zur Aufnahme der Musik.* 5 vol. Berlin: 1754–58.
———. *Versuch über die Musikalische Temperatur.* Berlin: J.F. Kirn, 1776.
Marx, A.B. *Die Lehre von der musikalischen Komposition.* 4 vol. Leipzig: 1837–47.
Mattheson, Johann. *Der vollkommene Capellmeister.* Hamburg: 1739.
Mayrberger, Karl. *Die Harmonik Richard Wagner's an den Leitmotiv aus "Tristan und Isolde" erläutert.* Bayreuth: 1882. The first part originally appeared in *Bayreuther Blätter* 4 (1881):169–80.
———. *Drei Wandtafeln über das diatonische und enharmonische Modulationsverfahren mittelst der verminderten Septimenharmonien (der sogenannten enharmonischen Akkorde).* Pressburg and Leipzig: Carl Stempel, 1880.
———. *Lehrbuch der musikalischen Harmonik.* Pressburg and Leipzig: Gustav Heckenast, 1878.
Mickelsen, William C. *Hugo Riemann's Theory of Harmony* (a study by Mickelsen) and *History of Music Theory, Book III, by Hugo Riemann* (translated and edited by Mickelsen). Lincoln and London: University of Nebraska Press, 1977.
Moser, J.N. *Johannes Evangelist Habert 1833–1896; Ein oberösterreichischer Komponist und Musiktheoretiker.* Graz: published by the author, 1976.
Müller, Carl Christian. *Tables for the writing of elementary exercises in the study of harmony. Arranged in conformity with S. Sechter's "Fundamental Harmonies," and adapted for the New York college of music.* New York: W.A. Pond, ca. 1882–86.

Munter, Friedrich. *Ludwig Thuille, Ein erster Versuch.* Munich: Drei Masken Verlag, 1923.
Newlin, Dika. *Bruckner-Mahler-Schoenberg.* Revised edition. New York: Norton, 1978.
Nottebohm, G. *Beethoveniana II.* Leipzig: 1872.
Orel, Alfred. *Ein Harmonielehrekolleg bei Anton Bruckner.* Berlin-Vienna-Zurich: Verlag für Wirtschaft und Kultur, Payer & Co., 1940.
Piston, Walter. *Harmony.* 4th edition, revised and expanded by Mark DeVoto. New York: Norton, 1978.
Preindl, Joseph. *Wiener-Tonschule; oder Anweisung zum Generalbasse, zur Harmonie, zum Contrapuncte und der Fugen-Lehre.* Vienna: T. Haslinger, 1827.
Rameau, Jean-Philippe. *Treatise on Harmony.* Translated by Philip Gossett. New York: Dover, 1971.
Reger, Max. *Beiträge zur Modulationslehre.* Leipzig: 1903.
Reich, Willi. *Schoenberg; a Critical Biography.* N.Y.: Praeger, 1971.
Reicha, Anton. *Die Kunst der dramatischen Komposition.* Translated by Carl Czerny. Vienna: Diabelli, n.d. Listed by Austrian National Library as 1830.
_____. *Vollständiges Lehrbuch der Harmonielehre, des Generalbasses, der Melodie.* Translated by Carl Czerny. Vienna: Diabelli, 1833.
_____. *Vollständiges Lehrbuch der Komposition.* Translated by Carl Czerny. Vienna: Diabelli, 1834.
Richter, Ernst Friedrich. *Lehrbuch der Harmonie.* Leipzig: 1853.
Riemann, Hugo. *Handbuch der Harmonielehre.* Leipzig: Breitkopf u. Härtel, 1906.
_____. *History of Music Theory, Book III.* See "Mickelsen."
_____. *Musicalische Syntaxis.* Leipzig: Breitkopf u. Härtel, 1877.
_____. *Musik-Lexikon.* Leipzig: 1909.
_____. *Das Problem des harmonischen Dualismus. Ein Beitrag zur Ästhetik der Musik.* Leipzig: Verlag von C.F. Kahnt Nachfolger, 1905. Article originally in *Neue Zeitschrift für Musik* (1905), no. 1–4.
_____. *Vereinfachte Harmonielehre, oder die Lehre von den Tonalen Funktionen der Akkorde.* London: Augener and Co., 1893. Translated by H. Bewerung as *Harmony Simplified.* London: Augener and Co., 1896.
Rummenhöller, Peter. *Musiktheoretisches Denken im 19. Jahrhundert.* Regensburg: Bosse Verlag, 1967.
Salzmann, Gottfried. *Lehrbuch der Tonkunst.* Vienna: 1842.
Schenker, Heinrich. *Harmonielehre.* 1st vol. of *Neue Musikalische Theorien und Phantasien.* Vienna: Universal, 1906. Abridged translation by Elisabeth Mann Borgese, edited and annotated by Oswald Jonas, appeared as *Harmony.* Chicago & London: University of Chicago Press, 1954.
_____. *Kontrapunkt. Erster Teil.* In 2nd vol. of *Neue Musikalische Theorien und Phantasien.* Vienna: Universal, 1910.
_____. *Das Meisterwerk in der Musik II.* Munich, Vienna, Berlin: Drei Masken Verlag, 1926. See "Kalib" for translation.
Schilling, G. *Enzyclopädie der gesammten musikalischen Wissenschaften, o. Universal-Lexicon.* Stuttgart, 1838.
Schoenberg, Arnold. *Structural Functions of Harmony.* New York: Norton, 1969.
_____. *Theory of Harmony.* Translated by Roy E. Carter. Berkeley: University of California Press, 1978. *Harmonielehre.* 1st edition. Vienna: Universal, 1911. 3rd edition, 1922.
Schreyer, Johannes. *Von Bach bis Wagner.* Dresden: Holze und Bahl, 1903. Later rewritten and published as *Lehrbuch der Harmonie....*
Sechter, Simon. *Generalbassschule.* Vienna: 1830.

_____. *Die Grundsätze der musikalischen Komposition.* 3 vol. Leipzig: Breitkopf u. Härtel, 1853--54. First volume edited and translated by Carl Christian Müller as *The correct order of fundamental harmonies: a treatise on fundamental basses, and their inversions and substitutes.* New York: W.A. Pond, 1871. 12th ed., 1912.
Sechter-Eckstein. *Das Finale von W.A. Mozarts Jupiter-Symphonie.* Vienna: Wiener Philharmonischer Verlag A.G., 1923.
Sessions, Roger. *Harmonic Practice.* New York: Harcourt, Brace, and World, Inc., 1951.
Seyfried, I. Ritter von, editor. *Ludwig van Beethovens Studien im Generalbasse, Contrapuncte und in der Compositionslehre.* 2nd ed. Leipzig/Hamburg/NY: 1853.
Shirlaw, Matthew. *The Theory of Harmony.* London: Novello, 1917.
Stockhausen, Ernst von. *Die harmonische Grundlage von 12 Fugen aus Joh. Seb. Bach Wohltempirtem Klavier sowie der As moll-Orgelfugue von J. Brahms nach den Grundsätzen von S. Sechter dargestellt und erläutert.* Leipzig: Breitkopf u. Härtel, n.d. (ca. 1901 according to New York Public Library).
Swoboda, August. *Harmonielehre.* Vienna: 1828.
Thomson, Ulf. *Voraussetzungen und Artungen der österreichischen Generalbasslehre zwischen Albrechtsberger und Sechter.* Tutzing: Hans Schneider, 1978.
Tittel, Ernst. *Harmonielehre.* Vienna: Doblinger, 1965.
_____. *Die Wiener Musik Hochschule.* Vienna: Verlag Elisabeth Lafite, 1967.
Türk, Daniel Gottlob. *Anweisung zum Generalbassspielen.* Vienna: Typo.-Musikalische Ges., 1807. Various other editions also exist.
_____. *Von den wichtigsten Pflichten eines Organisten.* Halle: 1787.
Vogel, Martin, ed. *Beiträge zur Musiktheorie des 19. Jahrhundert.* Regensburg: Gustav Bosse Verlag, 1966.
_____. *Der Tristan-Akkord und die Krise der modernen Harmonielehre.* Düsseldorf: Verlag der Gesellschaft zur Förderung der systematischen Musikwissenschaft, e.V., 1962.
Vogler, Abbé Georg Joseph. *Choral-System.* Copenhagen: 1800 and Offenbach: n.d.
_____. *Handbuch zur Harmonielehre und fuer den Generalbaß nach den Grundsaetzen der Mannheimer Tonschule.* Prague: 1802.
_____. *Kuhrpfälzische Tonschule.* Mannheim: 1778.
_____. *Tonwissenschaft und Tonsezkunst.* Mannheim: 1776.
Wagner, Manfred. *Die Harmonielehren der ersten Hälfte des 19. Jahrhunderts.* Regensburg: Gustav Bosse Verlag, 1974.
Weber, Gottfried. *Versuch einer geordneten Theorie der Tonsetzkunst.* 3 vol. Mainz: 1817–24.
Weitzmann, C.F. *Harmoniesystem.* Leipzig: C.F. Kahnt, 1860.
Wirth, Franz. *Untersuchungen zur Entstehung der deutschen Praktischen Harmonielehre.* Munich: 1966.
Zeleny, Walter. *Die historischen Grundlagen des Theoriesystems von Simon Sechter.* Wiener Veröffentlichungen zur Musikwissenschaft, vol. 10. Tutzing: Hans Schneider, 1979.
Ziehn, Bernhard. *Harmonie- und Modulationslehre.* Berlin: 1887. Rewritten in English as *Manual of Harmony.* Milwaukee: 1907.

Articles

Arend, Max. "Harmonische Analyse des Tristanvorspiels." *Bayreuther Blätter* 24 (1901):160–69.
Beach, David Williams. "The Functions of the Six-Four Chord in Tonal Music." *JMT* 11, no. 1 (Spring 1967):2–31.
_____. "The Origins of Harmonic Analysis." *JMT* 18 (Fall 1974):274–307.
Capellen, Georg. "Harmonik und Melodik bei Richard Wagner." *Bayreuther Blätter* 25 (1902):3–10.

Bibliography

Caplin, William Earl. "Harmony and Meter in the Theories of Simon Sechter." *Music Theory Spectrum* 2 (1980):74–89.
Christensen, Tom. "The Schichtenlehre of Hugo Riemann." *In Theory Only* 6, no. 4 (May 1982):37–44.
Dahlhaus, Carl. "Schoenberg and Schenker." *PRMA* 100 (1973–74):209–15.
──────. "Über den Begriff der tonalen Funktion." In *Beiträge zur Musiktheorie des 19. Jahrhunderts*, edited by Martin Vogel. Regensburg: Gustav Bosse Verlag, 1966.
Dunsby, Jonathan M. "Schoenberg and the Writings of Schenker." *Journal of the Arnold Schoenberg Institute* II (1977):26–33.
──────. "Schoenberg on Cadence." *Journal of the Arnold Schoenberg Institute* 4, no. 1 (June 1980):41–49.
Ergo, Emil. "Über Wagner's Harmonik und Melodik." *Bayreuther Blätter* 35 (1912):34–41, 138–49, 293–308.
Erwin, Charlotte E. and Simms, Bryan. "Schoenberg's Correspondence with Heinrich Schenker." *Journal of the Arnold Schoenberg Institute* 5, no. 1 (June 1981):23–43.
Federhofer, Hellmut. "Die Funktionstheorie Hugo Riemanns und die Schichtenlehre Heinrich Schenkers." From *Bericht über den internationalen musikwissenschaftlichen Kongress Wien*. Graz/Köln: Verlag Hermann Böhlaus Nachfolger, 1956.
──────. "Heinrich Schenkers Bruckner-Verständnis." *Archiv für Musikwissenschaft* XXXIX. Jahrgang, Heft 3 (1982) 3. Quartal: 198-217.
──────. "Heinrich Schenkers Verhältnis zu Arnold Schoenberg." Reprint from *Anzeiger der phil.-hist. Klasse der Osterreichischen Akademie der Wissenschaften*. Vienna: 1981, 118–23.
Flotzinger, Rudolf. "Bruckner als Theorielehrer an der Universität." In *Anton Bruckner in Lehre und Forschung*. Regensburg: Bosse Verlag, 1976.
──────. "Rafael Loidols Theorie Kolleg bei Bruckner 1879/80." In *Bruckner-Studien*, edited by Othmar Wessely. Vienna: Verlag der Oesterreichischen Akademie der Wissenschaften, 1975.
Forster, Walter von. "Heutige Praktiken im Harmonielehreunterricht an Musikhochschulen und Konservatorien." In *Beiträge zur Musiktheorie des 19. Jahrhunderts*, edited by Martin Vogel. Regensburg: Bosse Verlag, 1966.
Goehr, Alexander. "The Theoretical Writings of Arnold Schoenberg." *PNM* 13, 2 (Spring-Summer 1975):3–16.
Grant, Cecil Power. "The Real Relationship between Kirnberger's and Rameau's Concept of the Fundamental Bass." *JMT* 21, 2 (Fall 1977):324–38.
Grave, Floyd K. "Abbé Vogler and the Study of Fugue." *Music Theory Spectrum* I (1979):41–66.
──────. "Abbé Vogler's Theory of Reduction." *Current Musicology* 29 (1980):41–69.
Halm, August. "Heinrich Schenkers 'Neue musikalische Theorien und Phantasien.'" *Der Merker* xi (1920):414–17, 505–7.
Hynais, Cyrill. "Die Harmonik R. Wagner's in Bezug auf die Fundamentaltheorie Sechter's." *Neue Musikalische Presse* X (1901) 4:50–52, 5:67–69, 6:81–82, 7:97–100.
Jonas, Oswald. "Die Krise der Musiktheorie." In *Der Dreiklang Monatsschrift für Musik*, vol. 3. Vienna: Krystall-Verlag, June 1937.
──────, editor. "Heinrich Schenker: Über Anton Bruckner." In *Der Dreiklang Monatsschrift für Musik*, vol. 7. Vienna: Krystall-Verlag, Oct. 7, 1937.
Landon, Christa. "New Schubert Finds." *Music Review* 31, no. 1 (1970):215–31.
Leibnitz, Thomas. "Josef Schalk; Ein Wagnerianer zwischen Anton Bruckner und Hugo Wolf." *Bruckner Jahrbuch 1980*. Linz: 1980.
Lewin, David. "Inversional Balance as an Organizing Force in Schoenberg's Music and Thought." *Perspectives of New Music* (1967) 6, no. 1:1ff.
Louis, Rudolf. "Unsere Harmonielehre." *Süddeutsche Monatshefte* (1906) 10:430–37.
──────. "Zu Hugo Riemanns Besprechung der Louis-Thuilleschen Harmonielehre." *Süddeutsche Monatshefte* (1907) 5:614–20.

Mann, Alfred. "Schubert's Lesson with Sechter." *Nineteenth Century Music* 6, no. 2 (Fall 1982):59–65.
Mann, Michael. "Schenker's Contribution to Music Theory." *The Music Review* (1949) 10:3–26.
Mitchell, William J. "Chord and Context in 18th-Century Theory." *JAMS* 16, no. 2 (Summer 1963):221–39.
———. "The Study of Chromaticism." *JMT* (1962) 6, 1:2–31.
———. "The Tristan Prelude: Techniques and Structure." In *The Music Forum*, vol. 1. New York and London: Columbia University Press, 1967.
Morgan, Robert P. "Schenker and the Theoretical Tradition." *College Music Symposium* 18, no. 1 (Spring 1978):72–96.
Musgrave, Michael. "Schoenberg and Theory." *Journal of the Arnold Schoenberg Institute* 4, no. 1 (June 1980):34–40.
Reich, Willi. "Simon Sechter im eigenen Wort." *Neue Zeitschrift für Musik* 132, no. 10 (1971):539–41.
Riemann, Hugo. "Eine neue Harmonielehre: Harmonielehre von Rudolf Louis u. Ludwig Thuille." *Süddeutsche Monatshefte* 4 (1907):500–504.
———. "Die Natur der Harmonik." In *Sammlung musikalischer Vorträge*, edited by Paul Graf von Waldersee. Leipzig: Breitkopf u. Härtel, 1882.
———. "Ueber Tonalität." *Neue Zeitschrift für Musik* (1872) No. 45–46. Reprinted in *Präludien und Studien*, vol. III. Leipzig: Hermann Seemann Nachfolger, 1901.
Schalk, Josef. "Das Gesetz der Tonalität." *Bayreuther Blätter* 11(1888):192–97, 381–87; 12(1889):191–98; 13(1890):65–70.
Schenk, Erich and Gruber, Gernot. "'Die Ganzen Studien' zu Josef Vockners Theorieunterricht bei Anton Bruckner." In *Bruckner-Studien*, edited by Othmar Wessely. Vienna: Verlag der Oesterreichische Akademie der Wissenschaften, 1975.
Simms, Bryan. "Choron, Fétis, and the Theory of Tonality." *JMT* 19, no. 1 (Spring 1975):112–38.
———. "Commentary on Arnold Schoenberg's *Theory of Harmony*, translated by Roy E. Carter." *Music Theory Spectrum* 4 (1982):155–62.
———. "New Documents in the Schoenberg-Schenker Polemic." *PNM* 16, no. 1 (1977):110–24.
Seidel, Elmar. "Die Harmonielehre Hugo Riemanns." In *Beiträge zur Musiktheorie des 19. Jahrhunderts*, edited by Martin Vogel. Regensburg: Gustav Bosse Verlag, 1966.
Solie, Ruth A. "The Living Work: Organicism and Musical Analysis." *Nineteenth Century Music* 4, no. 2 (Fall 1980):147–56.
Spratt, John F. "The Speculative Content of Schoenberg's *Harmonielehre*." *Current Musicology* 11 (1971):83–88.
Sulz, Joseph. "Anton Bruckner als Didaktiker." In *Anton Bruckner in Lehre und Forschung*. Regensburg: Bosse Verlag, 1976.
Tittel, Ernst. "Bruckners musikalischer Ausbildungsgang." In *Bruckner-Studien*, edited by Franz Grasberger. Vienna: Musikwissenschaftlicher Verlag, 1964.
———. "Simon Sechter, zum 100. Todestag." *Osterreichische Musikzeitschrift* 22, no. 9 (September 1967):550f.
———. "Wiener Musiktheorie von Fux bis Schönberg." In *Beiträge zur Musiktheorie des 19. Jahrhundert*, edited by Martin Vogel. Regensburg: Gustav Bosse Verlag, 1966.
Waldstein, William. "Bruckner als Lehrer." In *Bruckner-Studien*, edited by Franz Grasberger. Vienna: Musikwissenschaftlicher Verlag, 1964.
Wason, Robert W. "Review of *Theory of Harmony* by Arnold Schoenberg, translated by Roy E. Carter." *JMT* 25, no. 2 (Fall 1981):307–16.
———. "Schenker's Notion of Scale-Step in Historical Perspective: Non-Essential Harmonies in Viennese Fundamental Bass Theory." *JMT* 27, no. 1 (Spring 1983):49–73.
Wintle, Christopher W. "Schoenberg's Harmony: Theory and Practice." *Journal of the Arnold Schoenberg Institute* 4, no. 1 (June 1980):50–68.

Unpublished Materials

Beach, David Williams. "The Harmonic Theories of Johann Philipp Kirnberger; Their Origins and Influences." Ph.D. dissertation, Yale University, 1974.

Bernhauer, Elfriede. "Gottfried von Preyer, Sein Leben und Wirken." Ph.D. dissertation, University of Vienna, 1951.

Bruckner, Anton. "Chromatische Anmerkungen." New York Public Library, *MNZ - Toscanini Memorial Collection.

_____. Untitled manuscript. Austrian National Library, Mus. Hs. 6072 A. Bruckner 197.

Eckstein, Friedrich. "Anton Bruckner System der Musiktheorie." Austrian National Library, Mus. Hs. 29.333/1–3 A. Bruckner 208d.

_____. "Anton Bruckners Universitäts Vorlesungen über Harmonielehre, gehalten 1884–86 zu Wien." Austrian National Library, Mus. Hs. 28.445 A. Bruckner 208b.

_____. "6 Notenheft zum Theorieunterricht bei Anton Bruckner." Austrian National Library, Mus. Hs. 28.447 A. Bruckner 208f.

_____. "Studien über Harmonielehre, gemacht bei Anton Bruckner. 5 Notenhefte." Austrian National Library, Mus. Hs. 28.446 A. Bruckner 208g.

_____. "Universitäts Vorlesungen und Nachträge zur Harmonielehre/Notizen zum doppelten Kontrapunkt." Austrian National Library, Mus. Hs. 28.444 A. Bruckner 208e.

Kalib, Sylvan. "Thirteen Essays from the Three Yearbooks *Das Meisterwerk in der Musik* by Heinrich Schenker." Ph.D. dissertation, Northwestern University, 1973.

Kreitz, Helmut. "Abbé Georg Joseph Vogler als Musiktheoretiker. Ein Beitrag zur Geschichte der Musiktheorie im 18. Jahrhundert." Ph.D. dissertation, Saarbrücken, 1957.

Proctor, Gregory Michael. "Technical Bases of Nineteenth-Century Chromatic Tonality: A Study in Chromaticism." Ph.D. dissertation, Princeton University, 1978.

Rothfarb, Lee Allen. "Ernst Kurth's *The Requirements for a Theory of Harmony:* An Annotated Translation with an Introductory Essay." Master's thesis, Hartt College of Music, 1979.

Schalk, Josef. "Aufsatz über die Chromatik." Austrian National Library, F 18 Schalk 410.

_____. "Ubungsheft (Harmonielehre); mit handschr. Notizen." Austrian National Library, F 18 Schalk 409.

Simms, Bryan. "Alexandre Choron (1771–1834) As a Historian and Theorist of Music." Ph.D. dissertation: Yale University, 1971.

Slatin, Sonia. "The Theories of Heinrich Schenker in Perspective." Ph.D. dissertation, Columbia University, 1967.

Yellin, Victor Fell. "The Omnibus Idea." 1976. Expanded version of paper read at AMS meeting in Dallas, November, 1972.

Name Index

Albrechtsberger, J.G., 3, 6-9, 27, 62-63, 140, 151n.14
Alembert, J.-d', 62, 155n.4
Asioli, B., 19

Bach, C.P.E., 21, 62, 63
Bach, J.S., 14, 63, 135
Beach, D.W., xii, 39, 151n.5, 156n.6, 157n.15, 162n.10
Beethoven, L. von, 9, 19, 79, 146n.10
Brahms, J., 135
Bruckner, A., xiii, 4, 27, 34, 48, 63, 67-84, 85, 86, 89, 97, 99, 100, 102, 105, 109, 115, 116, 119, 122, 128, 136-37, 138, 139, 140, 142, 156n.15, 174n.26, 176n.38

Capellen, G., 90, 97, 101, 115, 156n.14, 157n.19, 158n.3, 177n.1, 182n.11
Caplin, W.E., 49, 155n.22
Carter, R., 136, 163n.16
Castil-Blaze, F.H.J., 103
Catel, C.S., 11, 145n.1, 152n.26
Choron, A.E., 103, 147n.19, 174n.33
Czerny, C., 12

Dahlhaus, C., 13, 84, 105, 154n.11, 175n.42, 183n.25, 186n.51
Daube, J.F., 11, 156n.4
Decsey, E., 70, 76, 78, 79, 162nn.1,6, 163n.8
Drechsler, J., 25, 26, 27
Dürrnberger, J.A., 27, 28, 68-69, 70-71, 77, 97

Eckstein, F., 69, 72, 79, 80-81, 162nn.2,6, 163n.15, 164n.18, 166nn.45,49,54, 167nn.62,63,64, 173n.17, 176n.58

Fétis, F.J., 102-4, 123
Flotzinger, R., 79, 162n.6
Flotzinger, R./Loidol, R., 73, 79, 162n.6, 164n.25, 167n.62
Forster, W. von, 116, 159n.6
Förster, E.A., 21-25, 26, 27, 28, 53, 54
Fux, J.J., 4, 8, 62, 97, 134, 147n.17, 153n.6, 160n.1

Grant, C.P., 39, 40, 156n.10
Groth, R., 102-3
Gruber, G. See Schenk, E./Gruber, G./Vockner, J.

Habert, J.E., 97-99
Halm, A., 116, 121-23, 127-28, 131, 165n.29, 177n.1, 187n.54
Hartmann, J., 31
Hasel, J.E., 85, 99-100
Hauptmann, M., xi-xiii, 54, 61, 86, 90-91, 95, 104, 115, 116, 121, 122, 127, 139, 145n.1, 155n.4, 158n.3, 165n.38, 167n.63, 175n.35, 181nn.4,7
Helmholtz, H. von, 104, 105, 111, 176n.48
Hoffman, J., 5-6, 28
Hynais, C., 85, 97, 100-102, 111

Jadassohn, S., 95-96, 117
Jonas, O., 140, 149n.17, 185n.27
Joplin, S., 16

Kirnberger, J.P., xii, 11, 13, 34, 38, 39-41, 46, 47, 50, 61, 62, 63-64, 69, 83, 86, 123-24, 128, 129, 149nn.11,16, 151n.5, 152n.19, 153n.3, 156n.6, 157n.23, 160n.19, 160n.1, 161n.8, 164n.28, 165n.35, 168n.8, 175n.35
Kistler, C., 90-91
Kitzler, O., 69
Klose, F., 70, 77, 162n.6, 163n.12
Knecht, J.H., 11, 13, 73, 149n.16
Koželuch, L., 31
Kreitz, H., 14, 150n.18
Krenn, F., 28, 155n.19
Kurth, E., 15, 33-34, 90, 91, 92, 154n.11, 155n.22, 159n.12, 165n.29, 171nn.51,53, 173n.12, 178n.4, 181n.4, 183n.24

Lendvai, E., 205
Lewin, D., 136, 181n.7
Liszt, F., 78
Lobe, J.C., 61
Loidol, R. See Flotzinger, R.
Lorenz, A.O., 91, 171n.44

Louis, R., 116, 127, 177n.63, 178n.5, 179n.16, 180nn.18,20, 184n.38
Louis, R./Thuille, L., 80, 94, 99, 116-19, 121-32, 134, 142, 177n.63, 177n.1

Mann, A., 5, 147n.17
Marpurg, F.W., 5, 9, 13, 25, 34, 40, 62-64, 68-69, 73, 80, 149n.16, 153n.3, 155n.4, 165n.36, 166n.45
Marx, A.B., 28, 38, 61, 62, 68, 69, 86, 87, 145n.3, 165n.36
Mattheson, J., 62-63
Maxandt, J.N., 31
Mayrberger, K., 46, 85-95, 100, 101, 102, 108-9, 111, 117, 129, 173n.12
Mitchell, W.J., xii, 91, 93, 124, 170n.27, 171n.46, 182n.13
Momigny, J.J., 102
Morgan, R.P., 49, 148n.10, 156n.13, 160n.1
Moser, J.N., 97, 172nn.3,4
Mozart, W.A., 16, 18, 79, 146n.13

Newlin, D., 138

Oettingen, A.J. von, xi-xii

Pembauer, J., Sr., 116
Preindl, J., 9, 27
Preyer, G. von, 5, 85, 153n.9, 173n.9

Rameau, J.P., xi-xiii, 3, 8-9, 12-13, 14, 21, 24, 27, 34, 35, 37-38, 39, 40, 62, 63, 69, 121, 128, 134, 149n.11, 151n.9, 155n.18, 156nn.10,13, 158n.3, 162n.12, 165n.36, 175n.35
Reger, M., 105, 150n.23
Reicha, A., 4, 12, 62, 146n.9
Rheinberger, J., 116, 170n.28
Richter, E.F., 117
Riemann, H., xi-xiii, 13, 14, 33, 40, 69, 73, 90, 92, 104-5, 108, 109, 115, 116-19, 122, 123, 124, 125, 126-27, 128, 131, 134, 136, 139, 142, 146n.8, 150n.26, 155n.22, 155n.4, 156n.14, 158n.3, 166n.49, 178n.5, 181n.7, 182n.20, 185n.15, 186n.46
Riepel, J., 62

Salzmann, G., 4, 5, 27, 153n.9
Schalk, J., 79, 85, 97, 100, 102, 105-11, 117, 129, 166n.49
Schenk, E./Gruber, G./Vockner, J., 73, 162n.6, 167nn.62,64
Schenker, H., xiii, 14, 48, 84, 89, 96, 105, 115, 116, 117, 118, 119, 121, 127, 130, 132, 133-43, 148n.6, 157n.23, 160n.1, 165n.29, 177n.1,2, 179n.16, 183nn.24, 31
Schoenberg, A., xiii, 70, 72, 84, 115, 116, 119, 133-43, 152n.19, 172n.3, 173n.6, 177n.1, 178n.4, 179n.16, 181n.24
Schreyer, J., 115, 177n.1
Schubert, F., 5, 19, 146n.10
Schulz, J.A.P., 11, 38, 39-41, 63, 83, 124, 157n.2, 164n.28, 168n.8
Schwanzara, E., 70, 71-72, 73, 74, 76, 78, 80, 162n.6, 164n.18
Sechter, S., xii-xiii, 3, 5, 6, 8, 9, 12, 13, 14, 24, 27, 28, 31-84, 85, 86, 88, 89, 90, 91, 92, 93-94, 97-111, 115, 121, 122, 123, 124, 125, 127, 131, 133, 134, 135, 136, 138-40, 141-42, 146n.9, 149n.11, 168n.3, 169n.23, 182n.11, 186nn.46,48
Sessions, R., 48, 186n.42
Seyfried, I.R. von, 6, 8-9, 140, 151n.14, 152n.24, 153n.9
Shirlaw, M., 37, 168n.7
Simms, B., 103, 147n.19, 174n.33, 186n.51
Speiser, C. See Orel, A./Speiser, C.
Stadler, A.M., 31
Swoboda, A., 25-27, 49, 152n.28

Thomson, U., 5, 11-12, 13, 27, 28, 145n.1, 146nn.6,10, 147nn.15,18, 148n.26, 150n.18, 151n.1, 153nn.4,8, 162n.4
Thuille, L., 116, 178n.5. See also Louis, R./Thuille, L.
Tittel, E., 11, 27, 43, 68-69, 146n.7, 153n.1, 154nn.12,13,14, 162n.11, 162nn.4,6, 163n.12, 165n.35
Türk, D.G., 9, 11, 62-63, 68-69, 156n.15, 157n.17

Vockner, J. See Schenk, E./Gruber, G./Vockner, J.
Vogel, M., 92, 170nn.27,34,36, 171n.44, 172n.37
Vogler, A.G.J., xi-xii, 4, 9, 12-19, 21-22, 25-26, 27, 28, 38, 57, 61, 73, 81, 83, 126, 155n.4, 175n.35

Wagner, M., 3, 5, 11, 147n.18, 148n.4, 150n.18, 155nn.17,19, 155n.4, 162n.4
Wagner, R., 60, 69, 72, 78, 79, 85, 86, 90-96, 97, 100, 101-2, 106, 108-11, 174n.26, 176n.58
Weber, C.M., 4
Weber, G., xi, 11, 33, 34, 38, 51, 62, 126, 150n.26
Weiss, J.B., 68

Yellin, V.F., 16-19, 57

Zamazal, F. See Maier, E./Zamazal, F.
Zeleny, W., 32, 62-63, 147n.16, 153nn.2,3,4,5,6,9, 154n.14, 155n.18, 158n.1, 160nn.15,16, 161nn.4,5,6, 162n.12
Zenetti, L.E. von, 69, 166n.45

Subject Index

acoustics, 34, 104, 117-18
America, harmonic theory in, 116, 141
analysis, 25, 28, 33, 38, 59, 78-79, 85, 90-96, 99, 100, 105, 108-9, 115, 116, 131, 146n.13, 160n.20
  structural levels in, 50, 127, 130, 140
arpeggiation, 45-46, 88, 98, 129
"artificial" system, 134

"back alteration" (*Rückalterierung*), 80-81

cadence, 9, 14-15, 26, 56-57, 76-77, 99-100, 121-23, 128, 135, 155n.19
  "characteristic", 76, 128
  deceptive, 37, 107, 108
  "extended", 76, 122, 140
  "imitation of", 35, 38
Cecilian Movement, 97
chord
  "accidental", "incidental" (*zufälliger*). See chord, "non-essential" (*zufälliger*)
  "added sixth", 13, 149n.11, 155n.4. See also double emploi
  altered, 54-55, 99, 141. See also chord, "hybrid" (*Zwitterakkord*)
  "amphibilous" (*zweideutiger*), 23, 99
  "artificial" (*gekünstelter*), 26, 46, 47, 48, 57, 74, 77, 79, 82-83, 101, 123. See also chord, "non-essential" (*zufälliger*)
  augmented, 7, 22, 34, 51, 52
  augmented sixth, 7, 22, 26, 53, 55, 59, 63, 80, 90-91, 99, 186n.47. See also chord, "altered"; chord, "hybrid" (*Zwitterakkord*)
  "characteristic", 22
  chromatic, 7, 55, 94
  "common", 8
  consonant, 8, 22, 34, 130
  diminished 7th, 13, 26, 54, 85, 139-40, 149n.11, 168n.3. See also progression, "omnibus"
  diminished 7th, as incomplete 9th, 38, 40, 54, 108, 137, 139, 149n.11
  "directly related", 104
  dissonant, 7-8, 34, 84, 130
  dominant, 13, 52, 72-73, 129
  dominant preparation, 35
  11th and 13th
    as chords, 72-73
    as suspensions, 72-73, 87, 92, 157n.16
  enharmonic, 22
  "fantastic", 63
  "fundamental" (*Stammakkord*), 12, 22, 34, 63, 71
  "hybrid" (*Zwitterakkord*), 55-56, 80, 90-91, 92, 94, 99, 141. See also chord, "altered"; chord, "augmented sixth"
  "imperfect", 7-8
  "leading-tone change", 127
  linear derivation of, 123-25
  minor, 35, 156n.14
  Neapolitan 6th, 24, 57, 81, 109-10, 166n.49
  neighbor, 48, 125, 129-30, 141, 159n.6
  9th
    as fundamental chord, 71, 73, 74, 89, 101, 139, 141, 164n.26
    as 9-8 suspension, 8, 13, 23, 63, 71, 73, 86, 149n.16
  9th, 11th and 13th, by *supposition*, 8-9, 25, 26, 27, 165n.36
  "non-essential" (*zufälliger*), 84, 93, 107, 108, 123, 126, 130, 141-42, 176n.58, 187n.54
  "parallel", 127
  passing, 45-46, 47-48, 57, 63, 78, 85, 87-89, 93, 107, 108-9, 123, 125, 129, 130-31, 141, 142, 157n.2, 159n.6. See also chord, "artificial" (*gekünstelter*); chord, "non-essential" (*zufälliger*)
  "perfect", 7-8
  "plain third", 175n.42
  "primary", 76, 123, 126, 133, 134, 136, 138, 155n.22, 166n.49, 178n.5

Subject Index

"quality", in Viennese harmonic theory, 33-34
"second-degree" relationship, 104
"secondary", 122-23, 134-35, 136, 138, 155n.22, 178n.5
secondary dominant, 54, 55, 81, 139-40
seventh, 12, 22, 28, 51, 77, 102
$^4_2$, 7, 22, 46-48, 70, 74, 77, 79, 88, 93, 101, 125, 129, 183n.31
$^6_3$, 22, 103, 124, 129
subdominant, 35, 52, 133, 139
suspension, 7, 21, 26, 46-48, 57, 92, 93, 124-25, 165n.36, 172nn.57,58
Tristan, 90-91
chord identity vs. chord progression, 12-13, 33, 95-96
chromatic alteration, 21-26, 53, 57, 59, 81, 106, 140, 152n.19, 160n.12
chromatic harmony, 21, 23, 33, 34, 48-49, 53, 55-56, 64, 90, 97, 99-111, 131, 133, 139, 140-41, 158n.7, 167n.63
chromatic scale, 15, 21, 25-26, 57, 81. *See also* progression, "omnibus"
chromaticism
  harmonic, melodic, embellishing, 94
church music, 3-4, 6, 25, 27, 28, 61-63, 69, 97, 168n.1, 172n.1
"concealment" (*Verschweigung*) of fundamental, 40, 157n.16
conservatories, 4, 5, 31, 32, 67, 116, 146n.9, 152n.26, 178n.3, 178n.5
consonance, 34, 70, 135-36
  appellative, 103
  chord vs. interval, 77, 85-86
  "feigning", 126-27
counterpoint, 4, 5, 27, 31, 43, 71, 97-98, 111, 135, 160n.1

development vs. inversion, 133-34, 138-39
dialectic, xii, 116, 121-22, 143, 160n.3
diatonic scale, 33, 34, 56, 103, 104, 133, 136
displacement, 128
dissonance, 12, 34, 70, 73, 121, 125-26, 135-36, 141, 149n.16, 183n.31
  "essential" (*wesentlich*), 13, 84, 129, 164n.28
  harmonic, 13, 41, 75, 86-87, 149n.16, 161n.9
  "imagined", 41-42, 75
  "melodic", 13, 86, 95-96, 149n.11, 149n.16, 161n.9
  "natural", 103
  "non-essential", "artificial" (*zufällig*), 13, 63, 92, 164n.28
double emploi, 13, 38, 63. *See also* chord, "added sixth"
doubling, 7, 77, 134
"dualism", xii, 115, 117-18, 122, 136, 178n.5

elision/ellipsis, 40, 80, 93, 101, 157n.17
empirical science, 111, 115, 116-19
empiricism, 40, 104
enharmonic, 15, 21, 25, 34, 58, 62, 80, 81, 171n.45
extension of the fundamental, 45-50, 78, 98

fifth of II, as dissonance, 34, 35, 42, 76, 99
figured bass, 3, 6-9, 12, 15, 21, 22, 24, 25, 27, 32, 33, 37, 38, 46, 53, 72, 123-24, 136, 140, 141, 143
"free composition". *See* "strict composition" (*strenger Satz*) vs. "free composition" (*freier Satz*)
French harmonic theory, 3-4, 12-13, 33, 102-4
"function theory" (*Funktionstheorie*), 5, 33, 50, 91, 103, 105, 116, 126-27, 134, 155n.22, 155n.4, 166n.49, 172n.57, 179n.9
fundamental bass, 3, 13, 31-143 *passim*
  in chromatic harmony, 53, 80, 81, 93, 97, 99, 102, 107, 109, 167n.62

German harmonic theory, xii, 3, 11, 25, 33, 59, 80, 91, 94, 104-5, 115-16, 121-23, 125-28, 132, 139, 160n.2, 172n.1
Grundton, 28

"harmonic connective" (*harmonisches Band, harmonisches Bindungsmittel*), 38, 136
"harmonic figuration", 87-89
harmonic rhythm, 19, 50, 94
harmonic theory, and cultural/intellectual history, 61, 97-98, 145n.1, 180n.20
harmony
  and counterpoint, separation of, 71, 132
  "traditional", 3, 141
  vs. figured bass, 12, 21, 25, 28

"inferential bass", 40-41
"intermediate fundamental" (*Zwischenfundament*), 38-40, 43, 45, 50, 57-58, 74, 84, 85, 89, 92, 97-98, 101, 108, 138, 164n.19, 168n.3
"interpolated bass", 40
"interpolated fifth", 135
"interpretation dissonance" (*Auffassungsdissonanz*), 125-31, 142
interval, 7-8, 14-15, 70
  "directly intelligible", 86
inversion, theory of, 8, 12, 22, 24, 27, 37, 46, 63, 77, 88, 123, 124, 133-34, 147n.22, 149n.16
inversional balance, 136

Klangmischung, 104-5, 108

"law of the shortest way", 70, 136
leading tone, 14, 23, 33, 38, 51, 54, 59, 90, 134, 175n.35

Subject Index 201

major and minor, mixture of, 22, 26-27, 54, 59, 80, 100, 107, 108, 139
minor, 15, 34, 49, 54, 72, 82, 86
   progression in, 51-52, 150n.21
   scales, 21-22, 25, 51
"minor-interpretation", 117-18, 180n.18
modulation, 9, 15, 26, 34, 49-50, 94, 104, 106, 133, 140, 168n.3, 171n.45
   chromatic, 26-27, 80
   diatonic, 23, 49, 54, 58, 167n.63
   enharmonic, 34, 79
   "extended", 26, 49
   "implied", 123, 127
   pivot chord, 15, 49, 80
   pivot tone, 27, 152n.28, 160n.19
   "simple", 26
   "sudden", 26-27
"monism", 115
"monotonality", 140

Naturalistenstreit, 5, 153n.4
neighbor note, 48, 88, 101, 107, 108, 110, 125
"non-harmonic" tone, 124-25, 138, 141
notation, analytical, 13, 15, 24, 25, 27, 28

ordre omnitonique, pluritonique, transitonique, unitonique, 104
organ-point, 130-31
"overlapping" (*übergreifendes*) system, 90
overtone, undertone, 104, 117-18

passing tone, 35, 47, 57-58, 88-89, 92, 95, 107, 164n.22
   "altered", 95
   "irregular", 47, 74, 79
   "returning" (*zurückkehrender Durchgang*). See neighbor note
pedagogy, 145n.3
   of Bruckner, 67-71
   of Sechter, 31-33
   of Viennese theorists, 3-6
   turn of the century, 115, 116, 131-32, 136, 170n.28, 178nn.4,5, 179n.16
"plurisignificance", "polyvalence" (*Mehrdeutigkeit*), 14-15, 27, 58, 150n.23
progression, 13, 14-15, 32, 33, 37-38, 40, 43, 46, 48, 85, 103, 118, 122-23, 129, 136-39, 155n.22
   "artificial" (*gekünstelte*), "apparent" (*scheinbare*), 43, 45, 98, 138-39
   ascending, 35, 40, 42, 84
   ascending stepwise, 37, 38, 41, 74, 98, 137
   by diminished and augmented 5th, 52, 133-34
   "chromatic" (*chromatische Fortschreitung*), 53-54, 55, 57, 59, 106, 133, 157n.15
   circle of 5ths
      ascending, 123, 133

   descending, 8, 35, 45, 54, 55, 59, 76, 83, 122-23, 125, 133, 135, 136, 155n.22
   "compound" chromatic, 80, 167n.62
   descending, 35, 40, 84, 137-38
   descending stepwise, 37, 41, 54, 74, 84, 98, 137
   forbidden, 35, 70, 150n.21
   "irregular", 42-43
   "omnibus", 16-19, 24-25, 57, 81-82
   "root", 84, 141
   "simple" chromatic, 80, 167n.62
   stepwise, 35, 37, 39, 40, 43, 45, 50, 55, 57, 58, 70, 74-76, 98, 101, 104, 108, 122, 136-39, 166n.49
   "strong (ascending), weak (descending), superstrong (overskipping)", 137
   third and fifth ("natural"), 8, 37-38, 40, 45, 54, 98, 101, 109, 136, 138, 142

rationalism, 12, 40, 64
"reciprocal effect" (*Wechselwirkung*), 35, 121, 122, 135
Redukzion, 12, 149n.11
"related keys" (*Verwandtschaft*), 9, 15, 21, 26, 49, 54, 59, 80, 81
"romantic harmony", 9, 14-15, 59, 85-96
"rule of the octave", 7, 9, 15, 24, 58

"scale step", 48-49, 86, 89, 133, 135, 136, 139-42
sequence, 8, 54, 76-77, 135
"step theory" (*Stufentheorie*), 33, 50, 91, 104, 155n.22, 172n.57, 185n.39
"strict composition" (*strenger Satz*) vs. "free composition" (*freier Satz*), 4, 43, 61, 95, 98, 103, 169n.13
substitutes (*Stellvertreter*), 40, 76, 78, 98, 123, 127-29
suspension, 63, 71, 87, 95, 125, 130, 149n.16, 164n.22
   double, 8

theorists, as composers, 5-6
theory
   relationship to composition, 5, 19, 61, 84, 85, 115, 162n.2
   "speculative", 8, 69, 178n.5
   "speculative" vs. "practical", 116-19
third "divider", 138
"tonal direction" (*Tonleitung*), 15
tonalité moderne vs. *tonalité antique*, 103
"tonality", 102-7, 119, 133-34, 135-36, 181n.23
tonicization, 23, 48-50, 80, 90, 94, 133, 140, 141, 142
Tonverbindung. See interval
Tristan, 90-96, 100
tuning systems, 34, 49, 58, 76, 84, 97, 98, 154n.15, 169n.23

Vienna, cultural conservatism of, 3-6, 12
Viennese classic style, 3-4, 19
"voice exchange" (*Tausch*), 47-48, 57, 63, 78, 82, 83, 91, 101, 157n.2

voice leading, 16, 41-43, 47, 51-52, 70, 72, 75, 77, 78, 84, 90, 102, 111, 131, 134, 135, 141, 185n.27

www.ingramcontent.com/pod-product-compliance
Lightning Source LLC
Chambersburg PA
CBHW070337240426
43665CB00045B/2165